WHITE STORM

ACKNOWLEDGEMENTS

I would like to thank the following for their help:

Bill Campbell, Juanjo Moran, Jorge Valdano, Diana Lindsay, Mike Ticher, Cristina Velarde, Julia Gonzáles, Isabel Real, Begoña Agudín, Fundación Real Madrid, Julio Gonzáles Ronco, Loli López, Nacho Estefánia, Duncan Shaw, Mark Wilson and all at Mainstream.

MAINSTREAM *SPORT*

WHITE STORM

101 YEARS OF REAL MADRID

PHIL BALL

MAINSTREAM
PUBLISHING

EDINBURGH AND LONDON

To Harry, Lily and Diana

Copyright © Phil Ball, 2002

First published in Great Britain in 2002 by
MAINSTREAM PUBLISHING COMPANY (EDINBURGH) LTD
7 Albany Street
Edinburgh EH1 3UG

ISBN 1 84018 763 8

This edition, 2003

A catalogue record for this book is available from the British Library

Unless stated all photographs © Fundación Real Madrid

Typeset in Stone
Printed and bound in Great Britain by
Cox & Wyman Ltd

CONTENTS

Introduction 7
1. Home and Away 13
2. Madrid, Madrileños and Madridistas 29
3. Tall Oaks from Little Acorns . . . 43
4. Early Days and Early Ways 59
5. Life Before Alfredo 73
6. Dancing Behind Frosted Glass 103
7. The Famous Five 117
8. She Loves You 143
9. The Vulture Squadron 173
10. Raúl Madrid 191
11. Brand it like Beckham 207
Table of Statistics 213
Bibliography 217
Index 218

INTRODUCTION

'But many that are first shall be last; and the last shall be first' (Matthew 19:30). It seemed curious that after 101 years of hogging the sporting limelight for reasons generally connected to football, Real Madrid should have chosen to buy David Beckham, the latest in the series of the club's high-profile signings and a fine player of course, but the first representative of other tendencies in the post-modern game that up to June 2003 had been largely shunned by the famous club. As the Biblical quotation implies, the great names of both the distant and the more recent past may have cause to resent this sudden multi-coloured intrusion of marketing hype into the previously whiter world of Real Madrid – but they had better get used to it.

David Beckham has had little to do with the past of Real Madrid, but if the crazy summer of 2003 was anything to go by, he may well have plenty to do with their future. By signing the Englishman the club effectively sent the player and themselves simultaneously into hyperspace. Where they will land is anyone's guess, but the transfer triggered the seismic shift it was designed to bring about, causing scenes of bulb-popping hysteria rarely seen since The Beatles. Real Madrid and Beckham were always big, but the marriage of the two institutions seemed to change the world in some indefinable way, as though the dual powers of commerce and imagery had finally got together in a public takeover bid of the planet. Figo, Zidane and Ronaldo, three players signed almost exclusively on the basis of their footballing talents, were suddenly eclipsed. Real Madrid had done it again – albeit differently – with another reminder to the world that they set the template, that they alone change the rules. Look on my works, ye Mighty, and despair!

Nevertheless, there was life before Beckham. Real Madrid have always been around in some shape or form, and I remember them well as a kid. I was educated, in a manner of speaking, at a low-ranking English grammar school in a small provincial town on the north-eastern coast of England. The school tried its best to copy the manners of the public school traditions, dressing its masters in flowing gowns, teaching us the virtues of study and reminding us that the twin purposes of sport were participation and the team ethic, not the cruder emotions experienced in the aftermath of victory. The eccentric Headmaster, reading out the 5th Form soccer results one morning during assembly, lost his temper when several pupils dared to cheer the fact that some of their mates had won 8–0 over the weekend. The score seemed to be inviting some sort of comment from the groundlings below the lectern, but the Headmaster was having none of it. 'Be quiet!' he hollered. 'Why are you cheering? Our sympathies should surely lie with the losers,' he continued. And then he added in a quieter, more measured voice, 'The losers in such a game invariably learn more than the winners . . . and now, the Benediction,' as if his little aphorism brooked no challenge – as if it were a truth worthy of being followed by a religious ritual.

I've never forgotten that line about the losers learning more than the winners. It's a sentiment that would earn you short shrift from postmodern youth, and one that might also have got a frosty reception back then in many countries outside of Britain. When I look back, several of the teachers were clearly of a different opinion too, and coached the school football teams in an aggressive spirit that was hardly Corinthian in nature. I live in Spain now, and the idea that losing can serve some purpose in life is a notion so alien to the culture that it is simply not up for debate. The Spanish simply view the idea as idiotic, and have no time for it. And, of course, they may be right. In the not-so-distant past there were undoubtedly some feathery notions floating about the British sporting scene that it was undignified to proclaim that your purpose was merely to win. But, as far as I can gather, this decent but rather complicated attitude to sport has never been part of the Spanish scene. I'm unsure as to the reasons for this, but I could hazard a decent guess – Real Madrid.

This is the team that was rubber-stamped by FIFA as the best of the twentieth century, an accolade disputed by no one. Their statistics of victory are overwhelming: 9 European Cups, 29 league titles, 17 domestic cups, 2 Intercontinental trophies and 2 UEFA Cups, plus several losing appearances in finals and semi-finals, not forgetting the fact that when they were not *winning* the league title they were probably finishing as runners-up. The other curious fact to bear in mind, apart from all this largesse, is that a large proportion of it was won after 1953, when Alfredo Di Stéfano came along and changed the face of European football for ever. For those living outside Spain in the mid- to late-1950s, Real Madrid became synonymous with the country. Instead of the red and yellow sparkle of bullfighting, where the blood and the sequins mirrored the colours of the country's national flag, Spain became pure white, the colours of Real Madrid. When Don Revie took over at Leeds in the early 1960s, he changed their colours from blue and gold to all-white, in a superstitious nod to the powers of Europe's football kings.

The point of mentioning all this is to emphasise the extent to which Real Madrid have programmed the Spanish configuration for sporting attitudes. The rest of the pack, even Barcelona, can only dream of emulating their successes, but it doesn't stop them from trying. The fact that the Spanish league has become more competitive in the recent past, with various previously unknown sides coming to prominence through success in European competitions, should not obscure the equally important fact that 'La Liga', as it is now called in Britain, has always been a competitive, high-quality league. Real Madrid's consistent dominance of the scene is further proof, if any more were needed, of their status in the game. Their influence has rubbed off on the rest too, and there is precious little gentlemanly sentiment in Spanish football. It has turned into a dog-eat-dog league, a sort of roller-coaster experiment in the survival of the fittest. Real Madrid and Barcelona are the richest, of course, due to their massive membership schemes and lucrative commercial contracts, but the general spread of wealth in Spain over the last 20 years has seen the emergence of a new breed of rags-to-riches president keen on an attempt at seizing the crown, of usurping the traditional footballing monarchy. Deportivo de La Coruña and Valencia are recent winners of a league that is suffering from an outbreak of equality of opportunity – although there are still complaints that Real Madrid's relationship with central government and its close ties with the country's most important banks and municipal figures prevent a parallel outbreak of true sporting democracy.

But these rumblings have never cut much ice with the club. It is all part and parcel of the concept of *Madridismo*, a complicated notion whose central core is the glorification of indifference – an almost deliberate sense of narrow-minded commitment to the cause. If other folk don't go for the win-at-all-costs stuff, then that's their problem. And unlike their great rivals, Barcelona, Real Madrid's philosophy is uncluttered by the pretension that everyone loves and admires them, even though there is plenty of evidence to suggest that many do. But it probably doesn't matter to them. The club embodies the Spanish sporting concept of *Machacar* (crush without mercy), which relegates such decent notions as 'taking your foot off the gas' to the realms of weakness and foppery. You don't let your opponents off the hook, and you rarely allow the bull to live. There's no poetry in that. The Spanish soul is a complex one, full of generosity and violence in equal measure – a certain lack of self-control that has turned itself into a manly virtue. You have to *Machacar*, so that the opponent will fear you the next time. The bullfighter who permits a dull-witted beast to master him is soon chased off the stage. But no one admires the bull. He just hadn't read the script. Similarly, when Real Madrid lose, their opponents are rarely praised. The focus is on the Goliath, not the David. The big guy had an off day, and just didn't see that stone coming.

The spirit of the club resides in its trophy room, open seven days a week to the public, as a permanent testament to the glory of the institution. Great players come and go, but statistics never die. At the entrance to the *'Sala de Exposiciones'* (Exhibition Room) under the solid towers of the Bernabéu, a large blue mural assaults the potential unbeliever with the length and breadth of the club's achievements. Once inside the trophy room, the gold and silver of a hundred years – football's *conquistadores* rubbing the world's noses into the dirt – wink and shimmer in the tasteful lighting.

It's a beguiling scene that takes you in somehow, despite your better self. You cannot help but admire the sheer arrogance of it all. However, when I first visited the *Sala*, courtesy of the club, I was overwhelmed by the scale of what I was taking on. How on earth could all this history be condensed down into a smallish book? The task suddenly seemed enormous, impossible. But then I gradually came to see that no one had really taken the time to sit back and look at the institution through neutral spectacles, almost all of the literature on the club having been written through the rose-tinted variety. These books have their function, of course, and a club like Real Madrid has a strong need, both emotional and financial, to promote the writing of as many of them as possible. They are almost exclusively written by supporters, a genre created to avoid any awkward analysis. I can, however, boast the status of a neutral observer – despite the fact that when you write a book on some living phenomenon you inevitably warm to the subject after a while, and perhaps become more sympathetic than was your avowed intent. But I come neither to bury nor praise Real Madrid. I made this clear to the club from the outset, and they seemed perfectly happy to cooperate with all my requests. *White Storm* is not the first book published in the English language about them, Souvenir Press having published one in 1961, in the aftermath of the five consecutive European Cups. Long out of print, it has no authors, only editors. The chapters are a series of interviews with prominent figures at the club around the time, and prominent figures from football, with some exceptions, rarely say very much of interest about the game, conditioned as they are by their positions and their obvious lack of objectivity.

There are some interviews in this book, but they do not form its core. This is a personal view of Real Madrid, formed in part through my research into the club's history and shaped by my 12 years of residence in Spain, up in the north where the club's *peñas* (sympathisers) are thin on the ground. My 'neutrality' is therefore also conditioned by this fact, but football is so pervasive in this country, so all-encompassing that in the end my general perceptions of its ebbs and its flows are essentially the same as the chap next door. There are obvious limits on how 'personal' one's vision can ever be. But one important difference is that I'm English, and I was not a fan of Real Madrid. And although these struck me as important reasons for writing the book, I have to admit that the final clause of the previous sentence was written in the past tense. Familiarity breeds contempt? I don't think so. I've become a fan of sorts, and it would be nice to think that anyone who reads this book might also be tempted into becoming the same.

I feel privileged to have been asked to write this book, for the story of Real Madrid is as extravagant as it is captivating. I hope to have done it some justice.

Phil Ball
San Sebastián, July 2003

1. HOME AND AWAY

Real Madrid v. Las Palmas,
10 February 2002

On an unusually warm 10 February 2002, Las Palmas run out onto the patchy grass of the Bernabéu, canary yellow and blue against the tired green of the turf below their boots. They gather in the centre circle and wave to one corner of the enormous North Stand, where the entire Canary expatriate population of Madrid seem to be concentrated. They lie 15th in the table, with the best defensive record in the division, and are the last but one team to visit Real Madrid before 6 March, the date which will mark their host's much awaited centenary. The small programme in my hand informs me that this is Las Palmas' 983rd game in the Spanish First Division since their foundation. More ominously, their biggest defeat to date was in 1959, 10–1 on the very same ground on which they are now warming up their twenty-first-century limbs. Their illustrious opponents, in true rock-star style, are still down the tunnel somewhere, working up the expectation. Another glance at the programme yields the information that today's landlords are to play game number 2,117 in the top flight, and that they actually managed to score a record 11 against Elche the season after they pummelled Las Palmas all those years ago, a fact that might comfort any superstitious Canary fans over there in the opposite stand to where I sit.

The home side trot out and run to the centre amid mild applause. The club are undergoing one of their occasional 'crises' and have lost their last two games, ceding their beloved top spot to a tough-looking Valencia side. The crowd are showing their muted displeasure. At least I think so. The applause may actually be louder than I imagine, but whatever sound generated by the home supporters is being drowned out by the stirring baritone of Plácido Domingo, blasted out through the club's expensive sound system. Interesting that they chose not to use Julio Iglesias for the occasion, who in his younger days turned out as goalkeeper for the reserves. But the song, *'Hala Madrid!'*, is not quite Julio's style. The title ('Onward Real Madrid!') says it all really. Penned for the centenary by the young Madrid-born rock star José María Cano, it is an astonishingly traditional and emotional piece of music, building up to a Handel's Messiah-type crescendo, as if the entire cast of the holy host were flitting around the upper reaches of the stadium blowing their golden trumpets, and the Lord himself were looking down and smiling benevolently on the scene. When the din finally subsides the relative silence is slightly uncomfortable, as if an actual game of football were unworthy of such an introduction. Folk shuffle around on their seats, and try to refocus on the scene before them. A football match. The last-but-one of a hundred years, and the only one for which I could wangle a free ticket, kindly provided for me by the club on the strength of my writing this book.

Turn back the clock half an hour and I am wandering in off the wide Avenida Castellana into the Sunday-market bustle of the area immediately in front of the West Stand – the squat, imposing grey façade of the world's most famous club – outside of which I have decided to take in the atmosphere and pick up some hints from the groundlings, scurrying around like ants about to enter their nest. The scene smacks of what Rob James once wrote of the streets of Manchester on the day of a game at Old Trafford, back in the late 1960s. 'When Manchester United play,' he wrote, 'it is not a game but an event.' The whole city seems to be aware of it, and is either drawn towards it or must move away from it. But it is affected by the event, and cannot avoid its drama. Here in the wide open spaces of these plush northern precincts of Madrid, the atmosphere seems almost frantic – as if the seats inside the stadium have no number and it is a case of everyone for himself. 'Women and children first!' I try to walk against the tide towards the stalls which sell cheap club trinkets and memorabilia.

When I finally wade through and reach one of the *kioskos* I am surprised to see an expensively laminated calendar hanging from one of the sides, partly covered by the club's lilac scarves. The calendar announces 'Ultras Sur – 2002' and boasts a photograph of the area behind the goal where Real Madrid's infamous troublemakers tend to gather. For the photograph, they are posing with an enormous canvas on which is written 'Ultras', in a curiously pretty violet colour, the word itself cleaved in two by the Spanish flag. On the flag is a two-headed black axe, the neo-fascist symbol of Spain's Far Right. The shaven-headed youth in charge of the stall is clad in an olive-green bomber jacket and is selling a cigarette lighter decorated with a picture of Raúl. 'What's this?' I ask him, pointing to the calendar. He shrugs and looks away. 'A calendar,' he manages. 'I know it's a calendar,' I insist. 'But who has produced it?' At this he turns to face me, narrowing his eyes. I speak Spanish, but since I'm clearly a foreigner, I can't be a cop. He glances down at the laptop dangling from my right hand and I surmise that it's this that is making me look slightly official. *'They* have,' he attempts, waving in the direction of the West Stand. 'No, no,' I protest. 'That's impossible. The club can't have produced this. They wouldn't produce something like this, surely?' He is beginning to look nervous, especially as there is a veritable river of folks streaming past his stall, any one of whom could be nicking half of his livelihood whilst he debates the legality of a damned calendar with some nosey foreigner. He comes clean: 'I mean the Ultras. They've made it. They're on sale in all the stalls,' he insists, lifting his hands appealingly, as if God were his witness. But he fails. 'And what does it mean?' I persist annoyingly, pointing up at the axe on the flag. He looks cross now. 'It's the Spanish flag!' he splutters, waving his arms around and almost swiping a passer-by. 'I know,' I reassure him. 'But that. What's that axe thing?' This finally provokes a lesson in political history and several expletives: 'Fascists – fuck knows – nazis, hooligans, Franco . . . and all that stuff.' I nod an acknowledgement, ask him how much, and walk away with my booty for two Euros. Cheap at half the price.

Skinhead stall-owners notwithstanding, the rest of the scene looks like a family day out. Mums and dads with whole broods of kids, fathers and sons, husbands and wives, ticket-touts, the odd policeman – but there is nothing threatening in the air. The edginess that you get at the standard English game is entirely absent, despite the large numbers of Las Palmas fans, most of them – according to the morning's local newspaper, resident in Madrid. Groups of them loiter outside, clad in yellow, savouring the day. They wear their identity openly, a clear sign that they regard the stadium as safe.

Once inside the Bernabéu, your reaction at seeing first-hand what you have seen a thousand times on the television is always the same – you have come to the wrong place, a different stadium. The same thing occurs every time you enter a famous arena for the first time, but with this one there is that added touch of surrealism because of its reputation, because of its sheer presence in the annals of international football. This is where Di Stéfano trod, where Franco and his acolytes sat, where the immense figure of Santiago Bernabéu last waved to his adoring crowd before shuffling home and dying of cancer three weeks before the 1978 World Cup in Argentina. And yet in the weak light of a winter's afternoon, less than a month before the club's centenary, it is hard to appreciate all this and fit the emotions and the visuals satisfactorily into the current frame. The stadium seems awesomely tall, and more square than I was expecting from the outside. The five tiers of the North Stand opposite me are perched so giddily close to the pitch that the folk way up at the top seem to be looking down from on high in a vertical sightline to the crossbar, such is the steep gradient of the design. Up there you would want to be strapped into your seats, just in case. Whatever – the club's marketing department have perceptively noted from my apologetic tones on the phone that I'm no VIP, and have issued me with a ticket down in the 'Fondo Sur', to the left of the Ultras, affording me a view of the whole edifice. It looks imposing and self-righteous, boxing in the sky. It's slightly disappointing, but there are 90 minutes ahead. This is what I've come to see. A game. Perhaps someone will conjure up some magic. Zidane, Figo, Roberto Carlos. The probability seems reasonably high.

When Plácido's operatic belter dies away and the referee begins the game, the first player who catches my attention is actually a fellow Englishman, Vinnie Samways. At Las Palmas since 1996, I remember him in England as a pale, fragile sort of player, trying to gain a permanent berth in the Tottenham midfield and ultimately failing, but not for want of talent. He just didn't seem tough enough for the English scene, and it's odd to see him here, after all these years, with a reputation as a snarling, aggressive midfielder. Perhaps it's because he's called Vinnie, but unlike Jones, he still looks fragile and bony, his tiny face tanned and weathered, so that you'd easily mistake him for a middle-aged native. He's in exalted company, and it immediately shows. His first touch is to control a long punt downfield from Miñambres, Madrid's young debutant defender, but in doing so he unwisely decides to take on Figo, perhaps the world's second best player after Zidane, his teammate lurking close by. Figo anticipates Samway's slow feint and robs him, obliging Vinnie to race back and tackle the Portuguese midfielder, already intent on one of those lethal runs down the right channel. Samways concedes the throw-in and puffs out his cheeks. It's going to be a difficult afternoon.

As the game settles quietly into its pattern it is the pure simplicity of Real Madrid's all-white that begins to catch the eye. It is not so much a case of their playing any better as yet, but rather the strange threat that resides in the quiet dignity of their colours, as if the conscious decision to keep it plain has been based on some sort of inner confidence. Las

Palmas' garish yellow and blue strip seems, in contrast, to smack of the Sunday pub leagues – an awkward attempt to look flash which has been based on a proportionate lack of inner confidence. The movements of the Madrid players seem more elegant, more measured. When they have the ball, their probing and poking has an air of coherence about it, despite the absences of the home town favourite, Raúl, and the dark fearsome captain, Fernando Hierro. In short, they look a superior breed. It is difficult to imagine Las Palmas getting away with a result, their defensive record notwithstanding.

As the rays of the setting sun begin to paint the north-eastern tiers in an orange glow, I try to gauge something of the club from the folk around me. Some heaters above our heads are switched on as the temperature drops, and I am reminded that we are, despite the mild weather, in the depths of a Madrid winter. Nonetheless, the luxury of these radiators takes me back to my childhood and the freezing terraces at Grimsby, battered by Siberian winds off the Humber, against whose merciless claws we had only our duffel-coats as protection. Soft south. Kids nowadays! And talking of which, the family to my left are Portuguese, with a teenage daughter sitting beside me, glum faced. When Figo gets the ball, she shows some flicker of recognition, some sign of life, but it is momentary and fleeting. They probably represent not just the ethnic mix that is twenty-first-century Madrid but the sort of cosmopolitan pull of which the club can now boast. The Bernabéu is a place for the faithful, but also for the tourist. Blurb on the city claims that the stadium is the most visited 'monument' after the Prado and the Puerto del Sol. As if to prove this, outside the ground I had heard a surprising amount of English – a group of Liverpudlians had staggered past me drunk, I had intruded on a conversation behind me about Chelsea and Ken Bates, and had heard the distinctive tones of Geordie as I tried to buy the famous calendar.

Behind me, a thuggish-looking middle-aged man with a pockmarked face and a bald head in the shape of a dome is entertaining the folk around. Clearly the 'character' of this section of the ground, he sports the home club's shirt and keeps up a rapid-fire narrative of his four days in the mountains somewhere – '. . . great place – cheap food, cheap booze, good fishing – I only cut it short to come here . . .' which he punctuates with occasional fog-horn references to the game – '*Bloody Morientes! Get off the park!*' – sort of stuff. In fact he seems to have it in for Madrid's centre-forward, but his insults only seem to attract amusement. The husband and wife to his left are well dressed and wealthy looking, but the meritocracy of compulsory seating has brought these various types together, as it has all over Europe, and they would seem to be enjoying their fortnightly social encounter. They are from different backgrounds, I would guess, but the bald chap has the brash confidence of the self-made man, and his role as entertainer seems to cut across the class divide. Then the target of his one-liners opens the scoring on 20 minutes. Figo idles down the right-hand channel, in a direct line with my seat, swings the ball over with a whip of his instep and Morientes, flying in from outside the penalty area, connects with the ball like a speeding train and powers the ball into the net with his head. He runs over to salute the crowd immediately below us, but Baldy, not wishing to be outdone, shouts '*Imbécil!*' over the din, and breaks out into an alarming cackle.

The odd thing is that when you go to watch a side like Real Madrid, whose players are all household names, it comes as something of a shock to find that there are supporters who consider some of these demi-gods to have feet of clay, and who call them 'imbeciles'. Having been brought up on English lower-division fare, it seems inconceivable that here, in Madrid of all places, they can doubt their abilities, especially after such a fine goal. But everything is relative. I try to put myself in these supporters' shoes, bred on top-flight football, year in year out, and how they must inevitably develop a sixth sense for seeing the chinks in the armour, the hairline fractures in the players' temperaments, the smallest defects in their otherwise impeccable breeding. For that is how the players appear to me, especially the ones wearing white. They seem like shiny expensive racehorses, strong and sleek. They seem to inhabit a different dimension, as if their perfect bodies have been cloned to carry out to perfection this strangely captivating game that one plays with a leather ball. Those that I watched in my youth, in the old English Fourth Division, were of a comparatively scraggy biological composition, from a gene pond, as opposed to a pool. So if there is some problem with Morientes, I cannot see it. He looks pretty good to me.

Zidane looks even better. He spends an alarmingly short time with the ball for a player of such repute, and yet it is precisely this quality that lends him his greatness. I focus on him for several minutes as Las Palmas come out of their shells and begin to probe for an equaliser, and his long, elegant, slow-motion lope makes him look like a giraffe running with some calm intent. He keeps running into spaces that the others vacate, halting momentarily to assess the likely direction of the current move then adjusting his lope accordingly. Sometimes he simply stops, watches the play going on around him, and appears to take notes. His balding tonsure lends him an air of quiet, monk-like dignity, and I am reminded of Bobby Charlton, a player who operated in similar ways to the Frenchman. Like all the greats before him, Zidane's studious reading of the game and his instant relationship with the ball make him look as though he has all the time in the world – an observation made of all the best midfielders and defenders. But more interestingly, as the Las Palmas players flit around insubstantially in their gawky yellow and blue, Zidane appears to suit the Real Madrid colours to perfection. It seems inconceivable that he ever wore any other kit, even the blue of his national shirt. Whereas the black and white of Juventus distracted your eye from the player himself, in Madrid's simple uniform his qualities stand out, and match the clean, uncomplicated approach he has to the game. Cliché it may be, but he is a pleasure to watch. Every time he gets the ball there is a curious buzz that hovers around the ground, a slight shifting forward of bodies, a movement of feet. Zidane, just over the halfway line and moving over to the left, takes a long forward pass from Helguera and lets it run slightly, accelerating to the pace of the ball. He suddenly changes direction and heads diagonally for the goal, causing panic in the visitors' defence. Before they can regroup he cuts into the area in that curious lope and slots the ball gently with his left foot through a forest of legs into the bottom corner of the net. From nothing, he conjures a goal, and the wit behind me is more enthusiastic this time, with good reason. He stands up, applauding wildly: '*Así se hace coño! Así se hace!*' (That's how to play football! That's how you do it!) adding, just in case this were a shade too positive, '*Has visto eso Morientes? Así se hace!*' (Did you see that Morientes? That's the way to do it!).

Two minutes later, Morientes appears to take this advice. Figo, prowling down his favoured right channel, gets down almost to the byeline before trying to slip the ball around the Las Palmas defender Josico, to get in one of his trademark whipped-in crosses. As he shimmies, the ball runs loose, but Josico, tracking Figo's run, fatally turns his back on the great man, and the ball bounces off his ankle back to Figo. The latter immediately swings over a cross onto the penalty spot and Morientes, somehow anticipating the sudden arrival of the ball, hangs majestically in the air before flicking his neck and pounding a header into the net with murderous power. As the ball ripples the net it all seems too perfect, like one of those ridiculous goals drawn by a comic artist for an old-fashioned boys' magazine. I keep waiting for someone to turn on the lights, but the goal is for real. The whole incident seems beautiful in its simplicity, and Las Palmas wilt. There will be no way back for them.

At half-time, the other Englishman in the cast trots on in his tracksuit and plays keepie-ups with two of the other Madrid substitutes. Steve McManaman, though he owns a racehorse, does not resemble one, and looks oddly out of place in this solid arena of tradition and victory. The Liverpudlian looks skinny and undernourished, like a young boy who has borrowed the club tracksuit and sneaked onto the pitch to play with his heroes. He is playing near the dugout with Celades and Solari, but it is clear that he is perfectly comfortable in the surroundings. From a distance, he seems to be permanently laughing and recording the points scored by the three – the rules of the game appear to reward the last not to lose control of the ball and let it fall to the ground. Celades starts and flicks it to the Englishman, who controls it on his knee, lets it drop to his right foot then knocks it across to Solari, but a shade too far to be considered fair. Solari wags a finger, and McManaman turns to the crowd behind him and makes a mock appeal, waving his arms in true Spanish fashion. The noble, rather intimidating institution that is Real Madrid would appear to have accepted a little Anglo-Saxon eccentricity, and 'Macca', as he is referred to, looks happy enough. As their game continues, I tense every time the ball floats across to him because I am convinced, after several years of watching Spanish football, that English players have inferior technique, and I am horrified that McManaman may illustrate this every time it is his turn to deal with a pass. To my relief, he does surprisingly well, and as they go off, he is obviously comparing points with Celades and pointing mockingly at poor Solari. Whatever, if his teammates manage some more goals, he should see some action later.

A curious flute-like noise announces the half-time scores on the screen perched atop the Northern Stand, and it is interesting to note the crowd's reactions. Atlético Madrid, playing at home but out on the industrial banks of the Manzanares River against Salamanca, are a goal down – a score that produces laughter and wild applause. Atlético, who have had their moments historically, are currently leading the Second Division table, and should be back next year. Meanwhile, it would appear that there is little nostalgia felt for the absence of the city '*derbi*'. Real Sociedad are beating Zaragoza 2–0, and this one produces a low rumble of boos and some muttered '*Putos vascos*' (fucking Basques) as a little bit of politics comes into the reckoning.

Since the family to my right have gone off for a half-time coffee and left the coast clear for me to take a short stroll, I walk over to where a wall separates my section from the Ultras Sur supporters, gathered behind the goal. I peer cautiously down onto the shaven heads, as if peering over the edge of one of Dante's circles, about to witness the hellish scene below. But all is quiet on the southern front. There seem to be disappointingly few of them, but this is possibly an illusion created by the order of seating. Few of them, however, are actually sitting down, and several are waving an assortment of flags. I pick out a Union Jack, the lilac and white flag of the autonomous region of Madrid, the Spanish flag and an assortment of smaller ones whose colours and designs do not register with me. A shaven-headed tubby young man beats a drum from time to time and hollers 'Hala Madrid' in a half-ironic attempt to ape Plácido Domingo, but he seems happy. Another skinhead close to the wall and directly below me sports a lilac scarf with the anti-Barcelona slogan 'Club anti-Culé', to the side of which is a cartoon of a large boot crushing a Catalan head. But it seems to me, at a quick glance at least, that most of this allegedly fearful gathering look as though butter wouldn't melt in their mouths, and apart from one or two genuinely scary-looking individuals, they look as though they'll all be going home to mum's for supper after the game.

In the second half, Las Palmas dutifully wilt and show no stomach for the fight. With the score at 6–0 after 77 minutes and the crowd indulging in Mexican waves, McManaman replaces Figo. Within a couple of minutes, Morientes heads in the seventh, recording his fifth – only the 21st player to do so in the Spanish league since its inception in 1928, the first since Valladolid's Peternac in 1995 and, of course, the first to do it this century. Baldy behind is still playing to the crowd however, and when the applause dies down shouts 'Bueno hombre! Hoy has tenido suerte!' (OK man – you got lucky today!). There may be some truth in this, but astonishingly, four minutes later, the little Cantabrian, Munitis, on for a tiring Zidane, is pulled down in the penalty area. Just when the poor Las Palmas players thought it couldn't get any worse . . . the crowd begin to chant Morientes' name (he is not the usual penalty taker) and McManaman playfully pushes him over to the spot. The young striker shrugs and stands on the point of history. Only two players have scored six in a game in the entire history of the Spanish league, both in the early 1940s, and only Bata and the great Kubala have scored seven. But in the face of all this, Fernando Morientes seems apologetic, almost reluctant to heap more misery on poor Nacho Gonzáles in the Las

Palmas goal, and shunning history taps the ball to the keeper's left. The Argentine has all the time in the world to dive slowly down and thus recover a bit of the dignity lost over the previous 85 minutes.

No one has been booked, and no one has been sent off. A curious game, for that reason alone. Moments before the final whistle, the crowd begin to sing '*Así, así, así gana el Madrid*' (That's how Madrid win), deliberately mocking those around the country who chant these same lines in order to discredit the slickers from the capital, accusing them of being favoured by referees, being poor losers, and being downright lucky. But the centenary boys-to-be have looked rather good today, without ever moving into top gear. Every time they attacked, the ball ended up in the net. It seemed appropriate somehow, I reflect, as the folk disperse down the dark streets either side of the stadium and Las Palmas supporters drift past, trying to put a brave face on it. It really wouldn't do to see out 100 years with an ordinary game, to put too much pressure on the team to pull off one last thudding victory in the potentially awkward game against Alavés in two weeks' time. They have answered the call of history, going out with a bang and not a whimper. They've set themselves up nicely, and I was lucky enough to have been there.

Real Sociedad v. Real Madrid
27 April 2002

Ten weeks later, on a balmy April evening on the northern coast in San Sebastián, Real Madrid run out onto the colourful late-night floodlit scene dressed in an all-black strip. But they are not in mourning just yet. They can still win two of their three original objectives for the centenary year, the national and the Champions League. The painful blow of 6 March, when they were surprisingly taken apart on their biggest night by Deportivo de La Coruña (1–2) at the Bernabéu, has been softened somewhat by the events of four days previously when they outwitted Barcelona in a rare win at the Camp Nou in the first leg of the Champions League semi-final. Valencia are still a point ahead in the league, but with three games to go, the double is still on. But Valencia have an easy one at home to Espanyol this evening, and Madrid would probably have chosen a friendlier place to go for this league game – the one that is sandwiched between their two colossal heavyweight challenges with Barcelona. Due to regional TV broadcasting, the game is on late – 9.30 in the evening – giving the Basques the whole day to prepare their special welcome. Madrid wave rather lamely from the centre circle, but to whom? In other regions they can count on a certain number of friends, but here they are alone, isolated by historical events with which their current players have no connection, picked out by the floodlights in a glare of hostility, drowning in a sea of whistles.

Anoeta, Real Sociedad's newish municipal stadium, has a curving roof in the shape of a wave and looks very beautiful, the inky sky above contrasting with the riot of colour below. The old stadium, Atocha, backed onto the railway station and was a small, broken-down affair, but its intimacy put the fear of God into sides like Madrid. Anoeta is postmodern Basque, an attempt to smooth down the rough edges of their country-cousin reputation and present themselves as a more dynamic community of aesthetes. But it hasn't worked. The running track around the stadium has distanced the supporters from the action, and for all its beauty, the atmosphere is colder. Well, normally. Tonight the place is packed to the rafters, and as the home side run out, it's to a raucous, ticker-tape welcome. Whereas against Las Palmas in February, Madrid emerged to the traditional operatic strains of *'Hala Madrid!'* here they crouch for the press photograph accosted by the blare of *'Beti beti maite . . .'* (Always always love), a curious child-like ditty sung in a language that none of their players understand. As they break for the warm-up, the PA system hammers out an urgent message to the crowd, in Basque of course, reminding them that Real Sociedad need to win this game to assure themselves of top-flight football next season, and the continuation of this kind of spectacle. The threat of relegation still looms, after another poor season. The players are fired-up and there has been talk in the press all week of how the game plan will be to *Machacar* Madrid (pummel them, physically) and generally make their visit an uncomfortable one.

This is the city I have lived in for 12 years, and to some extent I understand its complicated culture. But the one-track hatred that always manifests itself when Real Madrid visit cannot help but depress me slightly, though I understand its function. Some of Madrid's players, particularly Zidane, look slightly bemused by the whole thing – which is saying something, four days after playing in the Camp Nou. I feel slightly sorry for them, in that feathery English way, but I desist from saying so. The man to my right, a well-dressed, bespectacled gentleman in his late 50s, with the white-haired dignity of a university professor, has already demonstrated exactly why it is best to keep quiet. Roberto Carlos, Madrid's Brazilian star, trips up the local boy Lopez-Rekarte, and the professor to my right hurls forth a barrage of abuse not just at Carlos but at the wider world in general, outside of the Basque Country. *'Book the black bastard! That's how they've come to play! That's how they always play. Bunch of tossers!'* I cast him a wan smile, but he's beyond subliminal messages. Tonight it's black and white, and we can forget the grey areas.

Madrid are without their hard-man captain Hierro, Guti is injured and Morientes, who ran riot the last time I saw his team in the flesh, has also stayed at home. The tiny Munitis is playing alone up front, with Raúl in the 'hole' behind him. But the tactic is a strange one, given that Sociedad's well-known defensive frailty resides in the manifest inability of their central defenders to head the ball. Munitis, a skilful but somewhat unpredictable individualist, is the sort of man they can cope with. He is a raggedy sort of player, with tiny legs and a huge head, like a cartoon caricature. Raúl would be better off leading the line, with Munitis behind him, and my know-it-all thoughts are confirmed when Figo at last gets to the byeline and swings the ball across. The Basques freeze, as they have done all season, and Raúl misses the curling cross by a whisker. The little episode quietens the crowd down, as they collectively recall that they are playing one of the best sides in Europe.

The game settles into a pattern on the half-hour, Sociedad concentrating their attacks down the right flank, so that Roberto Carlos cannot get free to do his thing. Lopez-Rekarte, the Basque right-back, is overlapping and causing him some problems, so that Zidane and Raúl are starved of the ball. Figo looks strangely out of sorts, and is wandering around in an inside-right position. He was absent from what was probably the biggest club event in Europe since 1960 – the last time that Real and Barça met in the European Cup, when the Catalans put paid to Madrid's unbeaten run of five European Cups on the trot. Getting himself booked for arguing in the second leg of the game against Bayern Munich, the rumours are that he didn't fancy another evening of abuse in Barcelona, where he has had to arrange for private security every time he visits his ex-employers. Against Las Palmas he was sublime, unstoppable. Here, he looks tired, as if he's a bit fed-up of the whole circus. It's a good sign for Sociedad.

Just before half-time, some supporters to my left have stood up and leaned down towards the lower tier, sticking up their middle-fingers in a friendly salute to a couple of Madrid fans who must have let their identity slip. Apart from the players and the technical staff, the only other followers of Madrid today are Jorge Valdano and Alfredo Di Stéfano, invited to partake of some Basque cuisine after the game by the host's sensible young president. But as for the supporters, even the Ultra Sur give San Sebastián (and Bilbao) a miss, and I once spoke to a family from Madrid who told me that when they drove to Paris they would take the longer route up through Catalonia and east of the Pyrenees, anything to avoid the fearsome Basques. The place terrified them, and they were at a loss to understand how I could possibly be living there. And now that a couple of foolhardy travellers have had their cover blown, two numbskulls appear from nowhere, and with nothing better to do with their testosterone begin to block my view as they lean over the railing and try to pick out the poor aliens below. Since the game is still in full-flow, I lean forward and tap one of the youths on the shoulder, indicating that I would like to watch the game. The boy, no older than 16, turns on me and starts to rant *'Es que no estas animando tío! Que te pasa? Venga!'* (What's the matter mate? You're not supporting us?), as if my objection has been based on some unacceptable neutrality. Not wanting to begin a fight I cannot win, I shout above the din that I can only support the team if I can see the game, an argument that seems to win the day. He skulks off with his friend, to await another opportunity to seek out the aliens and destroy.

Half-time arrives with the score at 0–0, but it has been an entertaining half. Madrid have not looked as comfortable as when I saw them last, but the circumstances are radically altered. Nevertheless, the general level of technique of their players and the lurking threat in some of their movements have presaged an interesting half to come, especially given the surprising announcement on the PA that Valencia are losing 0–1 at home to Espanyol. If Madrid can win this, they could be back on track for the league.

Two minutes into the second half and little Munitis, although he cannot know it, contributes to the further melting of the icing on the cake that the club has been so desperate to eat this year, after a century of gorging themselves on the stuff below. Raúl, at last given some space, runs at the home defence and panics them into a temporary disarray that leaves Munitis inside the box with an open goal. Inexplicably, he hesitates, as if waiting for the defence to gather round – and when they do he chips the ball adroitly, but too late, onto the top of the bar and down into the goalkeeper's grateful arms. The crowd jerk forward and backward as if one, letting out a low mutter of relief and laughing nervously, conscious of the enormity of the escape. Munitis, a bit-part player this year who will probably be on his way at the end of the season, has just blown the big chance.

Five minutes later, Michel Salgado, Madrid's solid if unspectacular right-back, is pulled off to avoid his collecting another booking. The affable and wise old campaigner, manager Vicente del Bosque – white blood pumping through his veins – has made an uncharacteristic mistake. He brings on Geremi, the Cameroon midfielder, and puts him at full-back, with the clear instruction to push up onto Sociedad's left flank and to bring Figo into the game. But Geremi's distribution is so poor that he immediately breaks up the links in the chain and puts his side on the back foot. Far from bringing Figo into the game, he gets in his way, apart from which he is leaving a whole empty motorway of space behind him. Sensing the sudden fault-line, Sociedad's left side, where its classiest campaigners Aranzabal and De Pedro reside, is suddenly freed from the shackles that Salgado's sensible positional play has been imposing on them. Aranzabal roars down the flank, cuts inside, and is shoved in the chest by Helguera. The ref points to the spot and the place goes wild. It goes even wilder when the Yugoslav Kovasevic drills home the penalty, low and hard to César's left. It's the beginning of the end. Over in Valencia, the league leaders, down to ten men, have equalised, and it would seem that the gods are conspiring against Madrid. The black shirts continue to argue with the referee, and the self-control is about to go.

Nevertheless, they try to get back on terms, but a whole section of their zonal strategy is simply no longer there. Javier de Pedro, the Basques' inconsistent but quick-witted midfielder, has drifted over to the left and is beginning to toy with the hapless Geremi. Zidane is lost in combat, presumed missing. It's not entirely his fault, of course, but every time he gets near the ball the Basques, roared on by a crowd sensing blood, simply hound him down and dispossess him. The contrast with his elegant dominance of Las Palmas is, as they say, eloquent. He starts to look tetchy, and his movements are less measured, less refined. Only when Raúl gets the ball do the home crowd begin to flutter, and he justifies their respect of him by suddenly breaking clear and rasping the bar with a shot out of nowhere. Europe's finest forward, whatever the English say of Michael Owen. But Europe's finest is not getting much of a touch, and Madrid's pack of cards is about to collapse. Khokhlov, the Russian midfielder, who has spent the season wandering whimsically around the park showing occasional touches of genius, reserves his best for poor Madrid. He too has seen that the left side is the place to be, and cuts in, pretends to shoot, then unleashes a quick-fire shot across Helguera that flashes past César and in at the near post. The normally reserved Russian does a jig and storms onto the running track, milking the applause. The black-shirted visitors look at each other, disconsolate. Time is running out on the dream.

Ten minutes later and it's all over bar the shouting. With Madrid reeling, completely disorganised and their right side cut open like a gaping wound, the substitute De Paula sticks out a foot at Rekarte's cross and the ball flies in off a post. The place erupts. Starved of goals all season, the home supporters stagger around, drunk with joy at this sudden and unexpected bonanza, all the more wonderful for coming against the demons from the capital. And of course, it practically saves them from relegation. A point from the next two games should see them home and dry. Over in Valencia, things have got worse. Playing with ten men for the whole second half, the league leaders have nevertheless beaten Espanyol 2–1. The cold arithmetic will not be lost on Madrid's players as they sit miserably in their dressing-room, since a four-point gap has now opened up, with just two games to play. Still, the Champions League trophy could be a reasonable form of compensation, just so long as Barcelona don't get uppity on Wednesday night and Bayer Leverkusen prove to be weaker than they looked when drawing 2–2 at Old Trafford.

Football – what a strange phenomenon. The way it can galvanise communities never ceases to amaze, especially in Spain. Through the darkened streets tonight, San Sebastián is buoyant, the dragon is slain, and everyone is smiling. It's a long way across the city so I hail a taxi, but the driver is in no mood for analytical chat. 'We stuffed them. I saw it on the telly. They didn't have the balls. They don't like it up them.' To this volley of conviction I suggest that if Munitis had scored, it could have been different. 'Well, he didn't,' he says firmly, thwacking the steering-wheel, 'and we stuffed them. God I'm happy!'

The two sides of the coin, the *cara* and the *cruz*. Madrid in the Bernabéu was a celebration of superior breeding, an arrogant and merciless display of power worthy of the club's reputation. Here, battered and shipwrecked on the rocks, miles from home, they suddenly looked small. The giant has feet of clay, and the taxi driver can work through the night with a contented smile. But I'm not so sure. I'm somewhere in the middle, closer to Madrid through the inevitable process of familiarisation that writing a book on someone tends to bring. I like them better for their weakness, but they probably wouldn't thank me for telling them so.

2. MADRID, MADRILEÑOS AND MADRIDISTAS

Modesty is not on the agenda at Real Madrid. Some clubs might choose to describe themselves as historic, homely, friendly, small or even successful, but only one seems to have the true derring-do to describe itself as 'the best'. Besides, the phrase has official backing. At the end of the twentieth century, FIFA decided, on the grounds of 8 European Cups and 28 League Championships alone (there is more), that the club had earned the title 'The Best Club of the Twentieth Century'. This endorsement of what Real Madrid supporters have always known, apart from mere statistics, cannot but help to further affect those who choose to support the club, and indeed the whole community of Madrid, whatever that is.

The folk who follow Real Madrid, either through choice or inheritance, cannot be wired in quite the same way as supporters of Getafe or Leganes, two teams from the working-class southern suburbs of the city who have never won a trophy between them. In fact they are unlikely to be configured in the same way as any other set of supporters, a fact immediately supported by the different scene over at Atlético Madrid. The very fact that the Bernabéu sits on the prestigious Avenida Castellana whereas Atlético's Calderón stadium edges the industrial banks of the Manzanares River, out by an old gasworks, tells you something straightaway. There are other clubs in Spain, and indeed, in most of Europe, who live off this social divide – Betis and Sevilla come to mind, Barcelona and Espanyol, as do FC Porto and Boavista in Portugal, Juventus and Torino in Italy and so on. But none of the more successful of these pairings can boast of the trophies that Real Madrid have locked into their cabinets, a fact that immediately sets their supporters apart. It is difficult to imagine them ever tolerating a trophy-less season. This has happened, of course, and the side even flirted with relegation in the 1947–48 season, but this tiny aberration, this little worm in an orchard otherwise groaning with fruit, has been the only occasion, to mix a metaphor, on which the giants displayed anything approaching feet of clay. In England, the relegation of Manchester United in the 1970s seemed seminal enough – as if the world were ending and the traditional order of the cosmos was being threatened, but the absence of Real Madrid from the Spanish top flight simply belongs to another space-time continuum. The proposition, such as it is, has no logic.

I vaguely remember the club as a child, and their exploits are recorded dimly in my head in the staccato black and white of the old *Pathe News* footage. They were certainly present in playground lore, and my contemporaries and I seemed aware that they were a great team, better perhaps than even the best English teams – at that time Manchester United and Leeds. My memories of Real Madrid pre-date my fear of Leeds and their seemingly white invincibility, but the colours of the two sides paired off in my mind, as if that solid choice of white had been something terribly exclusive and destined. To support the team, to actually watch and follow such an institution, seemed to me quite mysterious – bred as I was on English lower-division fare. As such, I have grown into a person who welcomes success (the relative type) but who does not expect it. Neither do I see it as a necessary or defining aspect of the friends I choose or of the games I myself get to play. It's not a question of losers and winners – a dumbed-down version of life, I'm convinced, but more a matter of keeping things in perspective. Twelve years in Spain have definitely taught me to be a bit more competitive, a little less forgiving and Corinthian (if that really is the English way) and a bit more abrasive, but it's partly a case of playing to the gallery, of wanting to be accepted. When in Rome, and all that stuff. But Real Madrid seem to have taken things a step further. What would represent a dream for most Spanish professional clubs can be a crisis at the Bernabéu, such as finishing runners-up in the league, or even worse, finishing below Barcelona on the last day of the season. Managers have been sacked for the latter crime, and for other slip-ups such as winning the European Cup (Jupp Heynckes), winning the league title (Vincente Del Bosque), being a little too well spoken (Jorge Valdano), or being 'too defensive' – an accusation levelled at John Toshack when he managed the team, with a rampant Hugo Sánchez, that won the Spanish league in 1989 with a record number of goals scored. A demanding public, one might say, and one so well fed and bloated on success that nothing less than the best will do. It is an odd mindset, and one that may not be entirely healthy, at least from the point of view of the outsider. Indeed, the Real Madrid supporter is not a popular being in the view of those outside of the church of *Madridismo* (Madridism), and the club is despised in the manner of most successful clubs, particularly in the areas of Spain that harbour regional nationalist sentiments.

FC Barcelona, another institution who consider themselves to be special and 'more than a club', to quote that tired phrase, are different in the sense that they appear to court popularity, and are convinced that the world loves and admires them. They are wrong, of course, but the idea is quite an endearing one. Manchester United, although they feign indifference, have never convinced me on this issue, and I'll swear that they too want to be loved, at the bottom of their brittle hearts. But both cities, although they are supposed to be exciting and although they are supposed to have recently signalled the more interesting post-modern cultural pathways of their respective countries, are a little cold, a little too full of themselves. In Spain, Barcelona may still be where it's at, but the citizens are a trifle too condescending for my taste, a little too convinced that they're at the centre of things. Madrid, on the other hand, which is seen as old-fashioned, more glum and staid, more right-wing, less avant-garde, is actually a friendlier, more open place. If its rather darker, more grandiose architecture seems to suggest a less friendly disposition, nothing could be further from the truth, down at ground level. This may have something to do with the make-up of the average *Madrileño* nowadays, much as one might comment on the contemporary make-up of London and Paris. Though a relatively smaller city in terms of population, it has been subject over the years to a gradual influx of citizens both from the provinces and from other countries that has changed its internal character forever. Being so much more of a pot-pourri than before, it has become more than a little facile to accuse the *Madrileños* of being *chulos* – that wonderful Spanish adjective that has a thousand meanings, depending on context, region, and what you are referring to. But those associated with the club, at any rate, are still seen as 'big-headed', and 'full of themselves', if these are really satisfactory translations of the word. Outside the Bernabéu on the day of the match against Las Palmas, I noticed a white T-shirt for sale hanging from one of the stalls. It proclaimed: '*No soy solo perfecto – soy Madridista también*' (I'm not just perfect – I'm a *Madridista* too).

There used to be a refrain from outside of the city's own culture that went '*Madrileño, culo pequeño*' (*Madrileño*, small arse) – although there seems to have been no great significance to this beyond the fact that it rhymed. No one has been able to explain to me satisfactorily why a person from Madrid having a small bottom is a problem, and indeed, one would have thought it was quite the opposite. Whatever, the refrain changed to *'chulo pequeño'*, which means 'small but cocky', slightly more meaningful but still rather strange. The classic image of the old-style *Madrileño* certainly contains the 'cocky', but not the small. Madrid, as we will come to see, has always considered itself as *castizo* – a loaded word related to 'caste' which speaks of a noble descent, of a pure blood-line uncontaminated by the later waves of more dusky foreigners. It is what certain old-style Madrid folk would still consider themselves to be, unashamedly right-wing and proud of it, church-on-Sunday, parochial and unconcerned with life outside the city walls. Madrid, after all, is at the centre of things. The area known as Chamberi, north of the centre of the city, is still considered to be the *barrio* (neighbourhood) from which the most *castizo Madrileño* hails, the male version a tall, well-dressed gentleman with a good crop of cultivated facial hair – not a dandy moustache like Dali's but one that bespeaks a respectable family man.

Juan Padrós, elected president of the club on 6 March 1902, was not from Chamberi but nevertheless fitted the stereotype perfectly. The sepia portrait of Padrós that dates back to the foundation year of Real Madrid shows a serious-looking chap with an alarming beard, wide enough to nest the brood of an eagle. He stares at the camera like a schoolmaster unwilling to tolerate fools. This is the stuff that men were made of, the portrait suggests, with expressions that would send undesirables scurrying back to the slums from whence they came. Whatever administrative or leadership virtues Padrós possessed as a president it was surely more relevant that the first man to take the official reins had a decent beard. His stern demeanour stares down through the generations, guaranteeing the club the importance of a serious *castizo* blood-line. The fact that Padrós was actually a Catalan is an unfortunate irony that tends to be swept under the carpet of the official histories of the club, but more of that later. For the time being, we are concerned with images. Padrós (and the decent fellows who turned out for those first games for 'Madrid Foot Ball Club', as it was then called) would have eaten their *callos y cocido* for Sunday lunch come hell or high water. Lashings of tripe and onions followed by a bucketful of chickpeas floating in a stew stuffed with sausages and veal. The stuff that champions were bred on, and ne'er a drop would have found its way onto those beards, perish the thought! This was an era, it should be remembered, in which Spain was still very much a backward nation in economic terms, a country that had retained intact its most prized value systems – those of austerity, sobriety and dignity – all three of whose elements formed the opposite of what a more materialistically oriented nation might have come to nurture. Madrid was in the centre, so Madrid marked the template. That slightly haughty, dignified look is the seed of the club, the old portraits imply, and the subsequent break-up of Madrid's more traditional social structure and ways of life does not mean that in the bricks and mortar of the modern Bernabéu, the old ways are forever buried. The centenary in 2002 was a ritual, an implication of continuity.

It follows from the above that the Spanish are keen on image and symbolism, and the Puerto del Sol, very much the historic symbol of the city, marks the very centre of Spain. All things emanate from this point, the heart of the country. The further away one travels from it, of course, the more distant this idea of Spain becomes, especially up in the wilds of the Basque Country or in the fashionable streets of Barcelona. The weather changes, the languages change, the smell and the texture of the air are distinct and Real Madrid metamorphose into something akin to the Great Satan. But the true *chulo* doesn't care. An essential part of *chulería* is being thick-skinned and proud of it.

Accusations that Real Madrid are favoured by referees, that they were favoured by Franco, that they kept the dictator in power, that they are propped up by a corrupt municipal council and fail to discourage the neo-Nazi element among their younger supporters are all water off a duck's back to the true *Madridista*. In the week leading up to the centenary date of 6 March, the Spanish President, José María Aznar, a centre-right politician with an occasional moustache that bears an unfortunate resemblance to the one sported by Hitler, was invited to dinner by the Real Madrid hierarchy. Barcelona's president that year, Joan Gaspart, over in Italy to see his side trounced 3–0 by Roma, made a fuss in the papers the next day about the dinner, implying, in the traditional Catalan style, that this was further evidence that the club was in cahoots with the government. This was an unfortunate accusation, harking back as it did to the days when Real Madrid and Franco were alleged to be intimate bedfellows. The Argentine Jorge Valdano, distinguished ex-player and manager, now turned spokesman and general manager of the club, replied smoothly that as Aznar had been a paid-up member of the club since he was seven years of age, and since he had never made a secret of his following the team, then what exactly was the problem? Several of Madrid's more prominent players also spoke out, claiming that Aznar had the right to follow the club he chose, just as his predecessor, Felipe Gonzáles, had been an unashamed supporter of Betis. Besides, both presidents, in following these clubs, were being true to their roots – a crucial factor in Spanish cultural rulebooks.

The official reaction from the club – that they were doing nothing wrong – is the key to understanding the *Madrileño* mentality. For them, the country's leader had every right to sup with his mates at the club's top table, as if the rest of the country were somehow not there – as if the rest of the country were being paranoid in their reaction to this harmless little example of *Madridismo*. The only possible English parallel would be to imagine how the rest of the Premier League would feel if Blair were to be seen to be openly courting Manchester United. The Old Trafford club do not represent Manchester culture in the same way as Real Madrid represent theirs, and Blair is not from Manchester, but nevertheless, the business and political implications of such an act on the part of a British Prime Minister would be far too serious to contemplate. Mancunians themselves would be unlikely to endorse such an act.

So the question has to be – what are the modern Madrid folk like? What is it that defines them, that gives them this siege mentality? In order to shed some light on the question I spoke to an 'expatriate' *Madrileño*, resident in the north in San Sebastián, about how the rest of Spain sees Madrid and vice-versa. Despite living in the Basque Country for 30 years, he still considers himself a *Madrileño* – a rather more loaded term that describes a person committed to a cause, in this case, the cause of Real Madrid. The exile's roots go deep. His brother was a well-known journalist on *El País*, Spain's most prestigious and respected newspaper, and he was brought up not far from Chamberi. Now a prominent businessman, he explained the issue to me apparently without bias, blessed as he was with the double perspective:

> People from outside Madrid, especially those up here – they've always said that we're obsessed with centralising everything, with bringing everything to the capital, to the centre. But down there they don't understand what all the fuss is about. Sure – the Basque Country and Catalonia were important economically long before Madrid, but now we all have to do things much more quickly, more efficiently. *Hombre* – it's logical. If your company starts to expand, you want to put an office in Madrid. It makes sense. Where are you going to stick it? In some two-horse town in

Extremadura? And once you get a foot into Madrid, you find that it makes things easier for you. It's in the middle of the country, and it's easier to get to. You try flying from Madrid to San Sebastián! You have to book months in advance.

I asked him if he missed living in the city permanently.

In some ways yes, but now I'm married, if you see what I mean. But there's no doubt about what I would do if I had my time again. You just can't compare it to a place like this. San Sebastián's very beautiful, but it takes years here to be accepted as one of the crowd. It's the same in Barcelona. You ask any young student which city is the more welcoming, in which city you can make friends almost immediately, and they'll tell you Madrid. Barcelona has this reputation for being trendy, for being an open, cosmopolitan sort of place, but it's a myth. I'm not just saying that because I support Real Madrid. They're all right, the Catalans, but they're like one big cartel. They don't really let you in. They just pretend to. They'd never do that to you in Madrid. And it wouldn't matter where you were from. I think *Madrileños* accept people as they are. They've always had to. It's a result of being there in the middle, of constantly having had folk passing through. The Basques here think that they spend all their time down there hating the provincials, but it's not true. They're just not that interested. They prefer to get on with having a good time. They're more hedonistic. They've got more *marcha* (get-up-and-go).

'But Real Madrid still have this *baddy* image,' I insisted.

Of course. But that's the same of most capitals. The French all hate the Parisians – they don't even consider them to be French. They've told me the same in England when I go there – that London doesn't represent the country in any way. My elder kid's at school in Yorkshire now. I've been up there, to York and around. It's a different planet, sure, but that doesn't mean London's got nothing to offer. It's a great city. Who cares about what it represents? It functions as a capital, and if the Londoners don't know what it's like in York then that's their problem. I didn't get the impression that York or wherever was damaged by this.

'But the club. Not the city so much. The club are the baddies, no?'

It's because people lump them together, and that's natural. They're probably right. But look at the club now. Pérez [the president] is a clever guy. He keeps a low profile, gets the club out of debt and gets Valdano and Butragueño to do all the talking, because they're better at it than him. He's smart. He keeps his head down. Gaspart [Barcelona's president] is an awful guy. He has no idea about PR, and you can see the results. The club's changed from being a flagship to a madhouse. They're all twitching uncontrollably. It's like a study in neurosis, like watching an Almodóvar movie. It was the same at Madrid a few years ago when Sanz was the president. All he wanted was to use the club to further his own business interests, and people knew it. They're not stupid. He had a poor public persona. He was *chulo* in the worst sense of the word and worse, he looked like a *mafioso*. The whole thing was a disaster, despite the Champions League stuff. That just papered over the cracks. But Pérez is bright, and he looks like a history teacher or something – like a decent guy. He doesn't look like a *chulo*. The other thing is that he means it. He has this idea, for the centenary celebrations, to load up a sort of travelling circus about the club's last hundred years and take it around the country, so that everyone can share in the glory. It's hilarious! He's either innocent or bloody-minded, but I think it's a bit of both.

'You mean it's not going to go down too well in Barcelona and Bilbao?' This provokes an outburst of laughter.

Go down well? They'd have to take it in an armoured car and surround it with *Guardia Civil*! But you see the point. There are some *Madridistas*, and I doubt that it was really Pérez's initiative, who would simply not see this. Despite everything that's gone on in this country, they still think there's no problem. Maybe they're right. Maybe it would be nice to do it – you never know.

'And the fascist thing?'

Look – the club's done a lot to throw off that *facha* [fascist] thing. There's not a lot you can do about kids who want to be Ultras, but you've been there yourself, you know it's OK. The Atlético [Madrid] thing is much worse, stabbing that guy from here*, and all the Nazi stuff that goes on around the stadium. Apart from Franco, they've got much clearer historical links with fascism. After the Civil War they were called *Aviacíon* [Air Force] for God's sake. They were stocked up with the best players from the military. The Atlético Ultras are proud of it too. They think that the Ultra Sur fans from Real Madrid are a load of *maricas* [poofs]. And yet if you talk to people from outside Spain, the only so-called hooligans they've heard of are Ultra Sur. The Atlético fans are probably right actually. Ultra Sur wouldn't last five minutes at Arsenal or somewhere. Real Madrid's a middle-class club. It's basically *pijo* [posh]. If you're truly working class and you support Real Madrid then you have to spend all your time apologising to your mates.

'But didn't the same thing happen as in Catalonia, when all the post-war immigrants saw Barcelona as the team to support, because by doing so they would be accepted? Espanyol was the working-class team, but they didn't go near them.'

Sort of, but not quite. What you had in Madrid was a much more gradual process of immigration. It didn't all happen overnight. So people set up their own cultures, like you get with Rayo Vallecano, in the Vallecas neighbourhood [of Madrid]. Now that's working class, and proud of it. They wouldn't be seen dead in the Bernabéu. Then again, Real Madrid have always tried to be a bit exclusive, to be fair to what you're saying. I mean that Madrid is an open city, but maybe the club has always been a bit snootier. You can't pack as many in as they do at the Camp Nou anyway! Look – Catalan culture is much more complex. You have to be Catalan or that's it. You've had it. That's why Espanyol only has about 16,000 members, because it never took off as a phenomenon there, as an alternative. Atlético and Rayo have got a lot more between them. There was always more choice in

---

* He was referring to the stabbing of the Real Sociedad supporter, Aitor Zabaleta, by a member of the now defunct 'Bastion', a self-proclaimed neo-Nazi group whose member Ricardo Guerra received a 20-year prison sentence in 2001 for the murder, committed in 1998 outside Atlético's stadium.

Madrid. You didn't have to be a *Madridista*. Real Madrid weren't really so big until Di Stéfano, despite what the history books might want to imply. You know that.

'And your kids? Who do they support?'

Well that was always going to be a problem. As a Real Madrid fan I obviously wanted to communicate that to my two sons, and it looks like I've succeeded. But it's difficult here in San Sebastián because despite the fact that most people are sensible there was always the possibility that some jerk was going to insult my lads, or worse beat them up if they went walking around openly in Real Madrid shirts. I felt that you just couldn't do that here. Politics have mucked it all up. I tell you – Real Madrid and Real Sociedad got on fine before politics intervened, before they decided here that you had to institutionalise the hostilities. But then my kids made it clear at school who they supported. They couldn't help it. But they never went so far as to actually wear the colours. Their aunts and uncles from Madrid never got the chance to buy them Real Madrid kit and all that stuff, and it became an accepted part of our family thing. And then when Iñaki was ten, all his mates from school put together on his birthday and bought him a Madrid tracksuit. It was the nicest thing I can remember, and you could have knocked me over with a feather. Real Sociedad fans buying their friend some Madrid kit! It must have been an historic event.

Of course, the Madrid fan who is brave enough to venture to certain provinces as an away supporter risks coming face to face with a great deal of hostility. I witnessed this several years before I came to research this book. In the late spring of 1993 I was lucky enough to get into the Heliodoro Rodríguez López Stadium on the grim industrial outskirts of Santa Cruz, Tenerife, on the famous occasion where Real Madrid blew the title by losing 2–0, handing Barcelona's so-called 'Dream Team' their third consecutive title. The ground was full to bursting, and I was shocked at the venomous reaction of the islanders towards the team from the capital. I hadn't been expecting it, but the historical reasons for the dislike are fairly well documented. Outposts like Tenerife, before they were developed for the British and German tourist markets, suffered throughout the Franco years as a result of being largely forgotten and neglected, both politically and financially. Now that they more than earn their keep, the resentment is fuelled further. Seated up at the top of the steep North Stand, I was sandwiched between a family from Madrid – young teenage boy and girl, polite and well dressed, brought over to the game by their comfortable, middle-class parents – and a tipsy Tenerife fan, male, mid-20s and out for a bit of bother. The family to my left had made the good-natured but innocent mistake of wearing their lilac Madrid scarves, and they were made to regret their misjudgement. When the bald Argentine Dertycia headed in Tenerife's first, the fan to my right stood up and leaned across me, jabbing the air menacingly with his forefinger: '*Putos Madrileños!*' (Fucking *Madrileños!*) he bellowed at them, swaying alarmingly. The family stared at the pitch stoically, determined to avoid eye contact. This seemed to annoy him even more, and after a loud lecture about what they were going to have stuffed up them he made to spit in their direction, pulling back from the brink at the last moment and instead just blowing air from his lips in a sort of raspberry. Again the family stared ahead like frightened rabbits but were at least spared their friend's attention until half-time when he leaned across and enquired if they were hot and, if so, would they like him to piss on them to cool them down? Afraid though I was of him (he was bigger than me) I made a gesture as if to suggest that he had gone far enough, and he went back to his drink, only to emerge again with a volley of insults when his team made it 2–0. No one else intervened, and the stoicism of the father in particular was impressive, since the Spanish male tends to fight fire with fire. My only conclusion from the whole regrettable scene was that in some ways the family had been expecting it, may well have experienced it on other away-days and were thus prepared for it, in their own disciplined way. They were martyrs for their cause on a miserable day when their team blew the league title for the third year in succession and on top of that they were abused and humiliated by one of their hosts. But their behaviour was of the stiff upper-lip variety. It spoke of a *castizo* mindset, of a quiet feeling of superiority, of some inner discipline manifestly lacking in their accuser – something that had not been lost on the Tenerife fan and which had probably angered him even more.

But it would be wrong to give the impression that Madrid was stocked full of stoical, middle-class types. It is an image that the older *Madrileño* is perfectly comfortable with, but the impression most recorded by a century of outside observers relates more to the city's busy bar culture, its preference for the late-night prowl, its drinking, eating and dancing, or just its fondness for the *paseo* – that curious Spanish ritual that sees folks taking a stroll in the early evening for no other reason than to be seen taking a stroll. Little wonder that foreign students take easily to the city. According to *The Rough Guide to Spain*, Madrid has more bars than the whole of Norway, a statistic that may have contributed to the traditional nickname for the male *Madrileños* of *los gatos* (the cats). No one in the city seems prepared to explain the provenance of the name, but if you suggest that it might have something to do with the fact that cats like to come out at night, they nod in vigorous agreement.

The city that they inhabit is an historical curiosity. Founded in 1561 by Felipe II, who had decided that flitting the court from place to place was a tiresome and expensive business, the symbolism, if not the climate, made Madrid the obvious choice. In an effort not to boost the power and status of any particular region, Felipe came up with the interesting idea of sticking the capital bang in the middle, so that no one could complain. If Felipe had not been such a do-it-yourself despot, somebody might have raised a few objections, however. The location has no natural advantages, lacking a harbour, for example. It does stand on an escarpment which made it fairly useful as a military post – indeed, in its previous village existence it had functioned as a look-out post, set between the Moorish south and the Christian north. But no one had thought of developing it further. It is suffocatingly hot in the summer and freezing in winter, and has to go down in geographical terms as an artificial city, like Canberra or Brasilia, as opposed to an 'organic' one like London. Artificial it may be, but that has not stopped its citizens from being proud of it and enjoying its alternative delights to the full. Canberra never came up with a team like Real Madrid or a museum like the Prado. Franco was born in Ferrol, an anonymous provincial town in Galicia, but he made sure that he came to be associated with Madrid. The city may lack the architectural and historical interest of Spain's great cities – Granada, Toledo, Salamanca and Seville – but it has made up for it with its other virtues. Besides, you can be in Toledo, Segovia or El Escorial in under an hour, a fact which has prompted some *Madrileños* to jokingly refer to these beautiful places as the 'suburbs'. So the folk do look outwards, but only so far. The dream of the working-class citizen of the capital, fulfilled by some of the middle classes, is to have, in order of priority, a chalet in the Guadarrama mountains for the winter weekend *escapadas* (escapes), a beach hut on the Costa Brava or up in cooler San Sebastián for the summer, and a posh flat right in the expensive centre of Madrid for the working week. Without a doubt, there are a number of well-heeled *Madrileños* who have managed to acquire all three, but their true Shangri-La might differ in one respect. The flat that they inhabit will be located at some point further north in the city, just off the Castellana and within *paseo* distance from their true pilgrimage site, the Estadio Bernabéu.

3. TALL OAKS FROM LITTLE ACORNS . . .

Most professional football clubs would more than likely argue that they illustrated the sentiment expressed by the chapter heading. None of the clubs founded in Britain way back in the nineteenth century could have envisaged what was to become of the football phenomenon. In the same way, the pioneering teams who kicked off the game in Spain in the latter years of that same century also began the venture as a wholly amateur pastime.

The first community to officially form a football club in Spain was Huelva, down in deepest Andalucía, on the night of 23 December 1889. They pre-dated the 'big three', Athletic Bilbao, Barcelona and Real Madrid (in subsequent order of foundation) by at least nine years – Madrid, in fact, not being formed until thirteen years after Huelva's emergence. This represented quite a long period in the history of a game which, by most historical accounts, had a tendency to spread like wildfire. But Huelva's foundation statutes give the game away. The expatriate English secretary, one E.W. Palin, records seven separate items on the agenda of the meeting that evening, none of which mentions the word 'football'. You can see that the expatriate club, formed for the purposes of providing social gatherings for the British employers and employees of the Rio Tinto copper mines (sold to the Brits for a song by an impoverished Spanish government after the Carlist Wars) was more concerned with cucumber sandwiches, lashings of ginger pop and jolly hockey-sticks than football per se. Tennis seemed to be the main attraction, but to be fair to the initiative of Recreativo de Huelva (as they came to be known), they did play a football match a week after the statutes were written, against the crew of an English ship docked in port.

After spending only one season of their 113-year existence in the top flight of Spanish football, Recreativo de Huelva finally managed to gain promotion to 'La Liga' by finishing a respectable third in the Second Division 'A' of the Spanish league at the end of the 2001–02 season.

Even so, it can hardly be said of them that their acorn grew into a 'tall oak'. A tree yes, but one of a less substantial variety.

This probably had to do with the fact that the foundation of Huelva was something of an accident. The actual sale of the mines to the London-based company who took on the development of the project took place in 1870, and as several football historians have pointed out, there must have been games around then between the expatriate workers and the locals. In other words, football was going on, imported from Britain – but it was going on in a town in the south-western corner of Spain, with a poor transport infrastructure into the north of the country. It needed to take hold somewhere else, and be less concerned with the cucumber sandwiches.

Bilbao were next on the list, although their foundation date of 1898 was never rubber-stamped like Huelva's. The easier maritime links between the Basque port and places like Southampton facilitated the toing and froing of a number of middle-class students studying Engineering, Maths and/or Accounting at the universities of Manchester, Oxford and Cambridge where, of course, they encountered their English chums practising the relatively established art of football. Bilbao, and the next on the list Barcelona, were two of the cities most at the forefront of Spain's second phase of industrialisation. It followed from this that the links with Britain, by then the world's foremost industrial power, would be considerable. FC Barcelona were actually founded in 1899 by a young Swiss expatriate, Hans Kamper, but he had been sent there by his father to work in a company that had trade links with Switzerland. Barcelona were actually beaten to it by their Catalan cousins from the Costa Brava, Palamós, set up by the Catalan, Gaspar Matas, who had been studying in England – the more typical pattern. But Palamós have remained a modest outfit, and obviously do not figure among the 'big three'.

The biggest of them all – not a phrase to pronounce too often in the streets of Barcelona – was founded on 6 March 1902 although, as always, there have been some disputes as to whether this should really have been the date. Pernickety as it may seem, the actual day (and minute!) is crucial to the club because of the nature of the celebrations that surround a centenary like that of Real Madrid. The club has always been slightly self-conscious of the fact that it allowed Bilbao and Barcelona to get in on the act before them, caused, of course, by a set of historical circumstances over which they had no control. But Real Madrid like to be in control, and the only way to compensate for this unfortunate accident of history was to make their centenary celebrations more lavish and *chulo* than those of the two clubs whose parties preceded theirs. Bilbao's was a surprisingly modest affair, given that the city's residents also carry a reputation for *chulería*, albeit of a different, more ironic variety to Madrid's. It's a complicated matter! But the Catalans went for it in a big way in 1999, and threw down the glove in no uncertain terms by winning the championship in the same season. Fortunately for Madrid, Barça were knocked out of the European Champions Cup that year in the group stage. It was a good job they were, because the final that year was played at the Camp Nou. Had Barça won it in their centenary year, in their own stadium to boot, the vibes from the symbolism would have eclipsed Madrid's pretensions of grandeur for at least the next millennium. It would have been easily as serious as Christ choosing the Camp Nou as the setting for the Second Coming.

Madrid's party had to be a bigger one because of many factors, but if you asked a club official for the real reason, they would probably reply to you that it was because Madrid is *El club de España* (Spain's Club). This is the bitterest pill of all to swallow for those provincial communities who resent Madrid's centralism, a factor already referred to. But again, the statistics tell the tale. Florentino Pérez, the president who resided over the centenary bash, claimed in an interview on Tele Madrid three nights before the Copa Del Rey final against Deportivo de La Coruña that 49 per cent of all Spaniards were *del Real Madrid* (supporters of Real Madrid). This was surely an exaggeration, but it nevertheless reflects the fact that an awful lot of Spaniards consider Real Madrid as either their 'first' or 'second' team. To prove the point, you could travel to deepest, driving-over-lemons Spain, find its most obscure village outpost and ask any suspicious-eyed resident which team he or she supported after their local side (assuming there was one). The reply would almost certainly include one of those two diametrical opposites – Real Madrid or Barcelona. Just in case, when Pérez took the reins in 2001, he commissioned a survey to find out what constituted the 'essence' of the club, to quote his phrase. Of the 2,000 people interviewed around the country, 29.2 per cent replied that they were white, as opposed to the 18.5 per cent who declared themselves to be of Barça's colours. There was no regional breakdown of these replies, but the figures make interesting reading. How did this come about? How did this team, whose first meetings took place among the cloth and linen of a boutique called *El Capricho* (Caprice), owned by a couple of Catalans on Madrid's Calle Alcalá, grow to become such a phenomenon?

There was plenty of space to improvise a game or two on the fields adjacent to the Manzanares River, out by Moncloa or the Puerta de Hierro. Spain's town planning has always favoured the gobbling up of all available urban space, leaving her outskirts relatively untouched and spacious. Sometime between 1896 and 1897 a gathering of friends that had become a weekly 'Foot Ball' ritual decided to name themselves 'Foot Ball Sky', although the reason for the curious name has never been fathomed. What is known is that the game grew popular in Madrid within similar social circles to Bilbao and Barcelona. Those who formed Sky were connected, in one way or another, to the *Institución Libre de Enseñanza* (Open Teaching College), a sort of technical college that offered a number of academic and vocational courses, and which seemed to have enjoyed a certain prestige back then, judging by the amount of students it sent abroad on work-study experience and the subsequent influence it is claimed to have had on education in general in the whole country. Again, this may be *Madridista* propaganda – you never know – but what *is* known for certain is that a group of students who had been on scholarships in Cambridge for a year had come back in 1894 and begun playing.

A certain Luis Bermejillo is a name that crops up frequently in connection with the foundation of Sky, but the more recent club historian, Ángel Bahamonde, claimed that when he spoke to the retired teacher Manuel Cossío, just before he died, Cossío claimed to have been responsible for starting and then organising games of football at the college. There seems to have been a lot of 'healthy body, healthy mind' stuff floating around masculine circles in late nineteenth-century Spain, particularly in the new middle classes, perhaps as a way of distinguishing themselves as a type. Athletic Bilbao grew up around a fairly posh city gym, as did Barcelona, and football was just another sport to add to those that were already available for the all-round development of a gentleman. There is some evidence, particularly from Barcelona, that the first kick-abouts provoked shock and horror among the chattering classes, but whatever tut-tutting there was seems to have faded fairly rapidly. Pictures of the early games in Madrid at the turn of the century all feature chaps with only a tiny speck of knee-cap showing, all bonding together in the wholesome spirit of sweaty bonhomie. Nothing to make the ladies faint.

The archives are then a bit vague about the relationship between Sky and 'Madrid Foot Ball Club', the name that most crops up as the direct predecessor of the team that Real Madrid claim as their heritage. There is a document dating from 1900 which refers to 'New' Football Sky as the only feasible opponents of Madrid Foot-ball Club, and please could they play against each other every week 'like they do in Barcelona'. The origins of Madrid Foot Ball Club are less clear, but it seems that various of the college graduates, once they had taken their first steps into their chosen professions, had come across other converts to the football cause from other parts of the city. Julian Palacios is another name that crops up frequently, and one who seems to have been the link between the two clubs. History deems him to have been Madrid FC's first president (pre-official foundation), and he is recorded as saying that when he was 'elected', Sky was virtually defunct. It's all a bit vague, but reading between the lines one can guess at what happened. Some of the early Sky players either got fed up or moved away, and another lot took over, less connected with the old college. Just to keep things strictly accurate at this otherwise rather foggy stage, there is a photograph dating from late 1900 which shows the team 'El New Foot-Ball Club' in all their glory. There are 21 players in the picture, 11 of whom sport a red jersey with a diagonal white stripe (presumably the *probables*) whilst the *possibles* had to make do with plain shirts. This team were clearly a continuation of 'New Foot Ball Sky', and their brief period of existence pre-dates the more important emergence of Madrid FC, about a year later. Just to confuse matters further, there was another side hanging around by the name of Espanyol de Madrid, a murky outfit that would be confined to the historical bins were it not for the fact that Palacios seems to have been their founder. But he didn't stay with them for very long, for in the period leading up to 1902 he is always referred to as Madrid FC's 'president'. He was also their centre-forward and lacked a bushy beard, but his moustache was more than adequate.

A friend of Palacios was one Arthur Johnson, an English expatriate businessman who had turned out for Corinthians. Quoted as the principal English link with Real Madrid, Johnson took responsibility for training and tactics, or as some books put it, 'showing the players the rudiments of the game'. It's easy to scoff, but the English game was relatively well established and developed by then. Johnson may well have been instrumental in simply showing folk how to kick, use space, attack, defend etc. The basics are by no means obvious, as a quick glance at any chaotic infant game will tell you. Johnson actually left for posterity a document in which he wrote down in Spanish four principles that he felt were the key to playing the game more effectively. The first – that each team should have a captain – is hardly radical stuff, but the second is quite interesting. He felt that '. . . players should always play in the same position, so that each comes to learn the position and tendencies of his colleagues'. Then comes the swipe at any early manifestation of total football: 'The system currently employed, whereby each player continually changes position is not FOOTBALL', the final word highlighted in the original by capitals. His third commandment was that the players should be more conscientious about running and fetching the ball when it went out of play, so that the games could be reduced by 'at least half an hour' and that there would consequently be 'less smoking and idle chat'. Stern stuff. As the fourth principle, Johnson thought, quite rightly one supposes, that the players should pay more attention to the art of 'COMBINATION' (written in capitals and in English) – a concept that he illustrates as comprising '. . . the passing of the ball back and forth between the players, a practice almost wholly absent at the present time'. He could almost be talking about the current English Premiership.

Some of the practices that Johnson was trying to stamp out, as well as the character of the Englishman himself, are evident in this extract from Julian Palacios, quoted from the club's archives:

> When I played at centre-forward I tried to make life as difficult as possible for defenders, but they left their marks on me as well. We had referees sometimes, but few of them agreed on the rules. They all had their own versions of the game, and frankly it was easier to play without them. And we wasted a lot of time smoking and drinking. Sky had a goalkeeper who used to sit on a chair in front of the goal-line drinking lemonade and just relaxing. When we attacked, he used to jump up and throw the chair behind the line, and put on this really serious expression. The only guy who really knew what he was doing back then was the Englishman Johnson. Lovely chap too, but he took the game very seriously. He got married here in Madrid on a Saturday, and turned up to play the match on the following morning. I don't know what his bride thought.

Palacios does not say, unfortunately, how or why the running of the club was suddenly taken over by the older Padrós brothers, Carlos and the aforementioned Juan of the alarming facial hair. It's not even clear how they knew each other, but the history of Real Madrid was to be forever associated from then onwards with these two Catalans, both born in Barcelona close to the mythical Ramblas. Juan was 32 and co-owner of the *El Capricho* boutique at No. 48, Calle Alcalá, then a busy shopping street full of coffee-houses and bars, now a display thoroughfare lined by banks, cutting across the Avenida Castellana at the point where the Cibeles fountain – later to become the gathering point to celebrate a league title or cup – spews up white water against the backdrop of the Bank of Spain and the Stock Exchange. Some have suggested that it was simply the back room of their shop that singled them out as useful. It was there that the prime movers of the club held their weekly meetings to plan a succession of events that would lead to the formation of the world's most famous football club. The fact that the Padrós brothers were Catalans is only significant depending on the cultural stance of those commenting on it. For *Catalanistas*, the brothers are either traitors or heroes, but for many Madrid apologists the presence of these two men at the earliest helm is positive proof of Madrid's tolerance and acceptance of all-comers, even back then. The awkward fact is converted into a virtue, as proof of *Madridismo* as a broader church than some would prefer to believe.

It's a nice idea, although not an entirely convincing one, given the very rapid development of the Madrid versus Barcelona cat-and-dog synergy. Those who claim that the hostilities only began under Franco ignore the fact that the Catalans had been getting bolshy right from the beginning of the twentieth century, and had plenty of reasons for disliking and resenting Madrid's growing centralism around the same time as the clubs were formed. Whatever the truth, another obvious thing that the brothers could provide was kit, or at least they had the contacts to get the materials at trade prices. This was important, since the proliferation of plain shirts or stripes on the backs of the early players was proof of the expense involved in having a full-coloured kit. Artificial dyes had only been in existence for some 30 years, and were still on the pricey side. Nevertheless, as proof of the Padrós' usefulness, in the year preceding the foundation the 'squad' members played each other as two teams, a red version and a blue one.

By this time they had moved from their first grassy residence near Moncloa to the Campo de Estrada, near the present-day José Ortega y Gasset – named 'Estrada' because it belonged to a marble-cutter of the same name, who, although he thought football a ridiculous pastime, was quite chuffed to have a field named after him by these young, middle-class bucks. Indeed, his name has gone down in history, but the field that bordered his workshop soon became inadequate for Madrid FC's needs and it was decided to move to a field adjacent to the old bullring, now in Calle Felipe II, very close to Alcalá and the Padrós' shop. Although this meant that they could have a game and then retire for a meeting, or vice-versa, the choice of this field was significant in the growth of interest in the club, for it meant that more casual passers-by were likely to see the games being played, and were thus more likely to emulate or encourage the proceedings.

The primacy of bullfighting was yet to be seriously challenged, but proof of the growing interest in the game in the capital was the appearance (and subsequent disappearance) of various sides to take on Madrid FC – the aforementioned Espanyol de Madrid, Club Retiro (who played in the famous Retiro park), Moncloa, Moderno and the Asociation Sportiva Francesa. But it was the former who finally and formally decided to take the plunge by electing, 'just as the light began to fade' on the evening of Thursday, 6 March 1902, a board of directors headed by Juan Padrós Rubió and one Enrique Varela as second in command. A secretary, treasurer and five committee members (*vocales*) were also elected at the same meeting, on an evening that the current Real Madrid decided some time ago to honour as the founding date of the club. One hundred years later, on Wednesday, 6 March 2002, Real Madrid, still clad in the pure white kit that Johnson first suggested they wear in 1901, lost 2–1 to Deportivo de La Coruña in the bright electric glare of the Bernabéu – half a mile north of Padrós' old shop. The final of the King's Cup, in which Real were making their 35th appearance since 1902, counted on the presence of 500 national police, 200 municipal police, 400 track officials and guards, 100 Red Cross volunteers, 612 journalists and 86 photographers, not to mention the 85,000 sell-out crowd. Tall oaks indeed. You'd like to bring Palacios, Padrós and Johnson back to life and show them what they began, to see their reaction, to see if they could even begin to understand the results of what they set innocently in motion. They might well be appalled, and certainly stunned. And what of the following day, with the Madrid flag at half-mast and the city in mourning. What on earth would they have made of all that? To us it is easy enough to understand – 100 years of triumphs stained on the biggest symbolic night of all, a night where the enormity of the occasion, begun that warmish evening a century ago, took the team by the legs and filled them with jelly. Poor Madrid could not function, and their Galician opponents revelled in pooping the party. The champagne corks may well have been popping over in Barcelona too, to celebrate the curtailing of Real's overweening desire in their centenary year to win the League, Champions Cup and King's Cup – an orgy of white triumphalism stopped dead in its tracks. Padrós would probably have glared above that enormous beard and asked for his *callos* and *cocido* (or *butifarra*), and Johnson would definitely have mourned the death of the Corinthian spirit that he had tried to instil.

The controversy regarding the date of foundation stems from the fact that the official document, signed by Padrós, was not handed into the municipal offices and rubber-stamped until 18 March, but no one has ever bothered to define exactly what type of act is required to constitute the true birth of a football club, or any other sporting institution for that matter. As Oscar Wilde pointed out, 'The one duty we owe to history is to rewrite it.' But the decisive act of administrative planning that took place on 6 March, whereby the club ceased to be merely a collection of friends and began to be an organised entity, surely marks some frontier in the development of Real Madrid. The fact that officialdom received the subsequent document 12 days later is of no consequence. The spirit of the club resides in that meeting in the back room of *El Capricho*, and anyway, if history had required them to play the centenary Cup final on 18 March it would have been held on a Monday – not a great night of the week for a match of such significance.

Three days after the board members were elected, Madrid FC played the first 'official' game of their new existence, although it was actually an internal affair to sort out who was to belong to the first team and who was to be a mere squad member. This was also the first occasion on which the players were obliged to pay their member's quota – the princely sum of two pesetas a month. All money was handed in to José Gorostizaga (elected treasurer three days earlier) in the bar *La Taurina*, just across the road from the new pitch by the bullring. The players were allowed to change in the toilets, so long as they agreed to use the bar for post-match refreshments. In the archives at the Bernabéu, the official care taken over the paying of the monthly quota can be seen in a receipt, preserved from 1905, where the new treasurer has signed and dated, in beautiful handwriting, a payment from the player Julio Chulilla.

That first game between the 'blues' and the 'reds' ended in a 1–0 victory for the former, the wonderfully named Spottorno (A) scoring the goal. His brother was on the opposing side. All 22 players are named in a report from the newspaper *El Heraldo de Sport*. Juan Padrós was on the victorious blue side, with Palacios, his unofficial presidential predecessor, playing for the reds. Curiously, the Englishman Johnson does not figure in either line-up. Perhaps after playing on the morning after his wedding he didn't want to push his luck too much for the next year. The newspaper records that several spectators were responsible for a variety of witticisms, one of them aimed at the bearded president: '*Mira aquel con barba – se parece a San Pedro*' (Look at that one with the beard – he looks like St Peter).

But at least they'd noticed, and they probably wandered down the next Sunday to see the Reds get their revenge, to the tune of 5–2. The planting of the seeds of the central aspect of Spanish football, that its clubs are essentially owned by the supporters – the *socios* (members) as they are called, was significant in the growth of both Athletic Bilbao, Barcelona and then Real Madrid. In the case of Bilbao, there were sufficient members by 1913 to fund the construction of the first purpose-built stadium for football in the country – the 'cathedral' of San Mamés, which quickly went on to hold 10,000 spectators. It cost 89,000 pesetas to build, which was a substantial sum. Madrid had built the O'Donnell Stadium a year earlier in 1912 which had a wooden stand for 200 spectators and which cost 13,000 pesetas – hardly comparable to Bilbao's investment in its new pilgrimage site – but important in the sense that it too had been financed by the 450 members that the club then boasted. In Madrid's case, there were still more members than room at the ground(!), but the point is that these people had seen that paying for the club's installations out of their own pockets was a valid investment, both in a financial and a spiritual sense. Football had by then reached the stage of no return, but this could not have been given such literally concrete expression without the open membership concept. The spectator making the witty aside that day back in 1902 may well have been paying his membership fees some months later – still going down to the bullfights of a weekend, but now beginning to take an interest in something else. And this something else may not have developed in quite the same way had it not taken root in the capital that year. For a mere two months after that practice match between the Blues and the Reds, the first national tournament was held in the capital, an event that marked the beginning of Spanish football as an expression of local culture, as a confirmation of regional identity. Once this was established, there was no going back.

Luis Bermejillo, mentioned earlier in connection with Foot-Ball Sky, had an interesting day job as secretary and accountant to the Conde (Count) de La Quinta de La Enrajada, recently returned from the games fields at Oxford and heir to an aristocratic line that was involved in horse-breeding and racing. Bermejillo, though no longer directly involved with Madrid FC by 1902, was the man who persuaded his employer and friend to rope off Madrid's Hippodrome and use its wide expanses for a football tournament to commemorate the coronation of Alfonso XIII on 17 May 1902. It seemed as good an opportunity as any to bring the fledgling game even more into the public eye of the country's capital. Eighteen years later, King Alfonso was to officially stamp his royal seal on the club, but Madrid's royal and governmental connections were essentially to begin back then, on the fields where the Conde de La Enrajada watched his thoroughbreds run.

Five sides turned up for the event, staged on 13 and 14 May, with the final to be played on the third day, two days before the coronation. Madrid Foot Ball Club, Foot Ball Club Barcelona, the other Catalan side Club Español de Foot Ball, Vizcaya (essentially Athletic Bilbao, but featuring some other players from their region of the Basque Country) and New Foot Ball Club, also from Madrid, including some of the old Sky connections and several of the players who hadn't made it into the Madrid FC first XI. The tournament was a great success, and its significance in the history of the development of Spanish football cannot be exaggerated. Bermejillo's initiative, eagerly taken up by the two best sides in the country, Bilbao (Vizcaya) and Barcelona, packed out the Hippodrome to such an extent that extra wooden stands had to be erected to accommodate the crowds. Coming only two months after Madrid's official founding, the tournament was proof of the pull of this sport-in-waiting. Unfortunately for Johnson and his charges, Madrid were drawn to play Barcelona, a side with three years' more experience, and considerably more competitive nous. And so it came to pass, on 13 May 1902, that the fixture that was later to become perhaps the most notorious in world football ended in a 3–1 win for the Catalans – not a bad result for Madrid, considering their opponents' greater pedigree at that moment in time. The record books, however, will always announce the unpleasant fact for all *Madridistas*, that a century's almost psychotic rivalry began with a Catalan victory. The line-ups show the cosmopolitan nature of the winners, with three Englishmen and their Swiss president in the team, whilst this time Johnson turned out for Madrid. More than that, he almost turned the game around in the second half when, with his side 0–2 down, he took a pass from Giralt and 'smashed' it past the opposing goalkeeper. Palacios then missed a chance, and with the smartly dressed public already smitten, our friend Spottorno gave away a penalty, which the Catalans duly converted. Strange to report, however, that the first man to score in an official competition for Real Madrid was an Englishman. Meanwhile, the powerful Vizcaya were stuffing Madrid's discarded 'New' possibles by the unfortunate score of 8–1, leaving Madrid to take third place by beating Español 3–1. Carlos Padrós refereed the final between Vizcaya and Barcelona, won 2–1 by the Basques. The standards were set. Madrid, as a capital and a football team, now had a clearer idea of what they needed to do in order to catch up and compensate for their three to four years of relatively innocent inactivity. They hadn't done too badly, and suddenly, from playing practice matches in front of a handful of gawping Sunday strollers, they were being cheered on by hundreds, even thousands, of paying spectators. The fact that Bermejillo had charged an entrance fee (either 10 or 25 centavos) had not deterred the crowds from turning up. Seeing the Prince at close quarters was obviously an attraction for the royal watchers, but whatever the reason for turning up, Madrid FC in particular and football in general were on the move.

On the second floor of the *Sala de Exposiciones* at the Bernabéu one is greeted by a large, rather garish mural of the players celebrating the Club's eighth European Cup success in Paris, 2000. The text arched around the mural assures us that not only were Real Madrid Spain's biggest side at the beginning of the twentieth century, they were also the first winners of the new millennium's first Champions League and Spanish league title. The latter is stretching it a bit, since it was strictly Deportivo de La Coruña who won the national title at the end of the 1999–2000 season, but one can see the poetic licence in the claim, Madrid's subsequent title win having been achieved in the year that began with the zeros. Of course, they are clearly wanting it both ways by claiming the same for the Champions League win over Valencia in 1999–2000, but it doesn't really matter. Such minor fibs in the face of the facts are all part and parcel of the legend. In the middle of the text, the author has instructed the graphic artist to highlight the following phrase in a larger font, in capitals . . .

Y SOBRE TODO, EL MADRID ES UN EQUIPO GANADOR
(AND ABOVE ALL, REAL MADRID ARE WINNERS)

. . . just in case we hadn't already got the message from the abundant display of a century's worth of booty on the floor below.

In some ways this is an extremely dangerous conceit to propagate, since it makes demands on the institution, at times surely unreasonable, to carry out this philosophy to the letter and continue to beat all comers with a regularity sufficient to preserve the essence of the boast. The problem, however, seems to have resided more in the rest of the country's lame attempts to hoist Madrid on the petard of their cocky claim. As we shall come to see, from the signing of Di Stéfano and the 1950s onwards, statistics smile roundly on Real. There is little to argue about, save the odd lapse and the occasional fallow period. But even when the field was being rested for the next year's crop, a trophy or two would still be finding its way into the groaning glass cabinets at the Bernabéu.

Other clubs have built their traditions on maybe a single golden era, a couple of outstanding players and something particular to their community, like Grimsby and their fish or Hartlepool and their monkey – or they may have converted their club into a form of politico-cultural expression, like Barcelona or the Glasgow sides – but looking at Real Madrid's records one cannot help but suspect that these other, more quirky features clung on to by the rest of the football world are somehow compensatory, attractive or meaningful as they may have become to those who inherit them. There is practically no other major club in the world that can base its whole culture around the word 'winner' and get away with it so comprehensively. This is, of course, the reason why one finds precious little neutrality expressed when opinions are solicited on Real Madrid. In Spain, they are loved and hated in not-quite-equal measure by everyone. No football supporter here will simply shrug his or her shoulders when quizzed on the topic of Madrid, and most people who would claim to have no interest in football whatsoever (there are precious few here) would nevertheless proffer an opinion on Real and everything that it implies. This is because its 'simply the best' boast is not an idle one – a fact which clearly intimidates. The accompanying swagger is too much for some people's tastes, and from a purely philosophical point of view the idea of being a permanent 'winner' is rather empty, since it would seem to contradict the very essence of sport.

A more reasonable view might be that sport's true pleasures derive from its ups and downs – from appreciating victory all the more for having understood the pain of defeat. Jorge Valdano, Director of

Football at the club in the current Pérez era, distinguished ex-player and manager and occasional 'philosopher' (his nickname in his native Argentina) expressed a rather more doubting Thomas's view of the issue in his *Libro de dichos* (Book of Sayings) when he wrote that *'Ganar queremos todos, pero solo los mediocres no aspiran a la belleza. Es como pretender elegir entre un imbécil bueno o un inteligente malo . . .'* (We all want to win, but the true loser is the one who does not aspire to beauty. It's like trying to choose between a good imbecile and an intelligent rogue.) But this is an unusual remark from a man at the heart of Real Madrid, and not one shared by many others at the club. Madrid take style for granted. There is no difference between a winning side and an attractive one at the Bernabéu. Victories, and oodles of them, are forms of beauty in themselves. Valdano is seen as a bit of an intellectual, a bit of an oddball who nevertheless lends the club a certain aura of dignity, with his Armani smoothness and educated, eloquent Spanish. But few of the players would get away with this sort of statement, more characteristic of Barcelona's obsessive insistence on style. Authentic *Madridistas* must be heard expressing the winner philosophy into the microphones thrust under their noses and to be seen carrying out these self-fulfilling prophecies on the playing field. Anything less is rarely tolerated.

Looking back over the club's history, it is interesting to try to fathom when this began, and why and in what circumstances this triumphant self-consciousness was born – given that it is more likely to be something particular to the Madrid mindset. Indeed, the design of the Trophy Room is intended to convey this very impression, that the soul of the club was lined with silver from the very start. This is apparent as you walk through the blue arch into the darkened ante-room, where your eyes are led past the first long wooden cabinet with a variety of minor 'warm-up' cups and medals to a more strongly illuminated patch to the left. Here, under tasteful spotlights, the club's first trophy, a large burnished silver cup, sits in dignified silence within a square glass cabinet. Given to Real by Alfonso XIII in 1908, it commemorates the club's first four King's Cup victories won on the trot between the years 1905 and 1908. Unfortunately for the trophy's guardians, the inaugural winner is inscribed in tastefully engraved italics at the foot of the cup – 'Athletic Bilbao', although when they actually won it they were still called Bilbao FC. Madrid took three years from their foundation to actually win this significant tournament (officially begun in 1903, the year after the Coronation games), but once they did they established the first consecutive run in their history, a phenomenon which was to become an important part of their legend in subsequent periods. Real were to have two consecutive runs of five league titles in the '60s and the '80s, a royal flush of European Cups in the '50s, plus several prials of three along the way. The Spanish are acutely aware of these runs, and attach great importance to them whether they support Real Madrid or not. It is as if they mark the signs of the times, as if they serve as important historical reminders as to the social and political goings-on during those periods.

4. EARLY DAYS AND EARLY WAYS

By 1903 Madrid FC felt that enough interest had been generated to justify playing an annual tournament in the capital, with the added attraction of the king's blessing and presence. A hundred years on, the Spanish equivalent of the FA Cup is still known as 'The King's Cup' (*La Copa del Rey*). In April of the second year of Madrid FC's official existence, the Hippodrome was once again witness to a national tournament, although the turnout was rather disappointing with only Español (from Barcelona) and Athletic Bilbao showing up. Madrid beat Español 4–1, whereupon Athletic went one better at 4–0, setting up the final for the next day (8 April). Five thousand turned out for the final, the attendance being recorded for posterity on the solid basis of tickets sold. Johnson turned out in goal for Madrid, and also the three brothers Giralt in defence, a fact which might explain why, in an excellent action photo of the final, the three white-shirted men to the right of the picture who are defending their goal all look exactly the same – with the same haircuts, the same moustaches, the same postures. Johnson, wearing a cap, has come out to the edge of the area but appears to have lost the flight of the ball, whilst an Athletic player behind him seems to be about to head the floating pig's bladder, frozen in time against the white sky. The players' shadows are long, and in the background a large crowd stands behind drooping ropes, with several white umbrellas shielding their owners from the late-afternoon glare. Madrid were 2–0 up at the break, but in the second half the Basques' greater experience showed, and they ended up 3–2 winners. The picture of Johnson with his back to the Bilbao forward was later to form the first cover of a weekly sports magazine accompanying the newspaper, *Nuevo Mundo*, although the artist responsible isolated him from the action and made it appear as though the Englishman knew exactly where the ball was. But in 1904, for 20 cents, you could share in a little piece of harmless revisionism, read all about the new sport and share in some of its already burgeoning tittle-tattle. The fact that *Nuevo Mundo* saw the need to cater for an audience was proof of the new market value of football. The fact that Madrid FC had come within a whisker of beating the powerful Basques suggested it was only a matter of time before they established themselves as peers to the northerners. A week after the defeat, Madrid FC showed how far they had left the local rivalry behind when they took on a combined Madrid XI in the *Trofeo Cordorníu* game – a match sponsored by the Catalan champagne company and further evidence of business interest in the fledgling game. Two games were played and Madrid FC won them to the tune of 13–1 and 7–0, leaving little doubt as to which side were establishing themselves at the top of the capital's tree. Besides, none of the other clubs in Madrid had come forward for the King's Cup, either out of deference, fear, or both.

Despite the appearance of the imaginatively titled song 'Goal', a paso doble dedicated to the club by the agricultural engineer Andrés Segovia, the next year, 1904, proved to be something of a transitional one when folks began to fall out and become suspicious of each others' motives – a sure sign that the game was growing in stature. It remains a simple historical lesson to observe that it is only when something becomes useful that it turns into an object over which people begin to squabble. One of the more obscure Madrid clubs, Moderno, complained that they had not been invited to play in a tournament the previous August to celebrate the fiestas of the monastery of San Lorenzo del Escorial (10 August 1903), and persuaded several of Madrid FC's players that they were playing for the wrong club. By Christmas of 1903, the Giralt brothers had left and taken Neyra and Pérez with them – all useful players and all part of the original *pandilla* (gang) that had formed around the turn of the century. But instead of joining Moderno they 'joined' the moribund Español de Madrid, reviving it temporarily and forcing the denuded ranks of Madrid FC, facing its first crisis, to fuse with Moderno. Carlos Padrós was by now the president, but had fallen out with the Giralt bothers over some issue connected to money. Having resigned as president of Madrid, he reappeared at the helm of the new fusion, but even he of the slightly thinner beard could not save the 1904 tournament. Madrid-Moderno and Español were obliged by the newly formed *Federación Madrileña de Fútbol* to play each other to decide who would represent the capital that year (a new arbitrary decision, allegedly plotted by the anti-Padrós wing). After a 'tense' game which ended 5–5, Madrid FC refused to take part in a hastily organised replay the next day, and the points were awarded to Español, Giralt brothers and all. But before King Alfonso could pin on his military medals and doff his bowler for the annual event that he seemed to genuinely enjoy, Español and Moncloa refused to play the reigning champions Athletic Bilbao at the beginning of the three-way tournament, for reasons never clarified. The Basques went home with the trophy, and perhaps the more cynical, awkward side of Spanish football's current boisterous personality was born that year.

Whatever the spin, the following year marked the first of the four annual wins that would see the initial piece of silverware transferred to the safekeeping of the club. The first three years (which secured the trophy for keeps) were all victories won over the previously invulnerable Athletic Bilbao, although the 1907 competitors were called 'Vizcaya' again, and contained elements of a regional representative side. But nonetheless, the oligarchy was broken and the spirit of democracy instilled. Moreover, it was ushered in by Madrid FC again, the club having dropped the 'Moderno' half of the compound in an attempt by Carlos Padrós to rekindle the intimate spirit that had reigned at the dawn of the century. The Moderno hangers-on were banned from the loos at *El Taurino* and discouraged from attending meetings at the shop. This sensation of clubs marking out their territory, of rejecting marriage and fusion, was all part and parcel of the growing identity of the game in the capital, and the process mirrored what had been happening over in Barcelona and up in the Basque Country.

Two months before the 1905 tournament, the infighting and the outfighting that had characterised this infant period produced yet another significant event in the history of Madrid's football. Two dissident members of Madrid FC, with some of the Moderno castaways, were invited to join the new side that had been formed by Basque students studying in Madrid in late 1903. They called their team 'Athletic Madrid', after the heroes they had temporarily left behind up in the Basque Country, and they dressed in blue and white stripes, originally the colours of Athletic. On the last day of February 1905, on a freezing Madrid afternoon, Madrid FC and Athletic Madrid met for the first time over by the bullring, and the 1–1 result was proof of the growing competitive health of the capital scene. The side, which was to later become known as Atlético Madrid and which would contribute to a clear division in the city with regard to its political and social following, was as yet in its pre-*Madrileño* phase, where the outsider (Basque) roots of the club attracted players as yet unconvinced by the growing *chulería* of Madrid FC and its cohorts. The very existence of Atlético still rankles in the Bernabéu circles, as though its 50,000 members are an affront to the more obvious attractions to be found on the Castellana. Atlético's rivalry with Real, though never as intense and psychotic as the one that has developed between the latter and Barça, is an interesting one, and crops up later in this book. Atlético illuminate by dint of contrast. They sit out now on an industrial estate, snarling at the aristos from the centre, never managing to portray a sufficiently friendly working-class face to attract a more silver-spooned socialist type of follower. But back then in 1905, only the tiniest seeds of this conflict-to-come were present. For the records, it was simply a measuring-up, another game to see how far each one had travelled.

Two months later, and this time not at the Hippodrome, Athletic Bilbao turned up with their chic cousins to the east, San Sebastián Recreation Club from the region of Gipuzcoa, close to the French border. Madrid FC were again the only side permitted to represent the capital, having beaten Moncloa 3–1 in the new 'qualifying phase' instigated by the Federation – but this time they were to justify this exclusivity. A fellow by the name of Prast scored the only goal of the final against Athletic, and the three sides went for supper in the *Café Inglés* on Calle Sevilla to celebrate (or lament) the engraving of a new name onto the trophy. Little were they to know that by 1909 a new silversmith would be gainfully occupied beating out the design of a new trophy, the original one having been rightly sequestered by Madrid FC as per the competition's original statutes. In 1909, the newly named 'Club Ciclista San Sebastián' (Cycle Club of . . .) won the day and the first of the 'Second Cup' as it has become known to history, and Madrid were destined not to drink from its fount at all. By 1916, Athletic Bilbao had quarried out a new and formidable line-up of giant redwoods from their fertile soil, and with the legendary 'Pichichi' (Rafael Moreno), the first great star of Spanish football, they made off with the trophy into the misty northern mountains. Whilst the lights went out in northern Europe and a bloody war was raging, they won the cup between 1914 and 1916, and it was not until the following year that Madrid were able to get their hands on the 'Third' version, beating Arenas de Getxo (from Bilbao) in the final.

But these were years in which football had reached a point of no return, war or no war. Before this period, Madrid's rise as a club was far from a vertical one, and there were times, particularly after their first consecutive run of cups, when all was far from rosy in the garden. One tends to view this period in terms of the King's Cups, but such a limited perspective obviously ignores the 11 months in each year when the tournament was not taking place. For this reason, it is worth mentioning events such as Madrid's first games against foreign opposition, matches against local rivals on Saints Day holidays and other initiatives that kept the pan simmering. The significance of games against the French champions Gallia from Paris in 1905 (1–1) and Internacional from Lisbon (0–2), both held in Madrid, show how the club were attempting to keep as many avenues as possible open, particularly considering the inconsistent nature of the King's Cup participation. In 1907, one of the better years, five teams turned up, two of them new to the competition – Salamanca and Vigo from the north, whilst Huelva from Andalucía made their second appearance. But the following year, for reasons unexplained, only Vigo turned up for the competition, and were beaten by the hosts 2–1. Barcelona had not participated since 1902, and were accused of being chicken in certain Madrid circles, especially considering the rumours that they had a decent side. The Catalan apologists argue, however, that Barcelona resented Madrid's monopolising the organisation of the tournament – which is a bit rich when you reflect that it was they who at least had the gumption to get the thing off the ground, finance it and then attempt to keep it going. When the tournament finally took a vacation up to San Sebastián in 1910, several teams refused to take part, whingeing about the sandy pitch by Ondarreta beach. So much for decentralisation.

A period of gloom seemed to have set in, with the resignation of Carlos Padrós and the defection of more players to Español, encouraged to leave by the wicked turncoat brothers Giralt. Yarza, Buylla and Neyra all left, and although their names mean little to a modern audience, they were allegedly important members of the squad. This turbulence gave rise to a crisis meeting of various clubs in October 1909, a sort of parley of chiefs in the wigwam, to smoke the pipe of peace. They came from as far afield as Bilbao, Vigo, Cartagena, Avilés, Huelva and Coruña and went away having formed the first *Federación Española de Fútbol*, effectively the national organ that exists today. Madrid's historians claim that theirs was the initiative, but the mere fact that the meeting was held in Madrid is hardly conclusive proof. Whatever the case, Madrid closed the first decade in a position not exactly reflective of their 'winners' label. Español de Madrid beat them in 1909 in the qualifying stages and thus supplanted them for the first time as representatives in the King's Cup, and the following year saw the tournament move north to San Sebastían (since the president, Vega de Seoane, was a Basque) – a healthy move in terms of sharing out the administration of the game, but a move resented by Madrid, especially since they had their noses pushed out again. Barcelona, possibly piqued at the barbs coming their way, turned up at last and shared the honours with Athletic Bilbao. From then until 1917, these two clubs would share the honours between them.

One might as well come clean at this stage and report that poor Madrid, apart from the cup win in 1917, were to play third-fiddle to the hegemony established over the early Spanish scene by the Basques and the Catalans, but particularly the former. It was not just Athletic Bilbao, but also Real Irún and Arenas de Getxo that strengthened the Basque hold on the sport. A sociological explanation for this phenomenon might maintain that it was not so much a case of the steak and beans in the northern diet as the fact that the Spanish industrial revolution effectively took place in Bilbao and then Barcelona, with Madrid looking on as an administrator desperate to hold onto the reins. The diaspora had settled, with the second generation of children from the waves of immigrant workers now beginning to have an impact on those urban populations. Madrid FC's staunchly middle-class roots were now beginning to look like a disadvantage in the face of this *mestizo* revolution. 'Pichichi', Spain's first great footballing star, was a *maketo*, the name reserved by the pure blood-line Basques to describe the product of a mixed marriage between a Spanish 'immigrant' and a Basque homelander. When he turned up at Athletic in 1913, down in Madrid they were still too worried about the *castizo* image they still like to portray nowadays, and it may well have been the case that the transfusion of a drop of working blood to dilute the pure-bred line could have made the side more competitive. It remains a theory, and one rarely discussed in the annals of the club's history, because in the end they emerged as the dominant force – by design or by lottery, an opinion you hold depending on which side of the political fence you reside in this country.

Despite the lack of trophies, the single most significant figure in the club's history took his first bow during this period. The man who was to lend the current stadium his name (reluctantly, according to his apologists) and who, more than anyone else, was to inculcate, design and encapsulate the very soul of the white spirit of *Madridismo*, Santiago Bernabéu, turned up in 1909 as a raw 14-year-old to play in

Madrid FC's junior side, established that year by the new president Adolfo Meléndez. Bernabéu thus began an astonishing 69-year relationship with the club, until his death in 1978, days before the beginning of the World Cup in Argentina.

The man whose name is synonymous with the concept of *Madridismo* – the idea that Madrid occupies a position at the centre of the universe – was born, oddly enough, in Albacete, a provincial city in the Manchego region, more famous for its cheese and Don Quixote than for its footballing stock. The man destined to bring to the planet its most famous and successful football team was brought screaming into the world in 1895, to a middle-class family background. His father was a Valencian lawyer, a profession that the young Santiago was also to take up, although he had apparently wanted to study medicine. Bernabéu thus reinforces the notion of these old middle-class characters of early Madrileño football, a creature of whom there were many more in the old, pre-professional days, when it was much more common to take up a normal job but combine this with some healthy sporting pursuits. Like the doctor Alcantará, one of Barcelona's first stars, he was a professional first, and footballer second. His family had moved to Madrid for work reasons, and by 1909, as mentioned above, he first turned out for Real Madrid juniors, immediately establishing himself in the side and going on to become a first-team player by the age of 17.

There is a rare photograph of Bernabéu in 1909, sitting in the centre of the front row, the ball at his feet, looking at the camera with a distinctly confident expression. He already looks like a leader. One of the stories of the time recounts how the young Santiago was the first volunteer to help dig up the land and help paint the lines at the new ground, the O'Donnell Stadium – Madrid's first purpose-built ground – in 1912. Fans of Bernabéu will recount tearfully how he allegedly painted the fences around the ground with his elder brother Marcelo, and never asked for a peseta. Four years later he was captaining the side, and to all intents and purposes should have been picked for the Spanish national team to travel to the Olympics in Belgium in 1920 – an important footballing event and the first time that many European sides had strayed beyond their borders – but he was not chosen, allegedly for complaining publicly about the system of regional 'quotas' that was used to determine which players would represent Spain for the first time in a major competition. Most of the players to travel were in fact Basque and Catalan, simply because Barcelona, Athletic Bilbao and Irún were the best sides at the time, but interestingly, Santiago thought otherwise and clearly felt that Madrid should have been better represented. In challenging this early version of what he clearly saw as 'political correctness' (appeasing the growing regional nationalist sentiments) he first showed his colours, unafraid to wade into turbulent waters, and clearly right of centre. Right-wing biographies of him refer to this incident as an example of his 'honesty, independence and firmness', but other readings might not concur with these sentiments. Bernabéu will obviously be mentioned again, but the introduction to him here is necessary because it underlines twin events that helped to secure the club in the firmament. With a real stadium – though it was no great shakes compared to their rivals in Bilbao and Barcelona – the idea of Madrid FC as a focus for a growing sentiment was effectively born. And with Don Santiago now in the ranks that sentiment would begin to take shape, albeit slowly.

The new stadium was a five-minute walk from the bullring, on the corners of Narváez and O'Donnell, the latter street lending the stadium its Irish flavour. It was actually designed by one of the players, the Basque 'Chefo' Irureta. Once again, to underline the point about the sort of men who were playing for the club at the time, Irureta combined his unpaid voluntary work in Madrid's defence with a day-job as an architect. Eighty years later, in the exact area where the old stadium stood, several flash apartments were built, one of which is occupied by Emilio Butragueño, star of the '80s and early '90s and one of the club's most emblematic figures. But a half-century before he was born, on 31 October 1912, Madrid FC proudly inaugurated their stadium with a blessing from the local priest and a game against Sporting de Irún, from the north-eastern corner of the Basque Country. The claim that they had invited 'the best' team from Spain to play them sounds rather unconvincing looking at the evidence. It smacks more of a snub to Athletic Bilbao, a side they probably feared might spoil the day for them. As it was, Sporting (later to become the better-known Real Unión in a merger in 1913) drew 0–0 with their hosts, impolitely thrashing them 4–1 later the same afternoon. Not an auspicious start, but as previously hinted, these were not to be the years of glory.

After the early flurry of trophies, the period up to the professional era in the late 1920s is referred to as a 'transitional' or 'developmental' period, which is probably easier than referring to it as a time of under-achievement. Perhaps the sense that one has now of Real Madrid is difficult to reconcile with these early years of relative uncertainty. There is certainly abundant evidence to suggest that things might have gone even more awry in those years, and that another side could have emerged as dominant in the capital. Madrid FC were certainly far from being considered the top dogs of the local scene, a fact underlined by the supplement *Nuevo Mundo* when it pointed out that in the regional championship game in 1913 against Gimnástica the match began with two of Madrid's players missing. After Gimnástica took advantage and scored early on, one of the 'disgraced' players, Aranguren, finally turned up, but too late to prevent a 2–0 defeat. In 1914, another regional tournament game between Madrid and a new local rival, Rácing de Madrid, was delayed at the start because there was no referee, and ended in scandal because of a punch-up. Rácing, another side who have disappeared into the mists of history, actually won the regional title the next year, and when the local Federation were then handed the responsibility of selecting a representative Castilian side to play in the short-lived *Copa Principe de Asturias*, only three of Madrid FC's players made it – Santiago Bernabéu, Sotero Aranguren and René Petit. The latter, who figures in most of the interminable 'greatest players' lists of the club, is an obscure figure whose appearance nevertheless coincided with something of a mini-revival in the ranks. Two friendlies against Sevilla, recently crowned champions of Andalucía, showed that there was nothing to fear from down south. Madrid put 19 goals past them in the two games, and when the grandads Huelva turned up for a benefit match to raise money for Rácing (rather curious, given that Madrid FC were supposed to hate them), they were also dispatched with some contempt, 9–0 and 5–0. Montenegro, Huelva's star in the firmament, stayed on and signed on for the victors, subsequently forming a useful attacking partnership with Petit.

This time, in 1916 the team once again reached the final of the King's Cup, where they lost 4–0 to Athletic Bilbao, at Español's ground in Barcelona. But in the semi-finals against Barcelona, in a game which was finally decided at the fourth attempt over at Athletic Madrid's ground, the seeds of a century of mutual antipathy were well and truly watered. After three draws, the last game saw Barcelona 2–1 up at half-time. Their first true star, the doctor Paulino Alacantará, was in the Catalan line-up and had scored the second goal, disputed by Madrid. In the second half, the eccentric figure who was to train Spain four years later in the Antwerp Olympics, Paco Bru, saved a penalty from Bernabéu after Zabalo had equalised, but from then on it was all Madrid. After Aranguren had put two more past Bru, the Barcelona players allegedly started to put the boot in, but seeing that the change of tactics was having no effect were ordered off the pitch by their captain, Massana. The complaints were of biased refereeing by the ex-Madrid player Berraondo, but the Catalans had themselves asked him to officiate from the first game. This was customary before the 1920s, and it was considered a part of gentlemanly protocol that a local would take charge of a game, as a symbolic act of mutual trust. The intervention of a 'neutral' referee from another region, standard now in world football, is a symbolic act of mutual distrust, and is rather a shame, but at least it avoids the sort of rumpus that accompanied the 1916 game, a rumpus whose echoes are still being felt almost a century later. The rivalry between these two clubs was always present, simmering below the surface of gentlemanly restraint, but this game seems to have been the beginning of the all-out warfare which has since characterised their 'relationship' – if such a word is appropriate. The Catalan press, as yet to be silenced by the later dictates of Primo de Rivera's republic, had a field day, accusing Madrid FC of all crimes under the sun, and unfortunately for Madrid, the final against Athletic de Bilbao was to be played over in the eastern port, at Español's Casa Rabía Stadium. The place was predictably packed to the rafters on the day with Barcelona fans, which was perhaps the first example in Spanish football of one group of supporters deliberately going along to cheer on another team. Such an act is a public announcement of cultural hostility, a marking out of territory. And even better for those Barcelona supporters who took the tram over to the other side of the city was the fact that Athletic, with the legendary Belauste, *Pichichi* and Acedo in their ranks, continued to impose their dominance over Madrid with a 4–0 win. Walking back to the changing-rooms, the Madrid players were showered with objects from the stands (another first in Spain?) and had to be escorted back to their hotel by police. Perhaps this was the beginning of the modern era? Whatever, poor Meléndez was relieved of his duties as Madrid's president after eight years' service, because the directors considered the decision to travel to Barcelona for the final a gross mistake of judgement, given the circumstances that had prevailed in the semi-final.

Meanwhile, Madrid the city continued to grow and modernise. By 1917 the population passed the 700,000 mark and the first metro line was opened, from Puerto del Sol to Cuatro Caminos. The Great War was almost over, after which Europe would be redesigned, for better or for worse, Fátima was having her visions of the Virgin Mary and Madrid FC were reacquainting themselves with the sensation of victory – in the

King's Cup again, for the first time since 1908. They beat Arenas de Getxo (now a posh suburb of Bilbao) 2–1 in the final, but only after another troublesome thrice replayed semi-final, this time against Español, in which the Catalan fans invaded the pitch at the end and bashed the Vizcayan referee over the head with a wooden chair, knocking him out. The following year they lost to Real Unión in the final, and apart from further occasional appearances in the final, the club would bring no further silverware home until 1932, when as the renamed Real Madrid they won their first professional league title with Zamora *et al.* in the ranks. However, 1917 was to be the shadow-line in terms of trophies, and the period in between is mostly significant for events that took place outside the actual field of play.

In 1920 Madrid FC became 'Real' (Royal) Madrid, an older Alfonso XIII accepting the club's invitation to bestow this honour upon them. Real Madrid still harp on about this event as if it had been somehow unique to them, a pretension that is of course nonsense. They weren't even the first club in Spain to be handed the royal seal, Real Sociedad and Real Unión beating them to it by several years. However, one has to bear in mind that this endorsement, completely meaningless nowadays, did serve to paint a certain political hue on the clubs that sought it. Real Sociedad, for example, are now a club more associated with Basque nationalism than with one seeking royal association, but the irony of their name seems to cause them few sleepless nights in the postmodern setting – as though they merely consider it a case of empty symbolism. San Sebastián, where Real Sociedad play, was a fashionable *Belle Epoque* resort for the Spanish royal family in the late nineteenth century and earned its endorsement largely for this reason. The troublesome events of the twentieth century had not yet strained its relationship with Madrid, and the royal family by extension. The granting of this title to Madrid FC, however, implied that by 1920 only they in the capital were worthy of it. In terms of infrastructure, trophies won and historical associations with the emerging middle classes of the city, there was only one choice. Athletic de Madrid, by then completely shorn of their Basque roots, were still a worthy rival on the field of play and won the King's Cup, ironically, the year after their royal neighbours had tacked on their blue-blooded title. But they had felt no particular urge to approach the city's aristocracy in this way, as if they were content to develop their own independent, more working-class identity. Interestingly, on the restoration of the monarchy to Spain after Franco's death in 1975, Don Juan set about making himself a man of the people by showing a healthy inclination to most of the appropriate sports, skiing in the fashionable resorts and being seen to enjoy football as much as the average Spaniard. His natural moth-like tendency to be attracted to the lights of Real Madrid (as if this might appease the more conservative elements in the transitional government) was a move he seemed to later regret, a political statement he presumably felt he needed to palliate by ordering his son, Felipe, to support Atlético Madrid. The prince has grinned and borne it with admirable stoicism, but the almost permanent scandals surrounding the club in the 1990s has shown how 'mere symbolism' can prove uncomfortable to at least one of the parties involved.

The roaring '20s do seem, however, to have been the period in which the *Madrileño* football scene took on the classic dual identity of a major capital, the rest of the rivals fading away into obscurity or simply folding. Indeed, as concrete proof of this, both clubs moved to new grounds within two weeks of each other in 1923. The granting of the royal title had boosted Real Madrid's membership considerably and there were really too many folk trying to cram into the inadequate spaces around the O'Donnell Stadium. So they chose a newly constructed velodrome in the north-eastern district of Ciudad Lineal, in truth too far removed from the hub of the club's support, which was at that time gathered around the city centre and a little to the north. But it held 8,000, as opposed to the paltry 200 who could huddle under the one stand at O'Donnell (the rest exposed to the elements), and the inauguration in April 1923 was honoured by Alfonso and the Infante Don Juan (the present King's father) with Real Unión once again the sporting guests. A couple of weeks later, the Infante Don Juan traipsed along to the Metropolitano with his mother, Queen Maria Cristina, to the inauguration of Athletic's rival stadium, Real Sociedad providing the opposition. Athletic may well have felt that official royal patronage was unnecessary for their development as a club, but the young Don Juan must have been particularly chuffed when he was invited to kick the game off. Perhaps he later told his own son, one night by the royal fireside, that if he too were to sire a son then he should oblige him to support Athletic Madrid, as a favour in return for the honour of that kick-off. You never know.

Whatever the case, Real Madrid realised their geographical mistake, and only stayed at Ciudad Lineal for a year, choosing the Chamartín district north of the Cibeles for an even larger stadium. They employed an ex-player as architect once again (Pepe Castell) and built the 15,000 capacity ground immediately behind the current stadium's east side. On 17 May 1924 the English FA Cup holders Newcastle United provided extremely prestigious opposition, but were sent home with a 3–2 defeat in their ear. Real Madrid, although by then more used to playing foreign opposition on friendly tours, were clearly delighted with themselves at beating Newcastle – the first proof that a team from Spain could live with a major team from the heartlands of the game. The inauguration seemed to presage a brighter future. Hence the consequent affection for this ground, which was only destined to last until 1945 and which was almost totally ruined during the Civil War. Older supporters still refer to the present stadium as 'Chamartín', and television commentators still let the old word slip, as if despite Bernabéu's reputation and standing they are somehow uncomfortable with the personalising of a stadium, as the man himself was also rumoured to have been.

The period after these important events was crucial in the context of the game's growing but still illicit professionalism. Players such as the famous goalkeeper Zamora over at Español, and the brilliant Samitier at Barcelona were receiving something more than fees for their appearances, and the fact that Real Madrid had embarked upon an aggressive policy of signings from other clubs could only mean that the colour of the peseta had entered firmly into the reckoning. Rácing de Madrid, still trying to oppose Real's growing hegemony of the capital's scene, had complained to the federation about their star player Valderrama's defection to Real, and there were further rumblings about the inclusion of a foreigner in their ranks, the Swiss defender Mengotti. This new wheeling and dealing had resulted in an upturn in Real's fortunes, and in the Chamartín year they managed their first final since 1917, although they were beaten by Real Unión.

Deaf to protests, they even tried their luck in England in 1925, setting off with a squad of 17 players to play a three-game tour against Newcastle, Birmingham and Tottenham, all of which they lost. Just before the tour they had managed to annoy the rest of the country by taking along Otero, Vásquez and Ramón from Deportivo de La Coruña, Esparza from Tolosa and Larraza from Athletic de Bilbao. All these players were subsequently signed, and in 1926 Real came clean with the purchase of the star forward from Arenas de Getxo, José María Peña. This signing is generally viewed in Spain's football history as the beginning of professionalism, since the player was actually offered a contract that specified a wage. The young Basque was not the first to receive money in exchange for his talents, but the pesetas on offer were paid to him above the table, as it were. Seventy-five years later, the Portuguese midfielder Figo and the Frenchman Zidane would move to this same club for transfer fees so relatively astronomical as to render any financial comparisons utterly meaningless. But it started back then, less in earnest than in experiment – and it was a sign of the times. There was no going back. The public were by now too demanding, and rivalries too important, to permit the amateur spirit of the game to continue along its more innocent path.

In the European summer of 1927, with Bernabéu working at the club as a sort of general manager, Real underlined their new financial status by extending their footballing horizons on a three-month tour of Argentina, Peru, Mexico and Cuba, returning to Spain from New York on the good ship *Alfonso XIII* the following September. As the expedition sailed the Atlantic back to Spain, the Argentinian journalist Julio Cunco wrote in *La Razón* that:

> Real Madrid are the most interesting and talented side to have
> visited our shores in recent times. They practise a superior brand
> of football to most European sides we have seen. They are more
> tactically advanced, and they like to entertain.

Real Madrid in particular, and Spanish football in general, was ready to organise itself in earnest. The Federation's big plan, to form a national league, was just around the corner.

5. LIFE BEFORE ALFREDO

A league is a many splendoured thing. Cup competitions featuring instant knockout, exciting though they are, cannot hope to match a championship whose measurement of success is based on the concept of long-term consistency, of eight months of toil through the changing landscapes of autumn, winter and spring. As the old cliché goes, the league table does not lie, come the end of the season. Leaving aside arguments of political favours, over-rich chairmen and the size of the hinterland from which teams originally quarried their players, it was more likely to be an accurate reflection of the relative qualities of the squads involved, since the argument that a team could be beaten on an off-day in the more randomised framework of a knockout competition became redundant within the context of a league competition. And curiously, though few people remember the losers in a cup final, they do, by and large, remember who were runners-up in a given year, or they can recall which side pushed the champions the most – probably because they view the achievements of the league's bridesmaids as more worthy than those of the defeated cup finalists. Just a theory, but one that would partly explain why the Spanish finally decided to set up a national league, in 1928. Certainly, the onset of professionalism demanded some sort of development in the infrastructure of the game, added to the fact that the national railway network, although still fairly poor, had improved considerably during the 1920s and was certainly considered adequate to support overnight travel for the teams in the two divisions that were to be established. Besides, as far as the top flight was concerned, of the ten teams invited to take part, nine came from only three regions of Spain – Catalonia, Castile and the Basque Country. The odd-man-out, Rácing de Santander, was from Cantabria, to the west of Bilbao, and thus hardly from the depths of beyond. Though Spain is a big country, and its modern-day football supporters are still relatively unaccustomed to English-style away-day travel, back in 1928 the longest trip any team had to make was probably Santander to Barcelona – a route facilitated by the fact that both cities were ports and were thus connected by rail.

For the record, the league finally got under way on 10 February 1929, after the traditional cup competition had been played and Real Madrid had lost 2–1 to Espanyol in Valencia's Mestalla Stadium, in the famous *Final del agua* (water final) exactly a week before. Zamora was in goal that day for Espanyol, and Bernabéu, elected onto a three-man board of directors two years earlier (he had also acted as trainer in 1928), was in the crowd. As he would do 23 years later on seeing Di Stéfano in the flesh for the first time, back then he knew that the talent and personality that Zamora possessed would be better off serving the image of Real Madrid than going to waste on a bunch of Catalans, a culture he had little time for. But he would have to wait for his first big coup. Meanwhile, despite the cup setback, Madrid looked to have put together a decent side capable of winning the prestigious first league title.

In the semi-finals in January, on another torrential afternoon, Madrid had put paid to the 'curse of Bilbao' and beaten the seemingly invincible Athletic 4–1 in San Mamés, the first time they had won there since the famous ground's inauguration in 1913. Coming after a 3–1 win in Chamartín, the psychological lift was palpable, especially considering the hostility they encountered, the appalling weather and the troublesome political backdrop of the oncoming republic. The game is a legendary one in Madrid's history, and Triana (2), Rubio and Lazcano the mythical scorers. Bilbao were far from broken, however, and went on to win the next four editions of the cup, beating Real in the finals of 1930 and 1933 in the process, but at the time it seemed like a case of good vibrations for our heroes from the capital.

The league, in truth, should have begun in the autumn of 1928, but the Spanish do have an unfortunate knack for fulfilling those stereotypes about *mañana*. Nevertheless, it is not always due to the indolence with which the country is unfairly associated, and was in this case more owing to a disease far more prevalent in the culture, that of being unable to agree on anything. As soon as one committee is formed, it seems to be par for the course to form another, just in case things are going too smoothly. It's not so much a problem of bureaucracy here as the simple need to express an opinion – to get your oar in. And this in a country that allowed itself to be ruled by a dictatorship for almost 40 years. The paradox has been noted before, but suffice to mention here that the delay of the league's onset was due to the disagreement between the Union of Professional Clubs and the Spanish Union of Clubs as to how many teams the two proposed leagues should allow in. The former eventually won the argument, and the ten sides invited in were the six cup winners since 1902, the three most common runners-up, and a tenth decided by knockout, won against Sevilla by the aforementioned Santander. Significantly perhaps, they were to finish bottom at the end of that first season.

The other nine pioneers were Barcelona, Español and Europa (Catalonia), Real Madrid and Athletic de Madrid (Castile), and Athletic de Bilbao, Real Unión, Arenas de Getxo and Real Sociedad from the Basque Country. In the original Second Division, sides who would later make some impact on the national scene included Valencia, Oviedo, Betis, Celta and Alavés. But the most interesting aspect of the First Division was the spicy mix of three regions, two of which were becoming increasingly restless in the political arena. Basque and Catalan nationalism had been around from the turn of the century, but they had been handed further justifications for their existence by the high-handed and shabby treatment meted out to them by Primo de Rivera's dictatorship – very much the shape of things to come. Madrid, as a growing symbol of right-wing political centralism, in so much as it was the seat of government, meant that the relationship between Real Madrid and any teams from the more unruly regions was increasingly strained. Add to this inter-city enmity the fact that there were also intra-city tensions between Barcelona and Español, Real and Athletic de Madrid and Bilbao and Getxo – not to mention the simmering hostility between Bilbao and Real Sociedad – and it seems astonishing now that this league was formed when it was, just three years before the declaration of the republic that would lead to the bloody Civil War of 1936. Maybe it delayed hostilities, by diluting them on the field of play, or was merely a form of practice for the real thing to come. Whatever, it was a seminal period in Spanish history, further underlined by the beginnings of a national league where players, and to a lesser extent supporters, could travel to other parts of the peninsula and experience first-hand the fact that Spain was a loose confederation of distinct cultures, a fragile entity about to explode in the face of the dizzying events of the '30s and '40s. It must have been fascinating for those players in 1929 to have been a party to this phenomenon, to have travelled to other cities with quite distinct cultures (and languages) and to have measured themselves up against other teams, just as the press itself must have welcomed the opportunity to spice up these new encounters.

Real's first game was at Chamartín, against Europa de Barcelona – once a side with vaulting ambitions but who now turn out in Catalonia's regional leagues. The league which Real Madrid would so dominate in later years began in auspicious fashion with a thumping 5–0 victory, with four goals from Lazcano, signed by Bernabéu from Osasuna the year before for 6,000 pesetas and of whom the great man is rumoured to have said, 'If he turns out to be a dud, I'll pay the 6,000 myself'. He was no dud, and now holds the honour of being the club's first scorer in the professional league. The following Sunday (Spanish games were played on the Sabbath from the outset) Madrid travelled to Barcelona and beat them – in some small way avenging that first encounter back in 1902 – and then did the same to Athletic de Madrid a week later over at their ground, in the first league *derbi* between the two. All in all, the first season was a successful one, but Barcelona stole Madrid's thunder when it most mattered for the history books, and pipped them for the first championship, finishing with two points more.

For those who look for the reasons behind the greatness of institutions, several of the factors that would eventually contribute to Real Madrid's hegemony of the Spanish scene were already clicking into place that first season. There was the simple matter of finance, and the fact that the club were already being followed by more folk than were watching Athletic de Madrid, for example. This meant that various signings could be financed, plus the fact that Bernabéu had already begun to fraternise with certain members of the Madrid banking community, people with whom he had had contacts in his lawyer days. Fifteen years later, when he was elected club president, these people would hand to him, on extremely favourable terms, the considerable credit he required to buy up the land upon which the Bernabéu was finally built. But first in 1928 and 1929, then again with the famous signing of Zamora, Madrid distinguished themselves as the market dabblers, the forerunners of the same club who would buy Di Stéfano, Puskas, Gento *et al.*, who would end the century by breaking the world transfer record to sign Luis Figo from Barcelona and later sign Ronaldo, Zidane and David Beckham, the latter in a flurry of market-driven enterprise. Bilbao, to highlight the diametrical opposite – the side that were to continue to dominate up to the Civil War – were already pursuing a Basque-only policy in their ranks, but Madrid were less fussy about the ethnic origins of their players, and were already a relatively 'cosmopolitan' set-up. Of the 11 players who turned out against Español in the cup final of 1929, only four were actually *Madrileños* born and bred. This is not to suggest, of course, that Madrid's subsequent history of big signings represents a more virtuous way of going about things than Bilbao's, but in terms of the relative post-war successes of the two clubs, there is little argument as to which policy has reaped the greater rewards.

However, more importantly than even this was the growing sense of continuity in the club, of something approaching tradition and patrimony, despite the fact that these were still early days. After 27 years of official existence, the three men at the helm, Bernabéu, Pedro Parages and president Luis Urquijo, were all ex-players from the earliest days. This organic sense that the club possesses to this day is crucial to any understanding of Real Madrid as an institution. Ex-players, notably Molowny, Muñoz, Di Stéfano, Valdano and Del Bosque would later return as managers, a public policy which often hid the more important incorporation of ex-players into the general coaching, administrative and executive branches of the club. In the centenary year, the most prominent figures of the PR machine were Jorge Valdano and Emilio Butragueño, both important ex-players. It's not exactly the policy of the 'boot-room', but rather the idea of a coherent and consistent line of people who have been, and who continue to be, committed to the cause. This is the type of club that Bernabéu, himself around for so long, had envisaged. Later on in this book Real Madrid's uncanny ability to replace their dying kings with fresh pretenders – especially when it comes to goalscorers – will be examined. But for now, suffice to underline the development of this general idea of continuity.

For the second season of the new league (1929–30), the Hungarian Lippo Hertza took over from José Quirante as coach – further evidence of Madrid's willingness to import foreign ideas. But the season was to be a disappointing one, at least as far as the league campaign was concerned. They picked up no more than a measly point from the first five games, ending the miserable run with a 6–0 thrashing of Santander, who had obligingly remained in the top flight because the Federación had failed to agree on the issues of relegation and promotion at the end of that first year. From that game on, things picked up a little, but at the end of the season Real finished a disappointing fifth with 17 points from 18 games, way behind the inevitable winners, Athletic de Bilbao who finished with 30 points. By the spring of that season the relegation criteria were at last in place, and it was to be Real's neighbours, Athletic de Madrid, who took the first plunge, Rácing de Santander going on to consolidate their place until they were to finally succumb in 1940.

Looking at the results from that season, one could be forgiven for suspecting that the factors which contribute to what we now understand as 'consistency' were relatively absent. How else does one explain an 8–1 reversal at Español in the 14th week of the season, a 6–1 victory two weeks later at home to Europa, a 5–1 reversal the following week up in Getxo, all concluding with a 5–1 win at home to runners-up Barcelona in week 18, to finish the season off? Granted, the Catalans were too far adrift of Bilbao to harbour any ambitions of the title that afternoon, but the rivalry between these two sides was by then sufficient to ensure that neither wished to lose. Maybe the explanation is prosaic, in that the undefeated Bilbao were so dominant that season that the rest were simply reduced to picking the bones and feeding off the scraps, a rather messy situation in which most of the teams were both physically and tactically short of the standards required to ensure consistency of performance over 18 games. Such a campaign seems short now, but one suspects that back then, with more primitive training methods, poorer diet and total lack of medical back-up, it was long enough. Suffice to mention that only seven years earlier, Rafael Moreno 'Pichichi', Bilbao's famous goalscoring star, had died suddenly of typhus at the age of 29. Spain was still a poor country, and its footballers, though fit men, were not immune to its endemic weaknesses.

However, once again, before the league campaign had got under way, Madrid had reached the final of the cup, this time coming up against the eventual league champions, Bilbao. The final was played in drier circumstances than the previous year, the neutral venue being the Montjuic Stadium in Barcelona, built back then as a possible Olympic venue and now home to Español. The game has gone down in Madrid's history books as the first one in which explicit Catalan hostility had a direct bearing on the result. Whereas Bilbao were applauded onto the pitch, Madrid were greeted with howls of derision. The Basques and the Catalans had by then formed a mutual bond of sympathy towards each other, due to the political similarities of their situations, on the surface at least. The game provided a good opportunity to make this explicit, and the choice of a Catalan referee, the unfortunate Sr Comorera, was hardly destined to allay Madrid's fears of an uncomfortable afternoon. Nevertheless, they made a decent stab at the game, twice equalising

Bilbao's opening two goals, until Triana, ten minutes from the end, scored what looked like a perfectly legal winner, hitting the ball through a ruck of Basque defenders. The reason for the disallowing of the goal has never been explained, but in the resulting extra time, Lafuente got the winner for Bilbao and Madrid left the pitch surrounded by a hostile Catalan public who had come along to show their displeasure at all things white. Peña, Quesada and Triana were all set upon by spectators who had invaded the pitch at the end, and the incidents caused a predictable furore in the *Madrileño* press. Real would find plenty of opportunities to get their own back, of course, and modern Spanish football lore is full of the tales of woe and victimisation allegedly suffered by Bilbao and to a greater extent Barcelona in the years after the Civil War. Some of these tales will emerge later in the book, and some of them, of course, have a great deal of substance. But back in 1930, Real Madrid were still small enough to be on the receiving end.

Bilbao, as mentioned, went on to dominate that second season, winning the first *doblete* (double) of the professional era and establishing themselves as fearful opponents with a passionate following in a true cauldron of a stadium, boiling over with regional nationalistic fervour. Despite Madrid's claims of robbery earlier that season, no one was in any doubt as to the identity of the kings of that early period in the league's history. Like Real Madrid, they had opted for foreign coaching, and were playing under the auspices of the legendary Freddie Pentland, an eccentric Englishman who had spent the whole of the First World War as a prisoner, coaching the German officers in the arts of the game. He had played for a number of English clubs before the outbreak of the Great War and had brought to Bilbao (a particularly Anglophile club) the 'Pentland Way', a philosophy of football that preached the superiority of the passing game, as opposed to the 'hoof and chase' that had predominated in the early 1920s. Barcelona publicly stole his ideas in 1928, since in their maestro Josep Samitier they had a player capable of translating Pentland's blackboard patterns into concrete expression on the field of play. But Bilbao also had Gorostiza and Lafuente, and the concept of the possession game that now so characterises Spanish football began to take root in these two sides. At Real Madrid, there was a distinct feeling that something had to be done in order to catch up.

Curiously enough, the solutions were not exactly classic Real Madrid. In the post-war period, their most significant signings were to be of charismatic forwards and attack-minded midfielders, but when the club finally got their act together in those early years, the reasons were of the more defensive variety. In the sunny October of 1930, the news that Ricardo Zamora – *El Divino* (the Divine One) had signed for Real Madrid took the country by storm. With the radio now a more significant feature of Spanish society and the press well practised in the art of sensationalism, the transfer caused an enormous kerfuffle, not least because it provided a rest from the problematic political backdrop. Six months later, Spain would become a republic and Alfonso XIII, the man whose initial enthusiasm had helped football to move into the public eye, would go into exile. But for now, the public, and particularly the *Madrileño* one, could talk about something else.

On arriving in Madrid by train, Zamora made a speech on the platform in the manner of a visiting statesman:

> I have come here to defend the colours of Real Madrid and to do everything that the directors wish me to do. I'm convinced that we can go far, not just because of my arrival but because the players here, are, by and large, the best in Spain. In Barcelona I still have many good friends but now that I've left I feel that I couldn't have chosen a better place to come – where the supporters understand their football and the warmth of the people is something that I really appreciate.

The defender who was to sign the next year, the great Quincoces, remarked in an interview in 1978 that in his time Zamora was 'more famous than Garbo and better looking'. It remains one of the great sporting quotes of the century and encapsulates its subject to perfection. Zamora was not given to idle talk, and his speech on the platform would have been designed to annoy as many people as possible whilst charming his new hosts to the brim. The stuff about Real Madrid's players being 'by and large' the best in the country was subtly qualified, but would nevertheless have annoyed the twin populations of Bilbao and Barcelona. But Ricardo was happy. He'd just taken a cut of 40,000 pesetas from the 150,000 paid to Espanyol by his new owners, and was no doubt looking forward to spending some of this enormous booty in the clubs and bars of the capital.

He made his debut a week later (5 October 1930) in the regional championship against Rácing de Madrid, and in the next game, against Athletic de Madrid, Chamartín was so full that spectators had to be turned away by mounted police. As if this commotion were not enough, in the second half, the star of the show dived at the feet of Buiría and remained there, motionless. You can hear the dumbfounded silence across the years. Zamora was carried off and would not appear again until almost halfway through the league season, by which time his new colleagues were still struggling with a mere three wins under their belts. He finally returned for the eighth game of the season up at Real Sociedad, the game after Madrid had been destroyed at home 0–6 by the old enemy from Bilbao.

Zamora, of course, had not just appeared from nowhere. All the fuss surrounding his signing requires some background, and the first thing to note is that the inclusion of Zamora as one of the most famous figures in Real Madrid's history may seem odd in some ways. This is because he is more readily claimed by the Catalans as their own – particularly by Espanyol, for whom he made his debut in 1916. He played through most of the '20s for them, having gone to Barcelona and then quickly returned – his detractors say for money to pay off his betting debts, his admirers because they say he felt most at home there. He only signed for Real Madrid 14 years after his league debut, and 10 years after his international debut at the Olympic Games in Ambères, Belgium. He was to play for the capital's club with distinction until the Civil War broke out in 1936, and after that would launch into his managerial career on the other side of town, at Atlético Madrid. But it is Zamora's association with Real Madrid that most people remember, due in some measure to the record fee paid for him back in 1930 and the fact that he was no *Catalanista*. However much Barça might wish to claim him as one of their legendary players, he was never happy at a club that wished to mark itself out as non-Spanish.

Espanyol, for whom he made his debut against, curiously enough, Real Madrid (0–0 of course), have always been a club that have stuck in the political craw of Barcelona, and have associated themselves, at times in their history, with the more fascist side of Spanish politics. Their foundation, two years after Barcelona, was a deliberate attempt to form a more 'Spanish' side within the city, since their founders considered Barcelona a 'foreign side'. Even today, when Real Madrid run out into the empty spaces of Montjuic Stadium in Barcelona, they are greeted like conquering heroes. The hostility encountered there in 1930 was generated by Barcelona supporters. Most Espanyol fans support Real Madrid too. It seems to be the tradition – so long as it annoys their neighbours over in the Camp Nou. It was no surprise, therefore, that

Zamora spent most of his time with these two clubs, and that he is remembered as Real's most famous keeper. So famous that when Stalin received news of the swearing in of President Niceto Zamora in 1934 for the occasion of the Second Spanish Republic, he is alleged to have said, 'Ah, that goalkeeper'.

If you look on several Internet sites for information on Ricardo Zamora, you notice that he is often included on pages that talk of other people who came to define their chosen sports – Jack Dempsey, Muhammad Ali, Don Bradman, Magic Johnson. This is exalted company indeed. Like many of these men, he was born into the working classes, in his case in a poor suburb of Barcelona in 1901 to Spanish 'immigrant' parents. The young Ricardo in fact showed little inclination to play football until he was 13 or 14, his favourite pastime being the Basque game of *pelota*, a game that requires strength and stamina, as well as an eye for the ball. Apparently, having seen a game live in 1914, he decided to turn his attention to football, because 'the ball was so much bigger, and I thought it would be much easier'. According to those still alive who saw him play, he did indeed make it look easy.

Zamora supposedly represents the classic divide in Spain, apparent for all to see when Figo left Barcelona for Madrid in the postmodern era. He who dares to play for both sides, like Schuster and Laudrup before Figo, is inevitably viewed as a suspicious character who cannot be trusted to understand, nor therefore act out, the classic cultural dichotomy of Spain. The player who swaps one of these cities for the other can only be doing it for money – the theory goes. Di Stéfano himself went on to play out the twilight days of his career at Espanyol, annoyed as he was with Madrid's treatment of him in his final year. Espanyol's infamous 'Blue Brigade' supporters' club signed up for the Falange in 1936 and fought savagely in the Civil War against the Communists, probably alongside Bernabéu himself. Zamora too was portrayed in the Catalan press as a turncoat in 1929 when he signed from Espanyol, but the truth was that he was moving from one right-wing institution to another. He knew perfectly well what he was doing.

Zamora's name still adorns the annual trophy awarded to the season's best goalkeeper in Spain, as does Zamora's early contemporary, 'Pichichi', the top scorer's version. Zamora, perhaps more importantly, came to represent Spain's first real version of the superstar syndrome, moving to Madrid at a time when the game was turning professional. The players were beginning to earn reasonable sums, at least at clubs where the public membership could pay the players a decent wage. He was also, lest it be forgotten, Real Madrid's first big star, signed by them at a time when both Barcelona and Athletic Bilbao were more successful. Barça had already had Samitier and Alcantará as big name players, and Zamora was Bernabéu's choice, in his first executive decision at the club, as the man to lead them out of the doldrums into the limelight. It was a big signing, and the fact that it took the country by storm was exactly what the club needed. Twenty-four years later, this time as president, Bernabéu would do it again by signing Di Stéfano. But Zamora was the first. At last, Real began to win things with him between the posts – the league in 1932 and 1933, and the cup in 1934 and 1936. Whilst he was with Madrid, he was voted best goalkeeper of the 1934 World Cup in Italy – some accolade, since they were knocked out by the hosts in the second round, courtesy of some very dodgy refereeing decisions and Zamora's non-appearance in the second round replay against Italy. Schiavo's famous thump at Zamora's throat as a corner was taken, and Ferrari's subsequent punching of the ball into the net were overlooked by a referee who was clearly under 'instructions'. Spain's most famous player could not make it for the replay, so brutally had he been singled out by the Italians. Italy won 1–0, and Zamora had made his final appearance in a major world tournament.

But in that first season, 1930–31, Madrid had not been able to count on his services until the eighth game. They had conceded 17 in seven games, but in the following 11 were only to let in a further 10, giving them the best defensive figures in the division. They finished a disappointing sixth, but at least avenged the Bilbao defeat by beating them (again the eventual champions) 2–4 in San Mamés. The fact that they only scored 24 in 18 games, only one more than the relegated Europa, seems to have passed by unnoticed, at least by the policy makers. During the summer, the offices at the ground were extended and the manager provided with a particularly posh one. When Lippo Hertza was shown his spanking new office by the press officer, Pablo Hernandez, the latter was somewhat taken aback by the Hungarian's silence. 'Come on, Lippo,' he allegedly began – 'even Pentland's lot haven't got installations like these' (referring to Bilbao). Lippo's acid reply – 'Yes. But he has a decent team' – seems to have been the spark for further reflection on the part of the directors, and later that year Madrid paid out 60,000 pesetas for two defenders who were making a name for themselves up in Vitoria, at Alavés. Jacinto Quincoces and Errasti Ciriaco were both full-backs, but could double as centre-backs when the occasion demanded. Besides, the term *defensa* was rather vague back then, especially at a time when full-backs rarely ventured beyond the halfway line. 'Defence' seems to have been defined by those who confined themselves to a certain area of the field, and 'centre-back' was anyone who was big and could use his head. Quincoces, proclaimed 'Best Defender' at the 1934 World Cup to accompany the accolade for Zamora, went on to win 25 caps and later managed the club, among others. The hard man of the time, he took to wearing a knotted handkerchief on his head during the games, claiming that it helped him to head the ball longer distances. When the football tabloid *Marca* recently entreated its readers to vote in a poll to decide on the order of the best 100 players to have played for Madrid, Quincoces was the highest-ranking pre-1950 outfield player to appear, coming in at number 20. Next to appear in the old-timers' hierarchy was his friend Ciriaco, at number 43. Since the poll was stacked in favour of those players who had actually been witnessed doing their stuff, their elevated positions in the hierarchy speak volumes.

The effect of their arrival in the capital was immediate. Madrid carried their bat and went the whole season undefeated, winning 10 and drawing 8, conceding a mere 15 goals. Bilbao were pushed into second place, and Barcelona came third, a pretty sight for all *Madridistas*. The team had also been reinforced by the arrival of the goalscorer Luis Regueiro from Irún (55th in the poll), but the tactical emphasis had been clear – build from the back, on solid foundations. Bilbao took the cup again, the third of a consecutive run of four, but in the league, the times seemed to be a-changin'. On the last day of the season, Bilbao could still have won it, but lost at Santander, whilst Madrid drew the final game 2–2 at Les Corts in Barcelona. The Catalans had failed to ruin their enemy's party, and Real returned to the ruin amid triumphant scenes. The tradition of jumping in the Cibeles fountain was yet to be established but the celebrations, coupled with the team's official invitation to the mayor's residence, all contributed to the growing feeling that Madrid's hour was nigh. Strange though it now sounds, this was their first trophy since 1917, and though it was not exactly won in style, it signalled the end of a fallow period. Little were those celebrating fans to realise, but after the retention of the title the next year, they would have to wait another 20 years for Di Stéfano before winning it again.

Meanwhile, Lippo Hertza left and the English connection of the days of yore was renewed with the arrival of Robert Firth, a Nottinghamshire man who had been managing Rácing de Santander with some success. Before Christmas, the cup had seen a repeat of the infamous 1930 final, although this time Bilbao won 2–1. The game was played in Montjuic again, and was refereed by a Catalan. No one invaded the pitch that day, but Madrid must have been happy to see the back of that stadium. Unfortunately, for the opening game of the season they were forced to return, losing 2–1 to Espanyol, the first league game they had lost since the end of the 1930–31 season, when they went down 2–1 in Barcelona, again! But they won the next four games, with Olivares scoring freely, and by the time they drew 1–1 at Barcelona in the sixth game of the championship, Bernabéu was once again working his magic behind the scenes. The signing that he came up with – that of Josep Samitier from Barcelona – was in some ways more surprising than the transfer of Zamora. Indeed, the whole issue of Samitier belongs more to the pages of Agatha Christie than a book on football, but it makes interesting reading nevertheless.

Of all the problems that the Catalans have had to deal with in the twentieth century regarding their troublesome relationship with Real Madrid, the *Asunto Samitier* (Samitier Issue) is one of the most mysterious and vexed. Just how he was persuaded to 'turn white' is a question that no one has answered satisfactorily, although like Zamora, *El Sami* was not averse to a peseta or two. The problem for *Catalanistas* far and wide is that whilst Zamora's right-wing leanings continue to be of comfort to them, Samitier was supposed to be the embodiment of the thriving Barcelona scene, another raffish society dandy whose style and contacts – he was friends with the Argentine tango king, Gardel – marked him out as the difference between the dynamic cosmopolitan city, refreshed by the breezes of the Med, and the supposedly more staid capital stewing in the arid centre of the country. But he changed sides! The first unthinkable act of a century's mutual antipathy whose counterpoint would be seen at its very end when Luis Figo did the very same, to similar howls of protest. But Figo has since been dismissed as a Portuguese mercenary. Samitier was from the heartlands. And just to make matters worse, when Barcelona visited Madrid nine weeks after the transfer, Samitier scored both the goals in a 2–1 win, and was celebrating with his mates three weeks later when the league title was retained and Barcelona finished fourth, nine points adrift.

Maybe it was Zamora's presence at Madrid that helped persuade him to change. They both made their debuts at 17, were both from similar social backgrounds, and coincided in the Barcelona team in 1919, playing together until 1922 when Zamora returned to Espanyol. By 1925, Samitier was the country's highest earner, his famous bicycle-kicks having earned him the rather curious nickname of 'the lobster', due to the eccentric action with which he accompanied these kicks. He certainly shared Zamora's taste for the high life, and though he never starred (as did Zamora) in any of the early 'talkies', he was another good looker, to which photos of the time can attest. Another more notorious photo of the time was snapped by a newspaper in the early hours down Las Ramblas, the hub of Barcelona's night-life, with Samitier leaving a club with his troupe of night-birds just as a group of Barça´s directors are passing by on the other side of the walkway, pretending not to have noticed their employee. It would seem that he was too important to the whole institution to rein in, and he continued his refuelling habits untroubled by anything resembling club discipline. Besides, in a less fitness-obsessed time, it all added to the legend. On the outbreak of the Civil War he fled to Nice where he joined Zamora in the French league, where the two of them found a society perfectly suited to their demanding social habits.

When Samitier died in 1972, there was mass mourning in Barcelona and scenes that resembled a state funeral – rather ironic considering that the man himself had been much closer to Real Madrid in his later years and had made no secret of his admiration for Franco and his friendship with Bernabéu. At the time of his death, Barcelona were going through a rough period in their history and probably needed a hero to mourn, a move criticised by several commentators but particularly by his widow. Certainly, those who are fond of conspiracy theories are keen on the idea that Samitier was the 'double agent' in the Di Stéfano affair in the early '50s, supposedly working for Barcelona but in fact on the payrolls of Madrid. This will be examined later, but for now it helps to partly explain the impact that the transfer had back in the '30s.

In strictly footballing terms he is important because he was one of the first players to orchestrate from midfield, although histories of Real Madrid insist on labelling him a *delantero* (forward). Until Samitier, the linchpins of the teams had been bruising centre-forwards, particularly up in Bilbao. This new emergence of the 'midfield general' was important, and was closer to Pentland's concept of style, which he introduced in the late '20s to the Basques. But *El Sami* was the first to come up with it alone, on the field of play. Bernabéu, traditionally reluctant to praise anyone with Catalan blood, made an exception of

Samitier, and described him as one of the best players he ever saw. He seems to have played in a position combining the roles of what we would now call the central midfielder and the sweeper, but with the licence to attack. By the time he arrived in Madrid he was 31, and perfectly suited to the role of provider for Olivares and Regueiro. Besides, his incorporation could provide the team with some style, and banish the idea that they were ultra-defensive. In two years, crucially, Real Madrid had poached the league's two most famous players, setting the template for the post-war years. All eyes were now on them, the way that Bernabéu had planned it.

Runners-up the next season to Bilbao, who simply refused to lie down and permit Real Madrid to take over, the Samitier-less Barça finished next to bottom in one of their worst seasons. At the end of the previous season, Alavés, shorn of their best defenders (Quincoces and Ciriaco), had gone a step further and been relegated. The smouldering resentment at Madrid's policy was beginning to have some justification. That season saw a change in the order of the two main events, and the cup final, as it is today, was played after the conclusion of the league championship. Once again it was in Montjuic, but this time Madrid broke the hoodoo and beat Valencia 2–1, on the sixth day of May.

The Catalan Paco Bru was by now the manager, Firth having left after one season at the helm. Bru was to stay until 1941, and was yet another character in the annals of the unlikely ones who turned up at the club during this period. Perhaps it is all evidence of Madrid's claim about itself – that it is the truly cosmopolitan club that welcomes all comers, and not Barcelona. Bru is certainly evidence of the continuing Catalan blood-line that ran through the earlier years of the club, something with which Real Madrid still seem to be fairly comfortable.

Born in 1885, he was playing for Barcelona during the first decade of the century. He went on to play for Español, hanging up his boots in 1917. On retiring, he decided to become a referee, and allegedly before his first game in charge walked into the dressing-rooms and pulled out a Colt pistol from his haversack. Saying nothing, he threw the gun onto a table in the middle of the room and began to put on his refereeing gear. Once he was changed, he picked up the gun and stuffed it down his shorts, explaining to a player who had had the temerity to ask him why he was carrying a pistol that he had merely wished to 'guarantee a pacific match, given that it is my first in charge'. They don't make 'em like that nowadays.

Bru had managed the first Spanish side to play abroad in an official competition, in the Antwerp Olympics of 1920 where they picked up a silver medal. He also managed the Peruvian national side during the World Cup in Uruguay, and in 1932 whilst taking Rácing de Madrid on tour to South America, had managed to get himself caught up in a coup in Peru. In actual fact, the coup would not have happened without him. When they docked in Panama, he was met by the Peruvian General Sánchez del Cerro, at that time in exile. Sánchez knew of Bru through the World Cup and promptly invited him to dinner, passing on to him various letters to deliver in Peru – letters which were actually military instructions to several of his loyal sympathisers. Four days later, Bru awoke to the sounds of shooting beneath his hotel window and was summoned to the presidential palace (by Sánchez) to be told that if he wanted to bring his family over to Peru to live, he would be given the freedom of Lima. Instead he came home, and a year later was managing the most fashionable side of the 1930s.

Betis surprisingly took the league title in 1935, their neighbours Sevilla winning the cup, but there was to be no significant shift in the balance of power since the migrant Basque workers who had made up that Betis side were in exile by the time the league programme was restored in 1939. The season 1935–36 was played out against a darkening political sky, and the famous cup final of 1936 took place only a month before the Civil War broke out. Madrid were again runners-up to Bilbao in that last, desperate season, but it was the cup final in Valencia that was to go down in history as a classic, not just because it was played on the very cusp of the war.

Real Madrid v. Barcelona that year, of all years, seems to have been the mischievous caprice of the gods. Though Barcelona was to become associated with Republican heroism and Madrid with fascism, these images are inevitably simplifications. Madrid, and then its football team, became Franco's pets much later on in the story, and only after Bernabéu had finally taken over as president in the mid-1940s.

What happened at that highly charged final was that Zamora, in Madrid's colours, finally had the chance to put one over on the former employers who, he later claimed, had turned their backs on him in the early 1920s. He was hit by a bottle before the game began, and was booed relentlessly by the Valencian crowd, back then pro-Barcelona. Despite the mood, Eugenio and Lecue each scored for Madrid in the opening 12 minutes but Escolá got one back for the Catalans before half-time. In the second half, Madrid's famous defence held out until three minutes from the end when Zamora pulled off a save rumoured to be up there alongside Banks's foiling of Pelé. It is certainly the most celebrated save of the country's football history, and most Spaniards know the facts surrounding it. There is actually a good photo, taken at close quarters by the side of the post to which Zamora had dived. The weather had been sunny for the period prior to the match and the pitch was dry and dusty. Ventorlá had taken off down the shaded right-hand side of the pitch and nutmegged Quincoces on the way – no mean feat – before switching the ball inside to Escolá. From just outside the area he hit the ball hard and low, aiming for the inside of the post. The stadium rose to acclaim the goal, upon which Zamora's dive sent up a plume of dust, obscuring the scene. In the photo you can see that Zamora's left arm has stopped the ball, just before his body hits the ground, but in the stands all that could be seen was the cloud. When the dust cleared, Zamora was standing there impassively, the ball in his hands. Comic-book stuff, but it adds to the legend – one whose last significant act on a football pitch in Spain was to deny his home town side some crumbs of comfort before a period in history that would see their culture attacked, their city all but destroyed, and most of their best players in exile abroad. When the league programme resumed Zamora carried on veering to the political right, trying his hand most successfully as manager of Atlético Aviación – later to become Atlético Madrid. Aviación, packed full of the top players from the airforce and army, won the first two titles of the post-Civil War period, and were clearly the first beneficiaries of Franco's new regime. Zamora, significantly, was at the helm.

Several months after his great save, he was smoking his three-packs and drinking his cognac on the street cafés of Nice, only weeks after newspapers reported seeing his bullet-ridden body by the roadside in a ditch in Madrid's Moncloa district. The reports of his death were exaggerated, but one can imagine the commotion that it provoked at the time. The fact that his namesake, President Niceto Zamora, had honoured him with the Order of the Republic in 1934 had led many to believe he was pinker than he really was. His death at the hands of Nationalist forces was therefore plausible, but he was instead portrayed as another heroic victim of the 'Reds', causing various memorial services to break out over the area, especially in those communities that had swung behind Franco. Whilst these were taking place, a group of militiamen, unamused by the reports and knowing of Zamora's real whereabouts, arrested him and took him to the Modelo prison, a dangerous place for anyone who had played for Español.

It's the stuff that films are made of, and over several days Zamora kept his potential executors at bay with tales of his playing days and an endless series of penalty competitions. His captors, politics aside, were simply the latest to fall for his charm, and could not resist the temptation to have a kick-about with him. When he finally slipped out, in disguise, he was driven up to the French border and on to Nice, where he met up with Samitier and signed for the local side. Samitier, who had hung up his boots in Spain and had been managing Athletic de Madrid, decided to resume his playing career in France during the Civil War years, but only after a lucky escape too. The fact that he was arrested in the early days of the Civil War by anarchist militiamen suggests that they were less than convinced of his Republican Catalan sentiments. He got away, on a French boat, but the story of how he managed it is very murky, and the experience seemed to embitter him, in his heart of hearts. There are those who attribute his alleged double dealings in the Di Stéfano affair to his close escape in 1936. Whatever, he and Zamora almost picked up a French championship medal between them, Nice finishing a close second to Girondins in 1937.

The Spanish Civil War was a complex and brutal event, a localised drama whose savagery was to be carried on faithfully by the perpetrators of the Second World War. But the idea that Madrid was somehow the fascist hothouse during the three-year period of conflict is wholly false. Madrid was very much on the losing side in the war, Franco having been halted at the city gates. The city suffered three years of bombardment and starvation, and, unlike Barcelona, was not occupied until the war was over. Its population, like any capital city, was spread across the class divide, so that the workers' militias were equally active there as in the more romanticised centres, such as Barcelona. Of course, it is not a retrospective competition to establish who endured the most, but it is worth making this point, just in case. And whilst Barcelona (quite justifiably) have recently resuscitated the memory of their president, Josep Sunyol, murdered by fascist militia outside Madrid at the outbreak of the Civil War – exposing a disgraceful state-sponsored cover-up that lasted for 50 years – it is still a lesser known fact that at the end of the war, Real Madrid's republican president, Rafael Sánchez Guerra, refused to flee from Madrid as it was about to fall, and was imprisoned for his pains. Later he was to go into exile to Paris, where he played an important role in the government-in-exile, before retiring to a monastery where he would die, some years later. Vice-president Gonzalo Aguirre was arrested then murdered in prison, as was the club treasurer, Valero Rivera. Even so, the divisions in families, clubs and among colleagues in the war were never better represented than by the fact that Bernabéu fought on Franco's side, and was decorated for bravery. This was to become significant when he finally grabbed the top job in 1944, for it was then that he could begin to mould the club more to his political liking.

On the outbreak of the war, Bernabéu, unsure of how the wind was to blow, went into hiding, taking refuge in the French Embassy. As a good example of how republican Real Madrid was at that time, Carlos Alonso, coordinator of the club's administration and an outspoken Communist, actually reported his colleague Bernabéu to the authorities. In this overwhemingly anti-fascist atmosphere, it was only the intervention of the Spanish Ambassador to France that saved Santiago's bacon. Little wonder that the legend-to-be fought with some ferocity on Franco's side, as soon as he could get hold of a uniform and a gun. In the official centenary book of Real Madrid, published by Everest, there is a picture of Bernabéu, in full soldier's kit, buying a newspaper from a street vendor. The city is unspecified, but is probably Barcelona, behind the Nationalist lines. The caption reads:

> During the Civil War, Santiago Bernabéu comes to a news-stand to read about the news that was devastating Spain. Before opening the paper he chats for a while with the vendor.

All very cosy stuff, and a perfect example of the problem faced by so many 'official' books on the club, with their awkwardly misty-eyed perspective. The fact is that Bernabéu had nailed his colours to the side who were to murder several of his colleagues at Real Madrid, whatever pleasantries he happened to be exchanging with the newspaper seller. And the authors of the book knew very well that in terms of modern political correctness, they could not go too far in specifying that Bernabéu was helping a bunch of thugs to win a nasty war and set up a brutal regime that would last for 40 years. Not that the Francoists were the only thugs, of course, but as the most common refrain from the playground goes – they started it. And then they won it!

Bernabéu, of course, returned as quickly as possible to his favourite nest. According to Julián García Candau in his extraordinary book *Madrid–Barça, Historia de un desamor* (History of a falling-out), Bernabéu was walking down the corridor on his return, only to come face to face with Alonso, under the protection of the general secretary Pablo

Hernández Coronado, a man who had kept his politics more under wraps. Alonso, whose tip-off three years earlier had almost done for Bernabéu, apparently confined himself to a '*Buenos días Don Santiago*', to which the future president replied, 'Don't worry. I forgive you. I forgive everyone.' Interpret that as you will. Bernabéu later managed to move Alonso downstairs, but incredibly, the red-under-the-bed stayed at the club until retirement, leading something of a charmed life.

However, even worse than this official tendency to sneak around the awkward bits, is that all the publications completely ignore the existence of Antonio Ortega, an interesting character who seems to have taken over as president between 1937 and 1938. All records of the club list Sánchez Guerra as president between 1935 and 1939, but there seems to have been a period in which he handed the hot potato to his communist friend, Ortega. In fact, brave though Sánchez Guerra was, it would appear that he had little to do with the club during the actual war, and that Ortega took over from another republican, Juan José Vallejo. Ortega was a colonel in the leftist militia that occupied the important strategic border town of Irún three days into the war, and three months later was sent to help defend Madrid, which he did with some honour. Finally arrested at the end of the war, it is still unclear what happened to him – whether he was shot or whether he emigrated to the Soviet Union – but he was Real Madrid's president, and a hero of the fallen republic. Facts like these would actually help the club shake off the neo-fascist accusations made by so many of those who worship outside the church walls of *Madridismo*. It would help to modify some of the simplifications bandied about as to the politics of the club. It cannot be denied that Real later became the 'Regime Team' (as opposed to the Dream Team), but even that was not strictly true. Bernabéu made no secret of his political and cultural preferences, but despite his massive presence at the club for 64 years, others less blue-shirted than him (Franco's shade of fascism was light blue, as opposed to black or brown) have made their presence felt. It is ridiculous to portray the club as one big iron fist, as too many Catalan and Basque commentators have sought to do.

As for the players, the brothers Regueiro and Emilio Alonso stayed on in Mexico, after travelling there to play with a Basque representative side (*La Selección de Euskadi*), Zamora decided he would be safer out of the heat of the kitchen, and Ciriaco and Eusebio faced up to premature retirement. Chamartín, though the rumour that it was used as a concentration camp is apparently false* was all but destroyed, its wooden stands converted into fuel. When footballers rather timorously re-trod the turf on 3 December 1939, Real Madrid were once again installed in Chamartín, but only because of the efforts of volunteer workers who had got the place into some sort of shape again, over a period of three months. The first games played in Madrid after the war were in fact for the regional championship in the October, and the homeless Real had gone begging to Vallecas (later Rayo Vallecano). Athletic de Madrid, in actual fact relegated in the last season (1936) under Samitier, were allowed back in 1939 because Oviedo, who should have replaced them, had not found so many volunteers to patch up their ground – in an even worse state than Chamartín. Eight of Athletic de Madrid's best players had died during the war (fighting on both sides), but enough of them had distinguished themselves to persuade Colonel Francisco Salamanca to merge his crack airforce team with what was left of the playing staff to have them renamed Atlético Aviación, the side which would win the first two leagues after the war. With Zamora as manager they snubbed Real's pleas to allow them to share the Metropolitano ground, sensing perhaps that they could emerge into the 1940s as Madrid's premier team. It certainly looked a reasonable bet. Of the squad that won Real the cup that day in Valencia in 1936, only Souto, Bonet, Lecue and an ageing Quincoces remained. Their president was gone, the ground was a mess, the new squad was of uncertain quality and their rivals were the apples of the new general's eyes. After the brief euphoria of 1936, Real Madrid looked to be on the crest of a slump.

In actual fact, after a few early hiccups the new-look side finished a respectable fourth, only four points behind the winners, Aviación. As in 1934, the top flight now boasted 12 teams, and the final positions that first year make interesting reading for any historians looking for a relationship between sporting performance and political context. FC Barcelona, shorn of their best players and submitted to a puppet presidency and rigid outside control (just in case the place became a focus of opposition), finished fourth from bottom. Sevilla, though they had won the cup back in 1935, had been the first city to be occupied by the Nationalist forces, and its more 'bourgeois' club were by then in favour, Betis struggling down in the Second Division. Sevilla finished second in the league and won the cup, spoiling the party slightly for Franco by beating his home town side, Rácing Ferrol. Franco was at the

---

* I quote from Joaquin Estafanía from El País Semanal, 3 March 2002: '*A pesar de la leyenda negra, nunca fue un campo de concentración*' (Despite the dark myths, it was never a concentration camp).

game to present the now renamed *Copa del Generalísimo*, and he would continue to do so, once he was convinced of the political usefulness of associating himself with the game. Bilbao, as ever, proved the exception to the rule, and finished third, despite being in a similar political situation to Barcelona. But you can't keep a good Basque down. Just to prove the point, they finished runners-up the next year, Madrid finished a disappointing sixth, and Paco Bru was sacked. Never one to go out with a whimper, he managed to come up with a curious departing speech, asserting that 'I leave this club with my head held high, and am particularly proud of the fact that during my eight years here, no player was ever sent off.' Good for him.

By and large this was one of the darker periods in Real's history, relieved only by the cup wins of 1946 and 1947 and the building of the new Chamartín Stadium. They were not even called 'Real' for most of this period, of course, and the name is only used, in historical reference, as a convenience term. The 'royal' part of the name was dropped in 1931 after Alfonso, their patron, went into exile, and the crown that adorned their shield was removed from the top of the famous circular design that contains the letters MFC. Franco gave them the crown and the Christian name back in 1943, as if he were beginning to sense that the club might be useful to him, whilst Aviación began to fall away.

At the end of 1942, Madrid finished second to a powerful new Valencia side, with Aviación third. With 14 sides now in the league Barcelona finished third from bottom, but surprisingly won the cup, beating Bilbao 4–3. It was the first time that Franco was obliged to hand them his cup, and so the conspiracy theory goes, he didn't fancy doing it again. Indeed, he was spared this little inconvenience until 1951, by which time he was more safely ensconced in his dictatorial chair, although Di Stéfano had not yet arrived to really broaden his smile. But as far as the '40s are concerned, no students of Real Madrid have satisfactorily managed to put their finger on the moment when Real Madrid suddenly became *El equipo del gobierno* (the government's team). However, the cup theory is a plausible one. Franco was smart enough to see that the presence of teams like Athletic de Bilbao and Barcelona in the top flight guaranteed some needle, some internecine interest that might keep popular protest off the streets and confine it to the football stadia. To have completely ruined Barcelona would not have been in his interests, but neither was it in his interests that they should be pre-eminent, for obvious reasons. In 1943 they were on the up, despite all the political control to which they had been submitted, whilst both Aviación and Real Madrid looked to be in something of a decline, finishing eighth and tenth respectively.

As fate would have it, Real and Barça were drawn together in the semi-finals of the cup that year. Madrid were to win the second leg of the game in infamous fashion, by the ridiculous score of 11–1, having lost 3–0 in the first leg in Barcelona. During the first leg, because of some particularly dirty play by Moleiro and Querejeta – the latter leaving his stud imprint on the stomach of Barça's captain, Escolá – the Catalan crowd had had the temerity to boo the opposition. Eduardo Teus, a former Real goalkeeper, was writing for the pro-Madrid paper *As* at the time, and claimed in his report that the crowd had thus been attacking 'the representatives of Spain' – a fairly provocative statement, and one that seems to have tarred Real Madrid with that particular brush ever since. It remains unclear whether Teus had this written for him, or if he really believed it himself, but before the return leg at Chamartín, Jimmy Burns (*Barça – A People's Passion*) writes that the Barça team were '. . . treated to an unannounced and terrifying visit by the Director of State Security, José Finat y Escriva de Romani, the Count of Mayalde'. In the changing-rooms they were apparently reminded that they were only playing due to the 'generosity of the regime' that had forgiven their lack of patriotism.

By half-time, the representatives of Spain, whether they liked it or not, were 8–0 up, and then managed another three in the second half. Again, the official history of Madrid does itself no favours by describing the players as *los heroes de una gloriosa tarde* (heroes of a glorious afternoon) and then applying the adjective *majestuosa* (majestic) to the result. The author of this obscene little piece of revisionism was either attacked by a moment of imbecility or simply could not resist the temptation to rub it in, 60 years on. The book is otherwise reasonable, but this is the darker side of *Madridismo* – the notion that such outrageously false strutting is either amusing or valid, just as long as it annoys the enemy. And after this event, there was no way back. Madrid lost the final anyway to Bilbao, and lost many of their friends in the process. Even this match, played in the Metropolitano, was not free from controversy. On the morning of the final a stranger managed to persuade the guard at the gates that he had been sent to water the pitch, given the sunny weather at the time. Later, the guard, forgetting that he had left the stranger alone for several hours, was horrified to find that he had disappeared and left an enormous pond in the middle of the pitch. The press muttered that it must have been a Basque, since it always rains 'up there'. The guard was sacked and Bilbao won 1–0.

The scene was set for Bernabéu who was finally elected president in September 1943, although he was not to take over until 1944. After more than 30 years' association with the club, he had finally made it to the top. Today, the presidents of Real Madrid and Barcelona are practically as important as the Head of State himself, and it has to be noted that Bernabéu was the man most instrumental in bringing this state of affairs to fruition. Curiously, his election was partly a political decision on the part of the Spanish Federation who seemed to be suing for at least a temporary halt to the hostilities between Barça and Real, although in retrospect, they might have made a more appropriate choice as their peace-broker. Nonetheless, Bernabéu's first act as president was to send a telegram to his rivals in which he extended the olive branch, pointing out that the clubs had always enjoyed good relations and that these could not be '. . . *turbadas por triviales episodios*' (disturbed by trivial episodes). Fine words, but the recipients of the communiqué might well have considered the episode to have been far from trivial. Indeed, 60 years on, you can still find scarves on sale outside the Bernabéu with the score 11–1 woven into the fabric. *Madridismo* was underway, and Don Santiago had a vision. He set to work straightaway, with a determination and an intelligence that were soon to transform the club into something resembling what it is today.

His next act, perhaps more significant, was to send a telegram to one General Moscardó, one of Franco's wartime thugs now promoted to the unlikely position of National Delegate of Sport. Bernabéu's wording of the telegram reflects more than simply a formulaic text of greeting. After the formal introduction, Real Madrid's new president writes:

> It is with honour that I fulfil my first act as president of this club, sending this message of greeting to our illustrious head of sport and *heroic soldier of the fatherland* . . . [my italics]

The message could not have been clearer. Bernabéu was using the occasion to establish his club's new Francoist credentials, to break ties with any vestiges of its Republican past and to invite Moscardó to join the party. And it follows that if you want to throw a party to impress your friends, you need a decent venue to carry this off. The folks who mattered were not going to turn up every fortnight to some broken-down ruin of a stadium. So within a year of being elected president, he had listened to the priest José María Soler read the blessing and splash the site with holy water before wielding a pickaxe and breaking the first ground of the mythical stadium that would eventually bear his name. The date was 27 October 1944, and the construction of the New Chamartín was under way. Since it was right next to the old ground, parts were roped off for safety, and by 1945 Real had to pack their belongings and move out, over to Aviación's Metropolitano Stadium, on the understanding that their members could attend Real's matches for free.

It should not go without mention, however, that after the infamous 11–1 Colonel Vendrell, the stooge president at Barcelona, had suggested to Moscardó (or vice-versa) that there should be two *partidos de la paz* (peace matches) in order to heal up the open sores of the semi-final. Bernabéu seemed keen enough, and before the first game at Chamartín (1–1) the two presidents walked out onto the pitch amid music, bouquets of flowers and an impressive ovation for the Catalan team when it took to the pitch. Given the incidents before and since, the scene must have seemed rather Pythonesque, and the cynics have never seen anything more than further conspiracy in this little pantomime. They may be right. Nevertheless, for the record, it is the only occasion, so far as is known, when Barcelona received an ovation in Madrid, and quite definitely the only occasion where the compliment was returned in Barcelona. It would make a good Trivial Pursuit question. Also for the record, it should be noted that Barcelona's goalkeeper was no longer the same custodian, Luis Miró, who had conceded 11 goals in Madrid. In fact Miró never played for the club again following that game. No one ever managed to get him to talk, but the inevitable rumours that he might have tried a bit harder have always had a certain edge to them. Was he paid off, and by whom? In the return leg in Les Corts, Barça won 4–0, but reports of the game suggest that this time Madrid may have been under orders. Bernabéu, still fresh in the director's chair, swallowed his pride and apologised for the 11–1 to the Marquis de La Mesa de Asta. But in the last league game of the 1943–44 season, the two teams were unfortunate enough to have to face each other again in Les Corts. Madrid won 2–1, the referee permitted rather too much hard stuff on the part of the winners, and Riba, Barça's dangerous winger, was kicked whilst down, sustaining a broken arm. Boys will be boys, and the ceasefire was effectively over.

Back over in Madrid, the land that Bernabéu had purchased for the staggering sum of 3 million pesetas – land that was then part of the old *Avenida del Generalísimo Franco* – represented a shrewd business move. He actually acquired for the club over five hectares, calculating, quite correctly, that any likely expansion of Madrid's old business district was likely to come north, through the land. Any mortgage – although he was alleged to have obtained credit on very favourable terms – would soon become insignificant when the Avenida, now the Castellana, indeed moved north in search of construction sites and new links to the airport. One glance at where the ground stands today in terms of Madrid's urban business development, and you see that the Bernabéu is on the city's most prestigious thoroughfare. As Simon Inglis puts it in his splendid book on Europe's football grounds, '. . . no other club in the world can boast such an esteemed address . . . home of museums, ministries, mansions and banks'.

This basic collateral has been one of the key factors in Madrid's success ever since, giving them the financial surety to approach willing creditors every time that a major purchase has been required. Whether or not the subsequent links with Franco's regime helped loosen the banks' purse strings or lessen the terms of interest remains mere speculation, but the new Chamartín was fact. It was inaugurated on 14 December 1947 against Os Belenenses of Lisbon. The hosts won it 3–1, and Sabino Barinaga was the man destined to score the first goal on the sacred turf. Interestingly, the game was played on a Sunday and coincided with the tenth week of the league programme. Bernabéu petitioned the Spanish Federation to postpone their game that weekend against Espanyol so that they could indulge in their celebrations. Curiously, the Federation agreed (an early sign of Madrid's new status) and it was the old foe, Athletic de Bilbao, who were to enjoy the dubious privilege, a fortnight later, of being thrashed 5–1 in their first league visit to the stadium, in front of an astonishing 75,340 spectators – the largest crowd to witness a game in the country up to that point in time. The money invested was already on its way back, and within three months of the inauguration, the club membership had risen from 40,000 to 48,000.

The figure makes interesting reading, because apart from the Athletic result, things were not going altogether well on the pitch, despite Bernabéu's steady labours offstage. A week after the first league game in the new stadium, the team were thrashed 7–1 at Oviedo, an adverse result only exceeded in the club's history by the 8–1 reversal at Espanyol, back in 1930. The result spelt the end of ex-player Jacinto Quincoces' first period of management. The week before they had been due to inaugurate the stadium, they were also hammered 5–0 by their temporary landlords, over in the Metropolitano. By the penultimate game of that 1948–49 season, with an awkward-looking visit to Bilbao looming, the threat of relegation was very real. It hadn't been quite what Don Santiago had planned – but it's a funny old game, and it was back then too. Bilbao decided to take their revenge for the earlier game and won 3–0, meaning that Madrid had to beat Oviedo in the last match to stay up. Up in the Basque Country that Sunday the Athletic fans had sung '*A segunda, a segunda!*' (going down, going down), much to the annoyance of Real's new champion, the football tabloid *Marca*. The Basques (and several others, it would seem) were to be ultimately disappointed, since Oviedo were beaten 2–0 on the final day, and Sporting Gijón and Real Sociedad went down, leaving Real Madrid 11th from 14. The final figures of 21 points, 41 goals scored and 56 conceded are their worst haul to date. Madrid's supporters know these figures and know of this year, as if by tradition it has been decided to hand down the terrible knowledge through the generations as a reminder that the club, though 'the best', are still mortal – lest it happen again.

The temporary gloss that the consecutive cup wins of 1946 and 1947 had painted onto Bernabéu's brave new world had been blistered and cracked by this dysfunctional season, made even worse by the fact that Barcelona had come roaring back into the frame and won the title that year. Five months after the assassination of Gandhi and three months after the initiation of the Marshall Plan – an aid package for Europe from which fascist Spain was to be excluded – Bernabéu, now aided by his right-hand man and PR chief, Raimundo Saporta, was exhorting the then manager, Englishman Mike Keeping, to sign anything that moved. This was not an era in which the philosophy of the *cantera* (youth policy) was particularly prominent, it can be concluded, and Barcelona, cannier in the market, were to win the league again in 1949 and then sign Ladislao Kubala, the Hungarian exile still considered to have been their greatest player. Madrid signed Muñoz and Molowny in this period, two players who were later to shine as managers, along with several foreigners who included the Frenchmen Luis Hon and Luciano, the Hungarian Nemes and the Argentinians Olsen and Imbelloni – but Keeping's team, though a vast improvement on the 1948 side, were no match for Barcelona. Saporta was undoubtedly the president's best 'signing' of the period, bringing the tough negotiator from the world of basketball, where he had established the Real Madrid team as world-beaters. Saporta was good with the journalists and allegedly knew people in high places, as did another administrative 'signing', the Anadalusían doctor Antonio Calderón, an ex-referee who was said to have several generals in his pocket and who knew all about the increasingly shady world of the referees' association. Or so the conspiracy theorists would have it. On the surface, he was employed as club spokesman, and acted as a link between the president and the players. Bernabéu kept at a discreet distance from the changing-room – and preferred Calderón to communicate his occasional dictums.

However, it was at the end of the decade when a most curious event occurred, one which was to have massive implications for the decade to come. A touring team of Hungarian exiles visited Chamartín, and although they lost 4–2 to Madrid, a certain Ladislao Kubala, a small blond playmaker, very much caught the eye. Bernabéu, so the story goes, wasted no time and offered the player a contract, upon which Kubala – in the bullish style that was to characterise his years in Barcelona, told his possible employer that he would sign if his brother-in-law, Fernando Daucik, could be taken on as manager. Although Bernabéu may well have welcomed this possibility (he was losing confidence in the Englishman Keeping) he could not be seen to be bowing to blackmail, and sent Kubala packing. That's the official tale anyway. Several months later, the old fox Samitier, back in Catalan employ as a scout, apparently had Kubala sign a pre-contract to play for Barcelona when the Hungarian was drunk – a state that he was still in when he travelled with Samitier to sign officially. Apparently on the train journey to Barcelona, Kubala, several sheets to the wind, looked up at a railway sign outside the carriage and enquired when they were going to arrive in Madrid. There seems to be ample anecdotal evidence that he actually thought he was finally destined for Chamartín, since his legendary fondness for the bottle caused him to have occasional lapses of memory – but once he was out on the pitch in the famous *azulgrana* colours, Bernabéu might well have regretted his earlier reaction to reject the Hungarian's cheeky petition. Indeed, such was Kubala's impact, along with César and Basora, that the new decade was dawning with grey mist and drizzle for Real Madrid. The new ground was built, the right men were working for him and the club was reasonably solvent, despite the country's ruinous economy – but the team, despite the goals of Pahiño, were still not firing on all cylinders. It needed a hero, a focus like Kubala. Two years later, on the night of the club's 50th anniversary, a man would come along to answer these prayers, a man who was to change the club for ever.

6. DANCING BEHIND FROSTED GLASS

The period following the Second World War was hardly a bundle of laughs for anyone, but for the Spanish, punished for their 'neutrality', the exclusion from the Marshall Plan handouts meant that times were particularly tough. The resentment of that generation still surfaces from time to time when the Americans and the British are mentioned, for the Spanish felt victimised, isolated and above all, undernourished. Rural Spain was hit particularly hard, but the suffering also cut across the urban class divide and affected prince and pauper alike, as anyone alive at that time will tell you. Spain's shock 1–0 win over England in the Brazilian World Cup of 1950 is one of the most famous games of all time in the country precisely because it stuck up a finger in the direction of its accusers (they also beat the USA in the opening round) and just as importantly painted some colour into the pale skies of Spain's post-war afflictions. In a similar vein, Neville Cardus, writing for the *Manchester Guardian* in 1947, described the cricketer Denis Compton's 18 centuries that summer as a blessed relief from:

> . . . the strain of long years of anxiety and affliction, which passed
> from all hearts and shoulders at the sight of Compton in full sail
> . . . each stroke a flick of delight, a propulsion of happy, sane,
> healthy life. There were no rations in an innings by Compton.

In the early 1950s, the population over in Argentina was comparatively well fed, thanks to the shipments of beef that Peron's government had been exporting to war-ravaged Europe. But such relative comfort had not been enough to prevent their professional footballers striking over pay and conditions in late 1948 – a dispute that led to the country's most promising star moving north to play for Colombia's richest team, the aptly named Millonarios of Bogotá. The 23-year-old Alfredo Di Stéfano, previously with River Plate, had joined a team consisting of seven other fellow Argentines (but only one Colombian) that was to contribute to the growing reputation of South American club football around that time – one of the reasons why the cartel of local barons who were financing the club had invested their money into the venture in the first place. By 1952, with the club pre-eminent in Latin America, Real Madrid had decided that their presence would make an attractive spectacle of the celebrations planned to mark their half-century, and promptly extended an invitation. The night before the celebrations kicked off, in March 1952, Bernabéu took part in a radio *charla* (chat) with the Millonarios' president and Di Stéfano, already earmarked as the club spokesman but practically unknown as a player in Europe. On emerging from the studio, Bernabéu turned to a local journalist and remarked, *'Este tío huele a buen fútbol'* (this guy smells of good football). What his nose suspected, his eyes confirmed the next evening, when the blond Argentine trod the Chamartín turf for the first time and scored twice in his side's 2–2 draw with the Norkoeping, the Swedish side who had also been invited in order to set up a triangular mini-competition. Di Stéfano's habit of almost always placing a ball in a net within the 90 minutes allowed him continued to good effect the following evening when he put another two past several of the men who would become his comrades-in-arms by September of the next year. His compatriot, Adolfo Pedernera, was also in the side that beat Real Madrid 4–2 that evening, the ageing forward whom Di Stéfano has subsequently cited as the best player he ever played alongside. The performance of Millonarios was impressive, but to any half-trained eye, the blond playmaker was the pick of the bunch. The sight of him that evening had Bernabéu really believing that his dreams of pre-eminence might one day come true. He knew, with the instinct of the proto-statesman that he was, that the Argentine's incorporation into the Real Madrid side could be the final piece in the jigsaw which would unite his own dream of national dominance with Franco's plans to centralise the country's power-base in a city whose football team would have to represent the white purity of power and victory. Meanwhile, Pepe Samitier, sitting some ten yards away from his ex-employer, was no less impressed. Trouble was, he had gone back to work for the enemy, and had only managed to get an invite to the game on the strength of his previous association with Real.

Samitier's role in the whole business has been questioned, as mentioned in the previous chapter, but to all intents and purposes, he was on a scouting mission for FC Barcelona that night. The Catalan club were enjoying good times, and part of his job was to make sure that things stayed that way. A quick glance at the period shows how dismal a time it was for Real's supporters, above and beyond the fact that there wasn't always enough to eat. Barça won the league title in 1948 and 1949, followed by the second worse option, the newly named Atlético Madrid, who won the next two. In 1952 and 1953 the Catalans returned to the podium – in short, six years of unremitting torture when Real's two biggest rivals trod their noses into the dirt. The period does not make pretty reading for *Madridistas*, and Bernabéu knew it. So it hardly needs to be said that the idea of Di Stéfano pulling on Barcelona's shirt became Don Santiago's worst nightmare, and the fact that he didn't – officially at least – has become perhaps the greatest football story of all time, and certainly one whose repercussions have never been remotely equalled in the history of the game. For depending on the spin you wish to apply to Di Stéfano, you might reasonably conclude that he changed the fortunes not only of a club, but of a country. Some have gone further and written that his benevolent influence on Franco's destiny changed the politics of Europe. That may be stretching a point too far, but his arrival in Madrid, after some tortuous wranglings, was in truth Madrid's 'year zero'. Before that they were a promising club. After it they were a colossus. Those coffee-table authors who insist on writing books about Real entitled *Cien años de gloria* (A Hundred Years of Glory) are simply suffering from the well-documented disease of 'white myopia'. Up to 1954, when the titles began to wash in like the Amazon in flood, the teacher's report would surely have read 'Good, but could do better'. But as soon as Di Stéfano was in the side, Real Madrid's swift conversion from also-rans to masters of both Spain and Europe puts one in mind of Hugh McIlvanney's great phrase when describing Muhammad Ali's so-called rivals, Frazier, Foreman and Liston. So poor were they in comparison to Ali that McIlvanney memorably described them as 'dancing behind frosted glass'. Suddenly, much of the light that had been shining on a resurgent Kubala-led Barcelona was deflected over to the capital, then out into a wider Spain to brighten the lives of those who would find it politically more comfortable to follow Real Madrid. And to paraphrase the post-war *Guardian* journalist – there were no rations in a game featuring Di Stéfano.

So much has been said and written about Di Stéfano – nicknamed *La Saeta Rubio* (The Blond Arrow) by the Madrid faithful – that it is difficult to know exactly where to start in order to get a fresh perspective on him; but just for a change, let's begin at the end. This is because as the club's honorary president and greatest player he was very much in the news in 2002, and was invited to the Zarzuela Palace in Madrid by King Juan Carlos to take part in the unveiling of Real Madrid's preparations for their centenary celebrations held in March. Di Stéfano lined up for a photograph with Raúl, Hierro and Butragueño, the young pretender Raúl having just equalled the old man's 23-goal haul for his adopted Spain by scoring the only winner in a friendly game with Mexico. *Marca* headlined the photo 'Four Kings' (of Madrid) and splashed it over their front page. The photo, curiously, was cut along the horizontal, so that only the upper halves of the dark-suited kings were visible. The reason for this became apparent when you opened the tabloid and found the full-length photo inside, which featured a shrunken and irritable-looking Di Stéfano with a cigarette in his right hand, hanging down below his waist. Where the three younger men wore Armani, Di Stéfano wore some sort of ill-fitting two-piece from the winter sales – and where the others looked immaculate, the old man had loosened his tie and the bottom of his shirt was hanging out of his trousers. It was typical of the legend who – at 76 as at 26 – if he wasn't on a football pitch, looked as though he simply couldn't give a shit.

Alfredo Di Stéfano, always referred to as 'probably the best player in the world', like an advertisement that is afraid of being taken to court, has always inspired great eulogies as a player, but not as a person. The two facts are significant, because men who acquire this sort of legendary status are inevitably judged on both counts. Maradona, whose ridiculous political posturing during the 2002 'homage' to him in Argentina (from which all intelligent footballers stayed away) and Pelé's own reputation for astonishing dullness off the field of play have all contributed to how we regard them – unfair though this may be. And this is probably because in our heart of hearts we feel that we cannot separate the player from the person, because it is not as interesting. George Best seems all the greater somehow, when you see footage of him at his peak, and you realise that he had probably been on the tiles until 5 o'clock the morning before. Di Stéfano, like Bobby Charlton, always smoked – a fact that seems impossible to contemplate now, in the more politically correct arena of sport – but he was no drinker and waster. As he himself remarked to the newspaper *El País* in an interview in 2000, '*Hombre, fumaba, pero nada más. Un futbolista tiene que cuidarse*' (Hey – I smoked, but nothing more. A footballer has to take care of himself). It would be wrong, therefore, to suggest that he was a maverick. Besides, according to Gento, the winger who supplied him devotedly for ten seasons, Di Stéfano only ever cared about two things – winning games and signing lucrative contracts. And although he is still revered in Spain as a player, and although Real Madrid made lots of noise about him during the centenary, there remains a distinct feeling that the club and the player tolerate each other for the public's sake. Di Stéfano never forgave Madrid for allowing his contract to expire in 1964, when he felt he still had two years left in him as a player at the highest level. His subsequent move to Español, Barcelona's more right-wing, anti-Catalan nationalist team, without the traditional 'golden handshake' from his former club, left him bitter for years. Ladislao Kubala, whose presence in the Barcelona team of 1953 probably guaranteed his move to Madrid, famously said of him: 'I admired him on the field of play – but he never bought me a single beer.'

The story of how Di Stéfano finally ended up in Madrid is a drawn-out one, but suffice to say that the man in question was actually signed by Barcelona and played three games for them – a little known fact. All three games were friendlies, but they probably served to demonstrate to Di Stéfano that the problem with playing for the Catalans was not one of money but of *protagonismo*, as they call it in Spain. The Hungarian Kubala was ruling the roost for Barcelona in those days, and although the two may well have proved an explosive combination, it is more likely that the midfield could not have accommodated two such difficult egos. Every now and then players appear on the scene around whom the rest of a team's tactics must be moulded. These players run the team, and the rest play the supporting cast. Kubala, widely regarded as Barcelona's greatest player of all time, could not have run things if Di Stéfano had been around. Similarly, Di Stéfano, much as he came to admire Kubala, would have been unlikely to have tolerated the Hungarian's famous drinking bouts and his somewhat lapsed version of professionalism. Saporta has since admitted, on an official Real Madrid video documentary, that he made several trips over to Barcelona whilst Di Stéfano was officially in the Catalan's employ, claiming that he simply wanted to point this out to him – that the town wasn't big enough for both him and the Hungarian. In the video interview, an elderly Di Stéfano sits quietly to Saporta's side, smiling wryly to himself when Saporta mentions the famous fudge that the Spanish Federation made, ruling that the Argentine would play one season for each side, alternately. Di Stéfano has since said that this was a lie, but he has never specified who was telling it – Saporta or the Spanish Federation. He may also have been smiling because, in truth, Saporta had slipped him a bulky envelope, with a decent amount of pesetas inside and a rough-draft contract, indicating the sort of money they were contemplating paying to him. It would seem that Di Stéfano also smiled that day – on reading the 'Total' column. Whatever the truth, it remains one of football's most curious facts that the two most prominent figures in the annals of the Real Madrid versus Barcelona story could each have ended up playing for the other side.

To cut a very long story a little shorter, Samitier had been working for Barça and had paid 4 million pesetas to River Plate, since they still officially owned Di Stéfano until 1954. Saporta had countered with 1.5 million to Millonarios in order to own the Argentine from that date, a clever move that effectively neutralised Samitier's payment. Unfortunately, FIFA had given their blessing to Barça's deal, so in a sudden flurry of legislation in the Spanish Federation, General Moscardó passed a law banning the further importation of foreign players – effectively blocking any chance of Di Stéfano turning out officially for the Catalans. Barça's president, Marti Carretó, travelled to Madrid to parley with Bernabéu, agreeing to release the player in question just so long as he went to Juventus! When Bernabéu surprisingly agreed, Carretó, like Chamberlain with his famous piece of paper, returned a semi-relieved man to Barcelona. At least Madrid were not going to get their hands on Di Stéfano! 'I believe it is peace for our time . . .' But he hadn't counted on Moscardó, who allegedly brokered the famous 'sharing' deal the minute that Carretó had left Bernabéu's office. Was it a lie, as Di Stéfano has claimed? Possibly. But it worked a treat. The Catalan press, fed the story the same day, went thermonuclear the next morning and howled their outrage at such a humiliating deal. Carretó, his tail between his legs, resigned, and the interim board of directors tore up the deal and rid themselves of the problem, handing Di Stéfano over to Madrid. Of course, they required Bernabéu to cough up the money Samitier had paid to River Plate, but the 5.5 million pesetas (about 35,000 US dollars) that Real Madrid ended up hauling from the coffers turned out to be cheap at half the price. Moscardó's previous legislation was suddenly inapplicable to Di Stéfano, since the small print of the law stated that any negotiations that had begun before the passing of the legislation were to remain exempt. Funny old coincidence.

And so Di Stéfano, with the puppet-masters of high power pulling the strings in the Ministry, finally pulled on the white shirt of Real Madrid, up to then a relatively under-achieving giant in the shadows of both Barcelona and Athletic Bilbao. He made his debut at home against Santander (4–2) in the third game of the season, scoring the third goal. Less than a month later he walked out onto the Bernabéu and scored four goals, against Barcelona of course. Talk about instant heroism. From that moment on, in 1953, the history of Spain, and to some extent Europe, was irrevocably changed. So great was the player's impact that Bernabéu, and more importantly Franco – a Galician who had decided to support the club whose city had in the end come around to his regime – suddenly found themselves riding a wave of success and image that neither could have dreamed of in the dark days of poverty-ridden, post-war Spain. About the time of Di Stéfano's arrival, Franco's position as a successful and long-lasting dictator was by no means assured. This extraordinary footballer ended all that. Real Madrid's outrageous run of wins in the first five European Cups acted as ambassador for the country, lending it a shine that it did not really possess. Franco had realised that football could be used to sway public opinion, provide the folks with opium during the hard times, and spread an image abroad of a nation of stylish winners, worthy of an invite back into the international fold.

Alfredo Di Stéfano was born on 4 July 1926, to Italian immigrant parents, in the Barracas neighbourhood of Buenos Aires. The family had a smallholding and ran a farm in the suburbs of the Argentine capital. Alfredo was to later attribute his legendary stamina to his days as a teenager, helping on the farm, shouldering a heavy workload as the eldest child in the family. Barracas is traditionally a Boca Juniors *barriada*, but at the age of 12 the young Alfredo joined a youth team called Las Cardales and whilst playing for them was spotted by River Plate, signing for them at the age of 15. Even then, his family allegedly received a pay-off, for other sides had heard of him too. At 16, he made his debut for the first team, in the legendary *La Maquina* side – so called because of their best-ever forward line consisting of Labruna, Muñoz, Loustau, Gallo and Adolfo Pedernera, the latter the man who would turn out with him that night in 1952 in the Bernabéu. Because of all these riches, River Plate loaned Alfredo out to Huracán, a decision they were soon to regret when their apprentice scored the only goal of the game against them, after 15 seconds. He stayed at Huracán for another two seasons, scoring an astonishing 55 goals in 66 games, whereupon his hero, Pedernera, was suddenly declared surplus to requirements and transferred to Atlanta to make way for the 20-year-old's return. River Plate took everyone else apart that season in 1947, with the country suddenly rich from its ever-increasing sales of beef to post-war Europe. Pedernera's Atlanta were relegated, and when Di Stéfano (inevitably) scored the only goal of the game at their ground, he was attacked by their fans and taken to hospital suffering bruising and shock. Three weeks earlier he had made his international debut for Argentina, scoring of course.

He only ever turned out seven times for Argentina, but most unusually (like Kubala) went on to play for two more countries – Colombia (4 caps) and Spain (31). For none of them did he ever manage to turn out in a World Cup – one of the reasons why he is rarely regarded by the present generation as better than either Maradona or Pelé, both of whom strutted their stuff on the world stage. With a similar background, the statistics alone suggest that the Argentine should take the vote; 2 Argentine championships, 4 Colombian championships, 8 Spanish league titles, 5 European Cups, 1 Intercontinental Cup, twice European Footballer of the Year, 5 times Spanish league top scorer – with something like 800 goals scored in all competitions – an astonishing number for a player who was not really a 'striker' but who was more often than not referred to as a midfielder.

Bobby Charlton said that Di Stéfano was the 'brainiest player' he ever saw, and Helenio Herrera, the controversial missionary of *catenaccio*, said that he was the greatest player of all time. Talking to the writer Simon Kuper he pointed out that whilst people referred to Pelé as 'the first violinist in the orchestra' Di Stéfano was 'the whole orchestra'.

He scored 49 goals in all European campaigns, making him the European Cup's top scorer. His overall total in the Spanish league competition of 228 is third behind Bilbao's Zarra and Hugo Sánchez, but he played fewer games than either of them. His account with Real Madrid is much greater, however, boasting 418 goals when cup competitions are taken into account. He even scored 19 more in the league after he had left Madrid for Español. As if this were not impressive enough, he managed an astonishing 267 in 294 games during his stay in Colombia and 23 for the Spanish national side, a figure now only exceeded by Butragueño, Hierro and Raúl – but the fact that Di Stéfano was only cleared to play for Spain in 1957 meant that if he had begun earlier, the current top-scorer, Madrid's iconic forward Raúl González, would surely still be chasing his shadow. In all official matches, his total exceeds the 800 mark, and some put it as high as 893. The Argentine's total is actually ranked fourth of all time, behind Pelé, Friedenreich and Binder, but when one considers the usual quality of the opposition, Di Stéfano's case looks the stronger. And he kept going longer than any of the other golden greats – Pelé, Maradona and Cruyff – who all retired earlier.

Despite the goals, there seems to have been a certain amount of reluctance over the years to describe Di Stéfano as a 'striker', a term that would seem to do scant justice to his overall repertoire. He was, as the Spanish put it nowadays, *Un Todo Terreno* (A Four Wheel Drive), capable of playing under any conditions in any position. If his colleagues were not supplying him, he would go and get it himself. The footage that there is of him rarely portrays this side to his play, since Spain's version of *Pathe News*, the black and white news programme *El Nodo*, had the equally annoying habit of cutting all action prior to the moves that culminated in the goals – resulting in a sort of staccato vision of the player, all sudden darts and pounces that give little hint as to how he really orchestrated the play. Be that as it may, those lucky enough to have seen him in action all attest to the same qualities – an upright stance, strength on the ball, *verticalidad* (directness) and an utter ruthlessness in front of goal to which no defences of the time seemed to have an answer. According to José María Zárraga, his captain during the 1950s, he wasn't bad in goal either. Football's first Renaissance Man?

At the end of the 1953–54 season Real Madrid took the league title, ending a barren run of 20 years. It was the last time they would have one. Instead, the era of the *trofeos seguidos* (consecutive runs) had begun, a sporting concept that has subsequently taken on a somewhat exaggerated importance in Spanish football culture, largely due to Real Madrid's post-war appetite for keeping their trophy-room employees busy. This also suits the Spanish sporting concept of *Machacar* (crush without mercy) mentioned earlier in the book. Occasional fly-by-night trophy winners have since had their 15 minutes of fame put brutally into perspective by Real Madrid's obsession with consistency. Valencia snatched the title in 1944, but had to wait again until 1971 to repeat the feat. Bilbao have had impressive runs in the cup, but as for the league, Madrid are the only Spanish side to have twice featured in five-year pig-outs, in the 1960s and the 1980s. These periods of *machaque*, to use the noun, were the very reasons why the Barcelona 'Dream Team' managed by Johan Cruyff became such a threat to what Madrid believed was their divine right to kingship. It has been the only period in which Barcelona have managed a run of four (1991–94) with a European Cup sandwiched in between, in 1992. The power-base seemed to be shifting, not for a single season – a normal occurrence – but for an agonisingly long period. The reconquest of the title in 1995 was, therefore, a joyous occasion for all *Madridistas*, for it was confirmation of their continuing role in the sporting cosmos, temporarily threatened by a sparkling celebration of *Catalanisme*. Lucky though Barça may have been to have won those four leagues, they played such sublime football that even the most hardened Madrid fans had to admit they were good to watch. In order to bury their memory, just for good measure, Real Madrid's basketball team won its eighth European Cup that same year of 1995 – *La Reconquista*.

Even the most casual student of Real Madrid will know where this is leading. Between 1956 and 1960, the club took exclusive possession of the European Cup, a trophy inaugurated in 1956 with considerable help from Santiago Bernabéu. Don Santiago was in on the planning of its original structure and was part of the famous meeting in the Ambassador Hotel in Paris, together with the head of the French Football Federation, Ernest Bedrignan, and the Hungarian Gustav Sebes, three delegates from the putative first participant clubs, who had been gathered together by *L'Equipe* journalist Gabriel Hanot to put the flesh onto the bones of his original idea. The previous year, a limited and unofficial competition had actually taken place, in which Wolves beat Honved 3–2 at Molineux in the final. Hanot simply saw this pilot as the model for an official tournament, in which the champions of various European countries could compete against each other. In a report for his newspaper, he praised Wolves for their defeat of the Hungarians, up to then considered the best side in Europe. Eight of their players had been in the famous 3–6 team at Wembley in 1953, and to the casual, pre-media hyped European football spectator, Honved would have seemed as good a choice as any for Europe's top side. There would certainly have been little reason to go for Real Madrid. But Hanot wondered, in his article, whether Wolves would have fared so well on neutral territory. Answering his own question, he initially proposed a tournament with the structure of a league system – shades of today – with midweek games, but the countries whose opinions were solicited favoured a knock-out competition. UEFA, reluctant at first, and somewhat cynical as to the value of the competition, passed the buck to FIFA, who finally gave the nod, but not before the ad hoc committee, chaired by Bedrignan, had met for a second time in Madrid – a testament to Bernabéu's new standing in the eyes of the delegates, and of the faithful Saporta's tireless string-pulling behind the scenes.

In the two years immediately preceding the birth of this life-changing trophy, Madrid had won two *seguidos* and begun to build up a balanced-looking squad to fit around the obvious talents of the new protagonist, Di Stéfano, who had scored 29 goals in his first league campaign. Barcelona's knocking them out of the cup in the semi-finals was the only real blot on a season in which extra tiers were added to the North and South stands and a young chap by the name of Francisco (Paco) Gento was bought from Rácing Santander up in Cantabria. Gento, voted seventh best player of all time by *Marca*'s aforementioned poll, was the surprise in the eventual package, for in his first season he was only saved from being loaned out by Di Stéfano's insistence that he stay. Four games from the end of the previous 1952–53 season Madrid had beaten Santander 2–1 in the Chamartín, the visitors badly weakened by a flu virus. The young Gento, already an accomplished national sprinter, was promoted to the first team for the visit, and so impressed the technical staff at Madrid that they signed him four days later, although he played out the season in Cantabria.

Gento is early proof of the old adage that great players such as Di Stéfano rarely prosper in isolation. The Argentine may have arguably been the greatest player of all time – but all great actors require a supporting cast. It is unclear what role the new manager Enrique Fernandez (who had won the league twice with Barça in the late '40s) had in the poaching of Gento, but the winger only played a bit part that first year. The next season, under the management of José Villalonga (Fernandez' face did not quite fit) Gento exploded into life. He was to become Franco's favourite player, but that was no fault of Gento's. Following the rather quaint Spanish tradition of awarding the greats with *apodos* (nicknames), Gento was soon called '*la Galerna*' (the gale) by the faithful – a rather apt description of his powers.

Everyone comments on Gento's speed, and there have been endless bar debates in Spain over the last half-century as to who was the quickest of them all – but in a sense this is irrelevant, since speed alone has rarely elevated footballers beyond the realms of the lower divisions. Exceptionally fast players rarely become greats, a truth well illustrated by the present European incumbent of the 'quickest' label, Barcelona's Dutch import, Marc Overmars. Dangerous player though he can be, his speed seems to have an inverse relationship to his effectiveness, for he rarely if ever seems to cross the ball successfully to his teammates. Gento not only crossed the ball with deadly accuracy for both Di Stéfano and Molowny, he scored plenty himself too, cutting inside with deadly speed and shooting powerfully with either foot, although he preferred the left. Getting the best out of him appears to have also been down to Di Stéfano, who was already wielding unofficial power at the club. In the close season of 1954, the new star in Madrid's firmament told Bernabéu that Gento himself needed a supplier, a left-sided midfielder who could ensure that the winger was more included in the play. Gento continued to astonish his teammates in training, but so far had done little where it mattered. Di Stéfano's eye for a player, later to be used to good effect as a manager, was already apparent back then. Seeing the need for this left-sided axis, he recommended Hector Rial, his old friend back in Argentina. Bernabéu in fact claimed that Di Stéfano had said to him 'Don Santiago – I need someone who will pass the ball back to me when I've passed to them' but whatever he said, Rial, born in Argentina but to Spanish parents from Galicia, came over and joined the party.

The signing of the elegant Rial was also evidence of Di Stéfano's infamous perfectionism in matters of football, and a testament to the old maxim that you can never have enough good players, even though you've just won your first league title in 20 years. Rial was to stay until 1961, a vital piece in the *época dorada* (golden period). Amazingly, Gento stayed on until 1971, bowing out after Real's Cup-Winners' Cup final defeat at the hands of Chelsea, which was to be the club's last European final for a decade. Given this longevity, Gento was to be the only player from that famous squad to play in all six European Cup finals, from 1956 to 1966. The youngest of the squad when he joined in 1953, he was the only one to go on to play with the 'Ye-Ye' generation, the subject of the next chapter. His record of six cups is unlikely to be beaten, although he has since declared that he thinks that Raúl (who now has three) could go on to do it.

Things were warming up nicely. For the second successive season, Madrid beat Barça 5–0 at home and finished one place above them again at the end of the season, taking the title with five points to spare. Di Stéfano, Molowny and Gento up front, with Rial prompting, had proved too much for the rest – the top flight by then containing 16 teams (from 1950). The champions finished with 46 points from 30 games, the highest total ever up to that year. Also, in January 1955, the General Assembly of club members had voted to rename the ground after Bernabéu, in honour of his contribution to the club's development over a period of 43 years. The man who had dug the ground and painted the fences of the O'Donnell Stadium back in 1912 had finally been transformed into a cult. It is said that he was never happy with the idea, and had initially intended to reject the initiative, but bowed in the end to the *vox populi*. Although he got used to it, he himself continued to refer to the ground as 'Chamartín', probably because it sounds a bit daft using your own name in reference to an institution, a phenomenon more associated with posthumous decoration.

Everything was settling nicely into place by the end of the 1954–55 season, and UEFA, as executors, had gone about the business of inviting the sides they thought should inaugurate the tournament. The original 18 sides who received an invitation were not all champions of their respective leagues, UEFA having taken into consideration distances, politics and solvency. The basic idea was, however, to eventually mould the competition into one where only the champions were represented, but first they had to convince the clubs and their respective national associations. Chelsea, for example, the 1955 title-winners in England, were on the original guest list but were not allowed to compete due to the legendary far-sightedness of the English FA. Hibernian were the only British side to actually go, but not as Scottish champions. Nevertheless, they were to give a good account of themselves and lost in the semi-finals to Stade de Reims, Madrid's first European Cup final victims.

As Disraeli noted, there is a problem with how you view statistics and, inevitably, there are those who have seen Madrid's famous run of five in a different light to the one that shines on the first floor of the club's trophy room. One of the arguments against Madrid's greatness is that the initial opposition was relatively poor – but if this was really the case, then it spoke volumes for the Spanish league at the time. It is true that the 16 sides who finally competed in the inaugural competition were a mixed bunch, but one can hardly maintain that Milan, Partizan, Sporting de Lisboa, Honved, Anderlecht, PSV and Rapid de Vienna, to cite but seven, represented 'poor' opposition. The tournament was exactly what Hanot wanted it to be, a sorting out of the sheep and the goats. The World Cup was already well established. It therefore made every sense to develop a competition at club level whose function would also be a rubbing of shoulders, an attempt to establish a hierarchy by empirical means, as opposed to hearsay and occasional friendlies. Looking at those sides quoted above, there was plenty of hearsay about them. But any notion that any one of them might be pre-eminent was about to be blown out of the water by Di Stéfano and company.

7. THE FAMOUS FIVE

Although Hanot never said as much, the bringing together of European teams, less than a decade after the ending of the hostilities, was not a bad political idea either. But politics were not uppermost in the minds of the 11 men who took to the field in Switzerland, on 8 September 1955, in the first game ever to be played in the European Cup.

Real Madrid had been drawn against Servette of Geneva – the country's oldest club – and were not quite sure what to make of them. What they encountered, unexpectedly, was a very physical side, one whose hunch that the Spanish 'might not like it up 'em' backfired miserably. Madrid could look after themselves, and Muñoz and Zárraga took no prisoners in midfield. Navarro and Oliva were very solid at the back, and although Madrid were still not the finished article, the crucial balance of flair and steel was sufficiently in place by that year to carry them through a game like this. At half-time, however, with the score at 0–0, the Madrid dressing-room was apparently suffering one of its occasional silences, because Di Stéfano was in a bad mood. The game had been messy, with no real pattern, and he had been unable to stamp his authority on the proceedings. Terrified of upsetting him, no one spoke. Suddenly the door opened and in walked Saporta accompanied by no less a figure than the exiled Prince of Asturias, now the Spanish King, Juan Carlos. The Prince was at finishing school in Switzerland, and had taken the day off to see some of his compatriots. The players shot to their feet, apart from Di Stéfano. The Prince walked over to the Argentine, shook his hand (upon which he stood up) and remarked in his faltering Spanish, '*Saeta – los emigrantes esperan una victoria*' (Blond Arrow – the emigrants are hoping for a win) – referring to the Royal Family. Di Stéfano, unmoved by the royal presence, simply nodded. The 17-year-old Prince, desperately trying to break the ice, came up with the famous phrase referring to Di Stéfano: '*Ese chico ahora es el rey*' (Now, this guy is the King).

In the second half, in the 74th minute to be precise, Miguel Muñoz scored Madrid's first ever goal in Europe, and Rial the second in the 89th. There was no reply from the obsessively defensive Swiss. In the second leg, Servette were shown the door in no uncertain terms, and the Bernabéu witnessed a historic 5–0 demolition of the visitors, a presage of things to come. Another ominous sign for the other teams competing was that Di Stéfano had opened his European account, scoring two of the goals. So far so good.

A curious anecdote to the first match was that on the morning of the game against Servette, Saporta, never one to miss a decent PR opportunity, had wangled an audience for the players with Queen Victoria Eugenia, the exiled monarch who was actually living in Lausanne. A photograph commemorating the presence of the Queen, Don Juan de Borbón and the aforementioned prince was taken with the players, and of course the shots appeared in the European press. Franco was not amused – one of the occasions that lend the lie to the old myth that he and Bernabéu were buddies. Ostensibly he, Saporta and Bernabéu shared the same political outlook, but the views of Don Santiago were probably more complex, and more tinged with a righteous moral streak that could transcend the limits of the party line. Besides, it was good publicity and Real Madrid were 'royal'. Not only that, but very soon, like the players in the photograph, Franco would be smiling too.

The second game (effectively one of the quarter-finals) paired our heroes with Partizan of Belgrade. Not only was this a much tougher prospect than the first game, but the political undertones of the first game were to surface in a much more serious manner in this match, given that the communist Yugoslavs were not exactly the great dictator's flavour of the month. Some of the fledgling UEFA's original worries about the tournament began to surface, and it was once again down to Raimundo Saporta, the arch-pragmatist, to set up a meeting with Franco and persuade him that it would only benefit the image of his regime to be seen to permit the first representatives of communist Europe to pass through the iron frontiers of Spain's central and fascist-tainted ideology. Posterity has not recorded the phrases he chose, but, as ever, Saporta emerged with his mission accomplished.

The game was played on Christmas Day 1955 – apparently a joke by Bernabéu to remind the Reds about the Christian birthday party that Marx had decided to boycott. The ground was packed with a happy festive crowd, keen on seeing this famous team from the nether world of Eastern Europe. The game kicked off at 3 o'clock in the afternoon, since the event pre-dated Madrid's floodlighting project. Alfredo Relaño wrote recently in *El País* that not only were Partizan a fine side, they were also '*educados*', a magical word of praise in Spanish culture which describes a state of genteel politeness from which the inventors of the word now feel sadly cut off – so radically has Spain changed in the last 30 years. The reason for their admiration of Partizan was that in the first ten minutes, with the crowd silenced and worried, the Yugoslavs scored twice, only to see both efforts dubiously disallowed by the French referee. Instead of arguing the toss, which would then, as now, be the required behaviour of any Spanish player, they shrugged their shoulders and got on with the game as if nothing had happened.

However, their sportsmanship went unrewarded. The winger Castaño, not a regular player, scored twice, followed of course by Gento and Di Stéfano. There is a wonderful photograph of the game's third goal, scored by Gento – one of the old black and whites which captures the light in a less cluttered way than colour. The picture is taken from behind the net, through which Gento appears in the right-hand corner, smaller, distant, with his right leg slightly raised – that little hop he would do when he hit the ball with his left – and a succession of Yugoslav defenders appear to have missed the ball, just about to cross the line. The thin winter sun is beginning to drop behind the West Stand, and the photograph catches the moment where it caresses the back of the stadium and sparkles over onto the pitch, catching the back of Gento and lighting the faces of the Partizan defenders in a split second of white December radiance.

On 29 January, a month after the Christmas party, Madrid ran out onto a rather less glittering scene, in temperatures of ten below zero on a pitch covered with hard-packed snow. It was the sort of legendary test that sorted the men from the boys, but which would be automatically postponed nowadays. Watching a video of the game, played in flurries of snow, the poor Spaniards seem totally incapable of standing up, let alone playing football. The Yugoslavs may have been *educados*, but this state of grace clearly did not extend to their postponing the game. They probably figured, quite rightly, that the snow would be there until April. It was therefore a good job that Di Stéfano scored that fourth one in Madrid, for Partizan emerged 3–0 winners, and Madrid were lucky to survive. As Juanito Alonso, the goalkeeper that day recalled:

> It was awful. They were used to it. They kicked off, came down
> the middle as if there was no one there and someone unleashed

this incredible shot. I never even saw it. It hammered off the face of the bar and loosened about ten kilos of snow that fell on my head . . . I was bloody freezing. We hardly got out of our area. They were all over us. We only attacked once in the whole game, and we got a penalty. Rial slipped as he took it and it went over the bar. I can't believe we only lost 3–0. We should have been stuffed out of sight.

But they weren't, and lived to fight another day. They drew Milan in the semi-finals, a game that was to be a preface to the epic final between them two years later. Madrid drew first blood in a tense game in the Bernabéu in April 1956, winning 4–2 after Milan had twice fought back and equalised. The game confirmed Real's place among the giants, and a conservative, pragmatic 2–1 defeat in the San Siro on 1 May on a bone-hard pitch booked the passage to their first final, to be played in Paris in honour of the country that had set up the competition. Stade de Reims beat Hibs in the other semi-final, and made sure that the Gallic hand was played to the last.

Stade de Reims, since fallen from grace, were then a fine side, and despite Madrid's obvious virtues were the favourites on home soil. The game was to prove an epic, a fitting finale to gild Hanot's fine idea with the kind of sheen that would guarantee its continuity. The winners were promised automatic entry into the following season's competition as an extra motive to win, and it was Reims, prompted by the lithe and skilful forward Raymond Kopa, who came sprinting out of the blocks and established a 2–0 lead. Ten minutes gone and Madrid were wobbling, but inevitably, Di Stéfano pulled one back on the quarter-hour and by half-time it was honours even, thanks to Rial. In the opening minute of the second half Gento had a goal disallowed, upon which Hidalgo put the French back in front. Madrid stormed back again with a rare goal from the defender Marquitos and won it in the final ten minutes with a close-range shot from Rial.

Up on the first floor of the *Sala de Exposiciones* at the Bernabéu, a narrow corridor leads you from a rather garish and cluttered collage of Madrid's 2000 win in Paris down to a wooden wall at the end where five small TV screens, set into the wood panelling, play the goals of the 1956 to 1960 games over and over for the eight hours a day that the *Sala* is open. The action begins to your right, with the 1956 match, and you move along, watching the scurrying black and white images re-enacting the five finals in a curiously cyclical ballet. Watching the first final,

Rial's is the clinching goal, but it is Di Stéfano's first – the goal that ignites the *remontada* (comeback) – that is the pick of the seven. It is classic Di Stéfano, and for a change, there is enough of the build-up to appreciate the goal. Muñoz moves forward in the right-hand channel, some 40 yards from the French goal and suddenly releases a vertical pass into the space behind the Reims defence, the ball arriving on the edge of the box where Di Stéfano, steaming in from midfield, collects it as planned and continues his run before firing home. The pass to him was measured perfectly, but it is Di Stéfano's intelligence that stands out. His run annuls the presence of five defenders, all watching Muñoz and backing off. The ball seems to be going nowhere until the Argentine appears in the bottom left-hand corner of the screen and lends the pass a deadly coherence. The defenders look at each other, perplexed. Dancing behind frosted glass.

The European press loved it, and especially Madrid's performance. *L'Equipe*, lest it be forgotten that the spectacle was their baby, awarded the medals to the two sides, whilst *France Soir* wrote that, 'The main reason for Madrid's victory was Di Stéfano, who took Reims' defensive system apart.' Spain was suddenly something bright and vital, with this wonderful team. Even referee Arthur Ellis, later of *It's a Knockout* fame, had his say. 'Madrid won because they had more bite and speed,' he told *Le Monde*. More bite and speed. From what one can see of the game, that observation would seem to be fairly accurate, with so much attacking quality in midfield that Reims, despite their own plucky performance, were simply overcome by their opponents' greater variety of attacking options. But all four goals were scored by midfielders and a defender, if one still dares to refer to Di Stéfano as the former. Real still lacked a 'holding' player, a reference up front. There was speed, creativity, defensive strength and finishing power, but no one to slow things down, to hoof the ball up to when things were getting hot so that they could take a rest. Joseíto (José Iglesias), signed from Santander in 1954, played in the final but did not quite convince. The local boy Enrique Mateos also played, and came to figure in the renowned forward line that won the second cup in the Bernabéu the following season. But Villalonga had seen the lack of a 'reference' and saw the solution in Kopa, the forward-cum-right-winger who had used the ball so intelligently in the final in Paris. He had Gento's ability to get behind the defence and cross, but he could also drift inside and operate as a 'holder'. Besides, Real were a little too reliant on their left channel for initiating attacks. The incorporation of Kopa could balance the attacking options, and give the forward line more width and more time.

In the close season, Di Stéfano took out Spanish nationality, thereby creating legal space for a further foreign player. The tournament and the swollen size of the Bernabéu had left the club flush, and there was money to spend on further reinforcements. Kopa – Raymond Kopaszewski, born in France to Polish immigrant parents – was presented to the faithful in October 1956 in a friendly against Sochaux, which ended with the ridiculous score of 14–1. A week later he confirmed himself as the new talisman, scoring twice in a 7–1 win over Jaén. The team, if it were possible, looked even more threatening, with a forward line that was simply frightening. Just as well, for there was more work to do. The season of the win in Paris, Real had run out of steam in the league programme and finished third, nine points adrift of Barcelona and ten short of the winners, Athletic Bilbao. Two teams supposedly disabled by the wiles of Franco and his cronies didn't seem to be doing so badly for themselves, and Bernabéu, though he feigned indifference to this little setback, was in fact keen on supremacy on all fronts. When Atlético Madrid and Athletic Bilbao walked out to play the Cup final in 1956 at the Bernabéu, Franco decided to show his appreciation for the new light that was shining on his regime by pinning the city medal to Don Santiago's lapel, with Spain watching on. It stole the two finalists' thunder and would not have gone unnoticed by elements of the Right who were looking for some clues as to how to curry favour with the dictator. But a lot still depended on Real doing the business again in Europe. Were they a team of fly-by-nights, a one-off? There were plenty of teams out there keen on proving just that.

The story of the five cups warrants a book in itself, and there is insufficient space to do the whole period justice here. Nevertheless, it seemed reasonable to describe in some detail the first campaign, since every game was suffused with some sort of historical significance. In the subsequent four tournaments, certain games stand out as icons to an age – games whose details any football fan from that period could still recount. There are other matches, on the other hand, that have become folklore at least within Spain, or within the walls of Real Madrid. They have influenced the Spanish language, and given it a specialised vocabulary exclusively associated with some of these resonant events. One such game was the second leg of the first game in defence of the title.

As winners of the trophy, Madrid were handed a bye in the first round, entering the draw in the last 16. They drew Rapid Vienna, one of Europe's most feared post-war clubs who boasted the famous midfield of Ernst Happel and Gerhard Hanappi. In the Bernabéu things did not quite go according to plan, the 4–2 result leaving the holders a little wary of what might transpire in the Prater Stadium. And they were right to be wary, since by half-time they were 3–0 down, Happel having scored a hat-trick and run a curiously sleepy Madrid ragged. Enter Santiago Bernabéu, literally through the dressing-room doors, large cigar in mouth. His words have been recorded for posterity not by the memories of witnesses but by a club official whom Bernabéu ordered to accompany him with a camera. It's a curious scene, with the shifty-looking players staring at the floor as their president delivers his broadside, flinging his cigar to the floor and grinding it to pieces with his shoe – the clear implication of aggression not lost on the audience. And it was an expensive cigar. Don Santiago only smoked the best. His speech has become famous, second only perhaps to his notorious words in 1966 about football having 'done a service to this country' – a phrase mistakenly attributed to Franco. It is worth reproducing verbatim his words that day in Vienna, since they have become the lyrics to the music of *Madridismo*.

> Aquí no se salva nadie, no hemos venido de verbena y hay que dejarse los huevos en el campo. No sé si lo entendéis: lleváis en vuestras camisetas el escudo de Real Madrid y he visto en las gradas miles de Españolitos que se están ganando la vida en las fábricas con enorme esfuerzo y sacrificios. A éstos si que no lo podemos defraudar de ninguna manera.

> (No one's getting away from here this easily – we haven't come here on holiday and I want to see more balls out on that field. I don't know if you understand, but you've got the shields of Real Madrid on your shirts and I've seen thousands of Spaniards out there in the stands who've come here to support us – people who work their hearts out in the factories to earn a living. You can't let these people down like this.)

It was typical Bernabéu, creating a myth through his own macho rhetoric, invoking a working-class spirit that he himself did not really belong to. The Spaniards he was referring to were expatriate workers, but his appeal to not 'let these people down' was also an appeal to patriotism. However much a pot-pourri of nationalities Real were becoming, they were representing Spain. The implication was clear. Go out and win for Real Madrid and Spain.

They didn't win, of course, but Di Stéfano dropped off deep and tried to wrest the initiative from Happel, who had begun to tire. With the midfield back under control, Di Stéfano stole forward and got the vital goal that made it 5–5 on aggregate. With extra time only applied to finals it was necessary to play a third encounter, meaning that Saporta would once again step from the shadows, his wonders to perform. He persuaded the Rapid directors that it would be of greater financial benefit to them to play the game in the Bernabéu with its huge capacity, an argument that he supported with the dangling carrot of 50 per cent of the gate money – a temptation that proved too difficult for the Austrians to resist. Perhaps they still fancied their chances. Given the overall pattern of the two games, they were maybe justified in their confidence. Bernabéu and Saporta obviously feared the possible consequences of a neutral venue, and wisely calculated that the short-term loss of gate money would be more than compensated for by the long-term prospects of continuing in the competition. They won 2–0, and the rest, as they say . . .

On such gossamer threads is fate determined. Having narrowly escaped from this particular trapdoor, the club rarely looked back. By the time they reached the semi-finals that season, another of the classic encounters, they were feeling cocky enough to make bullish noises about the draw against Europe's other emerging young side, Manchester United. Busby's Babes, who require no introduction, had already knocked out the other Spanish side in the competition, Athletic Bilbao. Bilbao, still officially called 'Atlético' by decree of Franco, had beaten United 5–3 in a snowy epic in San Mamés, but Busby's colts went on to win the second leg 3–0. The game against United was one of the reasons for Madrid becoming so famous in England – a sentence that one must extend to Britain by the time the side reached Glasgow for the epic encounter against Frankfurt in 1960. But this semi-final pairing has gone down in both countries' footballing cultures as a special occasion – in Spain because it was absolute and utter confirmation that Madrid's run was no fluke, and in England because less than a year later a tragic percentage of the same United team would lose their lives on a Munich runway. United were the first English side to enter the competition, and apart from beating Bilbao they had annihilated Anderlecht 10–0 at Manchester City's Maine Road. It was not only that their reputation went before them, but that the Spanish have always had problems with their attitude towards English teams and the cultural baggage they supposedly represent. The famous Spanish inferiority complex, hidden by bluster and noise, always seems to come to the fore against the English, as if the Armada were in danger of being permanently re-enacted. Busby himself added to the spice by declaring before the opening leg in the Bernabéu that his team were '. . . a little better than Madrid. Besides, I know we'll be champions. Maybe with the crowd behind them they could win this leg, but they'll have to score more than three if they want to survive Old Trafford'. With the crowd behind them! A capacity crowd of 130,000 got into the Bernabéu on that April day in 1957, and thousands more were turned away. There were running fights with mounted police outside the ground – one of the first outbreaks of this kind of trouble in the Spanish league. Inside the stadium, United put Jackie Blanchflower on Di Stéfano and held out until the 61st minute when Rial got the first, to be followed, as usual, by one from Di Stéfano ten minutes later. Taylor pulled one back for United – a goal bitterly disputed by the Madrid defence – but Mateos scored a third for the hosts six minutes from time. Madrid had their legendary five up front – Kopa, Mateos, Di Stéfano, Rial and Gento, whilst the United names were equally resonant – Foulkes, Blanchflower, Byrne, Colman, Edwards, Taylor, Pegg, Violett . . .

The return leg was keenly anticipated in England, and spawned some memorable photographs – a famous shot of Busby, back to the camera, alone with his thoughts, surveying the death of his early dreams as the new lords and masters in white took a 0–2 lead. The game was the first of the campaign to be played at Old Trafford, where work on new floodlights had been finished just in time to host the game. Another lovely shot is of a sunlit Manchester street, with an old *Manchester Evening News* delivery van to the right of the picture, propping up a headline board announcing the match that evening. In the centre of the picture a cloth-capped man squats alone on the pavement, reading the team news. The photo captures the whole point of football – the impact it makes on the individual, not on the crowd. Real Madrid were coming to town. The shot quietly records how it must have been that spring day in Manchester, with that delicious feeling of anticipation in the air, sparked by an event to come.

The event itself led to numerous repercussions in both the English and the Spanish leagues, since had United won, they would surely have stood a good chance against Fiorentina, a side packed full of Italian internationals but with a defensive instinct that would have played into United's hands. Had United gone through, Madrid's own future hegemony might have been affected, who knows? The whole significance of Celtic's first British European Cup final victory (over Inter Milan) and United's own historic win at Wembley in 1968 were all set up by this game. The Busby Babes were cut off in their prime, first by Real Madrid and then by an ill-fated refuelling stop at a snow-bound Munich airport. In a sense this is absurd speculation, but the way that the fates stack their cards often makes fascinating reading, with the benefit of hindsight of course.

United pulled two goals back, one each from Taylor and Charlton, but they never looked quite strong enough to turn the aggregate total around. Madrid, prompted by Villalonga's offensive outlook, had wisely perceived that United were a similar side to them, and that attack would be the best form of defence. The game prompted Bobby Charlton's famous observation that he was glad to have only played in one of the games, since Madrid were something that he had not witnessed up to that point – 'inhuman' was the adjective he chose. He did not mean that they were cruel but rather that their powers seemed almost supernatural. Charlton's comments are interesting because Madrid's performance that night in Manchester was not so exceptional. They played a fine first half, but understandably relaxed in the second and allowed United to strut their stuff. Three years later in Glasgow most of the journalists present were scrambling for their thesaurus in search of adjectives to describe what they had just been privileged to witness. But Charlton's astonishment at Real's tactical awareness, their individual skills and their fitness, put one in mind of the bomb that Puskas' Hungarian side detonated in Wembley in 1953 – a bomb whose surprising range of tones the English were still too deaf or arrogant to hear. By 1957 things were beginning to change, as evidenced by Busby's side itself. Nevertheless, Busby must have regretted his second pre-match analysis of Real Madrid in which he claimed that they:

> . . . tend to keep possession for too long in their opponents' area and, in general, rely too much on individualism. They're better than Bilbao, for sure, but we'll knock them out.

This assessment of Real is quoted with glee in all of Madrid's centenary publications, as if it confirms that the northern European suspicion of crafty Mediterranean artistry was based (and still is) on a mistrust of flair, a feeling that all that clever dribbling stuff was really a product of indiscipline and questionable temperament. *Plus ça change*. Madrid were booed off the pitch by the Old Trafford faithful, but at least the English press were big enough the next morning to accept that the better side had won.

The better side won the final too, 2–0 in the Bernabéu against Fiorentina, the Italian side having beaten Grasshoppers and Red Star. For all the fact that they boasted perhaps their most famous side ever, they were no real match for Madrid on Spanish soil, and their defensive attitude to the proceedings was unsurprising, to say the least. Curiously, the game was played on the afternoon of 30 May 1957, because, although the club had at last got their floodlights in place and working, Fiorentina refused to play in the evening, claiming that home advantage was one thing, but on top of that, to play in the dark! Whatever, the light did them few favours, and despite killing the game for 70 minutes in front of another 130,000 gate, they finally blew it by bringing down Mateos in the area for a penalty – a dodgy decision by the nervous Dutch referee, Leo Horn, and one still disputed in Fiorentina folklore. Di Stéfano put the spot-kick away, of course, and then Gento scored with a lovely chip, bearing down on Sarti and then delicately lifting it over the advancing keeper's head. Two down, and counting.

Each player was given 200,000 pesetas as a reward for the win, and because of the victory on home soil, *Madridismo* went up another few notches. Franco and several of his cronies had obviously turned up for the occasion too, and captain Muñoz was handed the trophy by the smiling *Generalísimo*. The white *pañolada* at the end – the ceremonial waving of hankies borrowed from bullfighting that can mean 'Rubbish!' or 'Brilliant!' (obviously the latter here) – apparently moved Santiago Bernabéu to tears, and also witnessing this spectacle from the stands was one José Emilio Santamaría, the Uruguayan bought days before to accompany Marquitos and Lesmes at the back. The policy of constantly building, of introducing new elements each year, of obsessively repairing even the most hairline fractures in the squad was evidence of a planning strategy before its time. The money that was flooding in was being put to good use, and the training facilities that were also bought that year, several acres of land baptised *'La Ciudad Deportiva'* (Sports City) north of the Bernabéu, were to prove vital 45 years later when its controversial sale to the city council wiped off the club's accumulated debts overnight (see final chapter). Santamaría, schooled at Nacional de

Montivideo, was actually born of Galician parents, and was to become another legend at the club. In terms of this theme of continuity, he also went on to play for and to manage Spain, although he had the misfortune to be handed the reins for the infamous home World Cup campaign of 1982.

Back at the ranch, Real made 1957 a golden year by winning the first 'double' of its kind, European Cup and league title. Even though there were not so many games to play in those days, the achievement still speaks volumes for the quality of the side, because as any Barça fan will tell you, this period also boasted one of their greatest sides, and Bilbao were always there or thereabouts. The league was no cakewalk, but that season Real won it with five points to spare, from Sevilla. Barça and Bilbao came in third and fourth respectively. Astonishingly, Real were to go eight years undefeated at home, from the 0–2 defeat by Atlético Madrid in 1957 until the same side beat them again in 1965, 0–1. The explanation, apart from the fact that Madrid were simply too good, might also reside in the fact that they had a large squad for those days, with 30 players to call on if necessary. Madrid used 24 of them that season, a figure that calls into question somewhat the idea of the team as a settled, fixed unit, but which does prove that they had already begun the process, much more characteristic of the postmodern football era, of settling in reinforcements to practically every position. None of the other sides, save Barcelona, had the financial resources to compete with this. Nonetheless, it was the surprising 6–1 defeat at Barcelona in the *Copa del Generalísimo* that season that soiled an otherwise perfect season and set Villalonga thinking about how he might shore up these occasional defensive lapses. Enter Santamaría.

Oddly enough, Villalonga was never to manage Santamaría, since he was destined to be the first manager of the club to depart after winning the European Cup. The same thing happened to Jupp Heynckes 41 years later, and as in the later case of the German, Villalonga's departure was an unhappy one. Despite all the plaudits and success, his relationship with his sergeant, the ex-player Juan Antonio Ipiña, had deteriorated to such an extent that they had ceased to speak to each other, and the situation was clearly intolerable for both the players and for Bernabéu. Nothing could be allowed to tarnish the new public image, and the dirty internal stuff was promptly dealt with. Pepe Villalonga, for all his contribution, was shown the door, and replaced by the Argentine Luis Carniglia. Ipiña remained as deputy-in-chief, a fact that left it pretty clear whom Bernabéu blamed for the trouble in the first place. Carniglia knew the European scene, having been in France as a player since 1951 with first Nantes then Nice, the side for whom he had taken over as manager when they met Madrid in the round before the tie against Manchester United.

The third cup was won in Brussels against Milan, 3–2 after extra time, where once again it was clear that Madrid could hack the pressure. Twice behind in the game, they nicked it in extra time with a scrappy shot from Gento that ended up in the net after passing through a forest of legs. Carniglia had done nothing to suppress Madrid's attacking instincts, but he did bring a more defensive mentality into the midfield, introducing central cover for the traditional three 'backs'. Marquitos lost his place, with Zárraga, Santisteban and Atienza all contributing to this concept of a midfield shield. The second game of that campaign had also provided something of historic interest in that Sevilla, allowed into the competition as league runners-up to Madrid in 1957, were drawn against their compatriots in the quarter-final. They were to regret it somewhat, beaten 8–0 in the Bernabéu and punished for their mistaken tactics of trying to dethrone their countrymen by kicking them to bits. Seville's Campanal and Madrid's Marsal were sent for an early bath after a spot of handbags, and Di Stéfano became the first player to score four goals in a European tie. The game definitely sent out a 'Don't mess with us' message, making it clear that the team could look after itself physically, as well as play a bit.

They took the double (*el doblete*) again that season but were denied the 'treble' by their old Nemesis, Athletic (Atlético) Bilbao, who had the effrontery to beat them 2–0 at the Bernabéu, with a typical show of Basque steel. Again, as if this defeat had robbed Real Madrid of the caviar at the end of an evening's sumptuous dining, they moved again in pre-season. On 1 August 1958, an odd little man of 31 years of age with an alarming little beer belly was presented to the Madrid faithful, and posed for the official photographs. Carniglia, who had had less to do with his signing than had Saporta and Bernabéu, took one look at the new player and declared: 'I don't know what I'm supposed to do with this guy, he's so overweight.' Bernabéu, within earshot, replied: 'That's your job! You're here to make him prettier!'

Ferenc Puskas didn't get much prettier, but he certainly contributed to the party. For an ageing player with a sagging belly, his figures with Madrid make for interesting reading. In 260 appearances he scored an astonishing 240 goals, and yet here was another footballer who is rarely referred to as a 'striker'. Such a noun does Puskas as little justice as it would do Di Stéfano, but it has to be acknowledged that his signing that year changed the way that Di Stéfano played. The Argentine was also 31, an awkward age for a footballer and acknowledged within the profession as the first year of the downward slope. Thirty is the prime of life for a player with Di Stéfano's strength, but at 31 you are past your peak, or may appear to be. Psychologically, it's a tricky year for a sportsman. Puskas was therefore the perfect signing, because his technique and style of play were not based on physical strength so much as guile and wile. Valdano once said of Puskas that he could have been a defender had the inclination so taken him, simply because his intelligence would have obviated the need for him to ever make a tackle. Puskas hung around up front, occasionally dropping into the famous 'hole', but Di Stéfano moved back more permanently into a less offensive role, charged with initiating the moves but not necessarily with finishing them off. Puskas was already known for his left foot, of course, but during his time with Madrid the 'Galloping Major' became known as *'Cañoncito Pum!'* (Little Cannon Bang!), a phrase which referred to his ability to generate extraordinary power in his shots with hardly a lifting of the leg. The ball arrived at his feet, a little swivel to adjust and 'pum!' as they say in Spanish. Most people remember the famous drag-back and shot at Wembley, but it should be emphasised that he kept on doing this, year after year, when he was allowed to.

Puskas' unexpected arrival changed the panorama again and provided the new 'most memorable line-up' phrase – the holy trinity of Puskas, Di Stéfano and Gento. Back in 1956 after the suppression by Soviet troops of the Hungarian uprising Puskas and the Honved squad had toured South America and Europe, voluntary exiles from the chaos and dangers of Budapest. In November 1956 they were in Spain and were invited to play against a Madrid Select XI, a game that Puskas actually claimed was organised by Franco's wife. Be that as it may, the 5–5 draw was witnessed by Bernabéu, and the president remembered Puskas when in 1957 the player refused to return to Hungary with some of the Honved players, preferring to try his luck in the west. Banned from playing by UEFA for his refusal to play for the new Honved, he was twiddling his thumbs in Bologna when Bernabéu sent two representatives to sound him out, one of them Honved's former treasurer and the other, Nemes, a Hungarian ex-player of Madrid. Saporta, in his usual role as Mr Fixit, paid a visit to certain UEFA officials and persuaded, or paid them, to lift the ban. As ever, Saporta's wish came true, and Puskas made his debut in the 1958–59 season.

He started rather slowly, as was to be expected from a player still unfit and suffering from over a year of inactivity. In January 1959, both he and Di Stéfano scored hat-tricks as Madrid pummelled poor Las Palmas 10–1. Barcelona were to pip them for the league title that year but in the fourth European Cup that season Madrid had other things to occupy them. For the second year running they were to be drawn against another Spanish side, this time from the same city, Atlético Madrid. Their neighbours had been relatively quiet since their league wins in 1950 and 1951 under Herrera, and had been very much consigned to the shadows. But their runners-up spot in 1958 gave them a crack at the throne over on the Castellana, and they certainly made Real sweat. In the previous rounds, they'd had a fairly easy time of it, apart from the game in Vienna against Wiener Sport Club (who had beaten Juventus 7–0) where during the 0–0 draw Puskas was sent off for reacting to a foul and Muñoz was wrestled to the ground by Austrian police as he ran onto the pitch to protest. Teams were out to beat them now, and they had to take it on the chin. Wiener took it on the nose in the Bernabéu, thrashed 7–1 as punishment for having been less than perfect hosts. But in the semis Atlético had come to prove that they could live with their illustrious rivals and took the lead in the Bernabéu with a goal from Chuzo. Rial and Puskas gave the meringues some leeway for the second leg (after Vavá had missed a penalty for the visitors) but in the Metropolitano, over on the less friendly side of town, Atlético had the nerve to beat them 1–0, and take the tie to a replay in Zaragoza. Real won it 2–1, with goals from the two new friends, but Atlético had emerged with a great deal of credit and were to gain revenge in 1960 and 1961 when they would twice beat Real in the domestic cup final.

This period, much to Barcelona's further annoyance, shifted the exclusive focus of rivalry away from Barcelona and back onto the streets of Madrid. It was, in many ways, an easier rivalry to cope with, and it made for a change. Of course, Barça were winning the league titles in 1959 and 1960, but these considerable achievements were buried in the Spanish consciousness by Real Madrid's European adventures. One of the greatest psychological scars on the very skin of *Catalanisme* is that their team of the 1950s has never been sufficiently appreciated by Spain's football historians. They are right, but no one cares too much about that, west of Lérida.

In the final, Madrid met their old friends Stade de Reims again, this time in Stuttgart. Five of the French players had been in the original final, and of course Kopa now lined up against some of his old friends too. It was to be his last game for Madrid. Vicent, who had not been in the side when Kopa was there, took him out in the first half with a nasty tackle, Mateos missed a penalty and the French side, as was becoming the pattern, had clearly decided to try to kick their way to the podium. As ever, it was a futile plan, especially since they conceded a goal to Mateos within two minutes of the start. Di Stéfano got the second and Zárraga once again lifted the cup to the applauding crowd. If it was all getting a bit too predictable, the final next season was to spread the icing on the cake so lavishly that it is almost impossible to recall a more sumptuous occasion. The match of the century? Probably not. Performance of the century is a more fitting description.

There have been some fine passages written on the subject of the Hampden final between Eintracht Frankfurt and Real Madrid, so this book cannot pretend to add to them in any significant way. Richard Williams, however, writing in *The Guardian* in May 2002, was more ambitious and entertainingly described the game in 1960 as:

> . . . Fonteyn and Nureyev, Bob Dylan at the Albert Hall, the first night of The Rite of Spring, Olivier at his peak, the Armory Show and the Sydney Opera House rolled into one.

The author of this book does not belong to that generation, and the game was long gone by the time that football caught my attention in the late 1960s. And yet every time I see footage of it, watch the sublime movements of the Madrid players as they simply bewilder their poor opponents, I am reminded of that documentary on The Beatles, *Let It Be*, where the painful break-up of the group only serves to highlight the sudden death of the wonderful musical era that they helped to create and fashion. Of course, great music and great football have appeared since, but I cannot watch that Beatles documentary any more. It fills me with too much sentimental regret. Had I been born during the Second World War, I might have felt the same about the Glasgow game. It seems to mark what the writer Joseph Conrad called a 'shadow-line' – an event that marked a change, a decisive shift. Not necessarily for the better or for the worse, but a shift nonetheless.

The date – 18 May 1960. The game certainly immortalised Real Madrid, and turned them into a concept as much as a club. After that it wouldn't have mattered to most clubs, and they could have sat back and relaxed. Madrid's almost neurotic desire to continue winning meant that there were to be disappointments, but the game is there, in glorious black and white, and it stands as a testament to an era, as the embodiment of everything good in the aesthetics of the game up to then. A crowd of 127,000. Then 7–3! A ridiculous score, put into further perspective by the fact that the Germans scored first and Real Madrid missed a whole host of chances, hitting the woodwork three times. It could have been much worse for the Germans and, watching the game, you cannot understand how they even got to the final.

In fact they had got there by beating Rangers, a side who would certainly have appreciated getting to the final on home soil, but who were themselves to fall calamitously in the semi-final, 1–6 in Germany and 3–6 at Ibrox. The overall score may have flattered the Germans, for the Rangers manager, Scott Symon, was so prepared for the first game that he actually enquired (apparently without irony) who Eintracht Frankfurt were, when his team landed in Germany for the game. When asked if he wanted to inspect the pitch, he apparently replied that it wouldn't be necessary, one pitch being very much like the next. Nevertheless, refocusing on the Germans, not many sides score an aggregate of twelve goals in a European Cup semi-final then go on to concede seven in the final. The fact is that after the game settled down and Real realised that their opponents had no defensive midfielders, they simply turned on an exhibition that had been five years in the making. Every great team does it from time to time, when everything clicks and the understanding between the players seems almost supernatural. At 4–1 the Madrid players were doing outrageous things, and the crowd were registering their astonished approval. Madrid, to use the unfortunate modern parlance, were 'taking the piss', and the German bull was staggering about, bleeding and confused. If it hadn't been such great football, you would have been pleading for the referee's whistle to put the losers out of their misery. The goalkeeper Egon Loy, however, has to take some of the blame. Three times Di Stéfano beats him, and Puskas goes one better with four, but Loy, like the goalposts behind him, seems to be made of wood. At 4–1, he looks as stiff as a guardsman, watching the ball fly past as if he were drugged. Stein actually pulled back two near the end, a tribute to some fighting spirit in the Germans – and Domínguez goes so far as to shout crossly at Marquitos when his poor pass gifts Frankfurt their third, as if there were time for a comeback!

However, perhaps the most curious aspect of this singular game is that it might never have taken place. Puskas had claimed that the

German side that surprisingly beat the great Hungarians in the 1954 World Cup final were 'doped', prompting the German football authorities to ban its teams from playing against any that featured the Galloping Major. After the semi-final results, Puskas wrote a letter apologising for his previous indiscretion, meaning that the game could go ahead. Of course, the prime mover in the climb-down letter was the trusty Saporta, who had seen the problem coming and had persuaded the reluctant Hungarian (actually of German parentage) to put 1954 behind him. Bernabéu's trusted servant almost certainly composed the letter himself, to which Puskas added his signature.

History simply accompanies Real Madrid on their travels. Forty-two years later, they were back in Glasgow to win their ninth European Cup, this time at an all-seated Hampden, in front of a much reduced capacity of 52,000 but a worldwide audience of mind-boggling proportions. The opponents were German again, but Bayer Leverkusen were never likely to concede seven goals. Of the two that did cross their line, one will remain a classic, and no doubt warmed the cockles of Di Stéfano's heart, present at the game. At a grumpy 77, the old man retains a cynical silence about the figures of the modern game, but he likes Zidane. The Argentine's habit of calling him 'maestro' is praise indeed, and the delicious left-footed volley that the Frenchman struck in the 45th minute of the game will have only confirmed the reasons for the elder maestro's endorsement. Poignantly, the other man whom Di Stéfano considered a maestro, the man whose presence in the Barcelona team of the 1950's had a lot to do with the Argentine's final destination – Ladislao Kubala – died in Barcelona the day after the Glasgow final, after a long illness. Di Stéfano, himself looking frail, stepped off the Iberia flight from Scotland to be told the news that his old sparring partner had passed away.

But Real had won their ninth Champion's Cup, on the night of San Isidro, the patron saint of Madrid, back in the Scottish city that saw their greatest night, in the year of the centenary. The close win over Leverkusen was more than compensation for the loss of the King's Cup and the disappointment of third place in the league. The anti-Madrid lobby described it as a last desperate attempt to save the centenary season from farce. *Madridistas* described it as winning the only one that mattered anyway.

In a similar vein, 1960 is seen as a golden year for the club, despite the fact that it was also a blank year on the domestic scene. But what a wonderful campaign, coloured even more brightly by the fact that the semi-final had itself been a fairly apocalyptic occasion. Real Madrid and Barcelona had been drawn together, in an eerie preface to the following season's tournament in which the Catalans would finally put the brakes on their great rival's escapade. An historic game and the third consecutive season in which Real had met a Spanish league side in the tournament. And it was surrounded by various controversial events at the heart of the club. Carniglia had gone and been replaced at the helm by the Paraguayan Fleitas Solich, but he was to last less than a year, victim of Madrid's new victory paranoia. After beating Elche 11–2 and Oviedo 8–1, the side lost 3–1 to Barça four weeks from the end of the season, a result which eventually saw the Catalans champions again. In a curious fit of pique from the Madrid press, Fleitas was shown the door, some three weeks before the semi-final against Barça. Fleitas' loss was Miguel Munoz's gain, and the ex-player was to be the manager for the next 14 years, ushering in a new era of stability and establishing the post as one that benefited from longevity, not from constant changes. The famous Helenio Herrera was in charge of the Catalans for the semi-finals, but Madrid won it 3–1, with two from Di Stéfano and another from Puskas. Bernabéu, before the game, came out with another of his Churchillian rabble-rousers, and told the players pointedly that they were to '. . . defend the prestige of the club and everything that the supporters wanted from the game – and not only those in Madrid' – the implication being that the 'faithful' outside of the secessionist regions were all behind Madrid – a loaded statement, but one that had some truth to it.

Barcelona had Suárez, one of Spain's all-time home-grown greats, Kocsis and Villaverde. The referee was the Englishman Reg Leafe, a man whose face was to become famous on the dartboards of Madrid seven months later. But for now, Madrid won 3–1 in the Camp Nou too, silencing the Catalans and particularly Herrera, who had boasted that 3–1 would be easy to turn around. He paid for his prediction, and was hounded out by press and fans alike. Shrugging his shoulders, he travelled to Italy and changed the world . . . and would exact his revenge in 1964 in Vienna – in Di Stéfano's last game for Madrid.

It is tempting to describe the post-1960 period as a 'decline', but the bubble had to burst sooner or later. Nevertheless, the remarkable aspect of the end of the run is that it occurred in controversial circumstances, in the November of this famous year against Barcelona once again. Before briefly examining the circumstances of this so-called decline it is worth mentioning some of the changes in personnel and the fact that

Madrid's cup was more than overflowing. There had been talk in 1959 of the possibility of an intercontinental challenge – The World Club Championship, as it came to be called in Britain. Peñarol of Montivideo, Santamaría's old side, were South American champions in 1960, and FIFA decided to give it a go. Spain, Europe, the World. It seemed a logical progression, a further assessment of how great Real Madrid really were. The Uruguayans, Argentines and Brazilians were best known and well respected, but the logistics of the tournament were not as simple a matter as nowadays. When Madrid finally arrived in Montivideo, in the early July of 1960, the Uruguayan winter was in full force and the game should never have gone ahead. The 0–0 draw, played on a pitch with more water than grass, was an utter farce. Madrid managed one shot on goal, a miskick by poor Puskas as he tumbled backwards into a large lagoon.

The return game in Madrid in September was more recognisably a footballing event, and the Europeans ended up comfortable 5–1 winners in front of 120,000 spectators, keen on witnessing further testimony to their greatness. Another trophy for the groaning shelves. The five-year run had yielded some impressive statistics; 27 wins, 4 draws and 6 defeats, with 112 goals scored to 42 conceded.

By the time the draw landed them with Barça again that November, Canario was a fixture on the right wing and Kopa was forgotten. Canario, although not as fast as Gento, gave Madrid further individual flair on the right, and his contribution to the Glasgow massacre has often been underplayed. Didi, the famous Brazilian midfielder, had come and gone, staying only a season and never reproducing the form that he had shown in his native country. His wife, unhappy in Madrid, wrote a monthly column in a Brazilian newspaper, in which she claimed that her husband was unpopular with the *Madrileño* press for the simple reason that he was the only player in the squad who had refused to pay them for their sycophancy. The suspicion that the player himself had fed this to his wife did not exactly contribute to his popularity at dressing-room level.

No matter. Luis del Sol had been signed in 1960 from Betis, and reinforced the midfield with 25-year-old legs. These were now ten years younger than those of Di Stéfano and Puskas, but the two warhorses were not finished yet. They were certainly not to blame for the November defeat, the historians of Real Madrid preferring to point the finger at two English referees who have become notorious in the black books of the club – Arthur Ellis and Reg Leafe. Ellis had officiated during

Madrid's first win over Stade de Reims, and was later to enjoy the dubious privilege of blowing the whistle for the eccentric *It's a Knockout* television series in England. In charge for the first leg in the Bernabéu, Madrid were soon 2–0 up and it looked like business as usual. But in the second half the Catalans came out fighting, and when they protested fervently to Ellis for disallowing a goal by Kocsis, the suspicion has remained that the subsequent free-kick and the penalty, both tucked away by Suárez, were the Englishman's way of avoiding any more arguments with the visitors. But if Ellis is looked at sideways in Madrid's history, then Reg Leafe is still very much in focus, usually on the capital's dartboards. The return game in Barcelona was always going to be tough, but Madrid were not expecting to have to play against 12 men – an accusation so ironically levelled at them by their opponents down the years.

The significance of these two games was enormous, not simply because they represented the first European (aggregate) defeat for Real Madrid since the inauguration of the competition, nor because they showed the giant to have feet of clay, but because it is practically the only occasion in the history of the virulent rivalry between these two clubs from which Real Madrid have emerged claiming that they 'wuz robbed'. Barcelona's version of Real Madrid's hegemony of the Spanish league from the Bernabéu period onwards is that it was all due to state-sponsored favouritism, and bent refs – accusations dismissed by the Madrid camp as *victimismo* (victim complex), Barcelona's excuse for never really matching Real on the field of play.

Whatever, a fortnight later in a heaving Camp Nou – back then just three years old – the kings lost their crown in a tumultuous affair. Of the terrible twins it was the turn of Mr Leafe to officiate, and looking back at old footage of the game, it has to be said that Madrid's protests had some substance. Leafe disallowed four of Madrid's five 'goals', and yet none of them appears in any way illegal. The two scored by Barcelona were, however, jotted down as legal in the ref's notebook, and the 'Regime Team' were out. Bernabéu came out with one of his better lines after the game, remarking that Mr Leafe had been Barcelona's best player.

Poetic justice was seemingly done in two ways after the game, with Madrid hammering Barcelona 3–5 in the league just 11 days later in the Camp Nou. Maybe they were proving a point. Barcelona, on the other hand, saw the cup win as proof of what they had been saying all along – that when the referees were outside of the bent orbit of the capital's fascist politics, the results were fair. Maybe so, but watching the black and white images of the disallowed goals, one is tempted to conclude that dear Mr Leafe did not have one of his better days. Anyway, the second aspect of 'justice' resided in the fact that Barça blew it in the final that year in Berne, losing 3–2 to an emerging Benfica. Madrid continued to snigger up its collective sleeves until 1992 at Wembley, when Koeman's free-kick finally broke the Catalan's European duck.

But the next few years, before the arrival of the 'Ye-Ye' side, were hardly the stuff of tragedy. For the five consecutive European Cups, read five consecutive league wins between 1961 and 1965, the first time that Real had surpassed a run of two from the inception of the league in 1929. Curiously enough, the 1960s were a *Madrileño* wipe-out, the title staying in the capital for the decade from 1961 to 1971, when Valencia stopped the party. Real won it eight times in this period, with Atlético chipping in twice for good measure. And Real were hardly silent on the European front.

In the next season's quarter-finals – Madrid won the league in 1960–61 – there was another classic encounter, this time with Agnelli's Juventus, who boasted John Charles and Omar Sivori, the 1961 European Footballer of the Year, in their ranks. Madrid were worried by their opponents' pedigree, and played a conservative game in Turin, nicking a 0–1 win nevertheless, the work of Di Stéfano. Agnelli, in the days before agents, requested an interview with Gento and offered him an enormous sum to leave Real and come over to Turin to play provider for Charles and Sivori. But Gento was happy where he was. The Italians returned the compliment in Madrid and the game went to a replay in Paris, Agnelli promising each player a Fiat if they won the game. They were forced to hang onto their bikes as Madrid won the game 3–1.

After cruising past Standard Liege in the semi-finals, Madrid were to register another first with regard to European Cup finals – by losing one. They came up against Benfica in Amsterdam, a year after the Portuguese had put paid to Barcelona, by all accounts rather luckily. But this time they had the young Eusebio, signed from under the noses of Sporting Lisbon, and, in another magnificent final, the two sides were trading punches at 3–3 until Eusebio twice beat the Basque goalkeeper Araquistain to settle the matter. And when they went out to Anderlecht the next year in the opening round, it began to look as though the rest of Europe – some of them at least – had discovered a real heel of Achilles in the collective boots of Real Madrid. Even their first *doblete*, won after they beat Sevilla the season before in the domestic Cup final could not allay the fears that the average age of the squad should have been brought down sooner. Del Sol went on his way, but perhaps in response to this demand for more youth the Galician forward Amancio had been signed (he was to stay until 1976) along with the Navarran defender Ignacio Zoco – a significant member of the younger brigade who were to form the backbone of the 'Ye-Ye' squad.

Time's winged chariot was to grant Di Stéfano two more significant acts on the stage, although the first one was hardly in the genre he was expecting. In August of 1963, with Real Madrid healing their European wounds in the Venezuelan sun and taking part in a pre-season tournament in Caracas, Di Stéfano received a phone-call in his hotel room at 6 o'clock in the morning ordering him down to the lobby to be interviewed by two policemen. Santamaría, sharing a room with the Argentine, blinked and told him to shut up – he was sleeping. Di Stéfano asked them up and demanded to see their credentials – they obliged – upon which he left the now rather more concerned Santamaría and accompanied the two men into the street. Once in the car, they blindfolded him and took him to a flat where the leader of the NLAF (National Liberation Army Front) was waiting to inform him of exactly why they had decided to kidnap him. 'Publicity' was the word that Máximo Canales, the group's leader, used that morning, and publicity was what he got. By the next morning, almost all the major European papers were running the story, and every single Spanish paper ran it as their headline. The incident even prompted a show of tanks on the street by the Venezuelan government, just to remind folk of who was in charge. Whilst the world's press was proving, as if it really needed confirmation, that sport had moved onto a new level as far as the public's view of it was concerned, Di Stéfano was playing cards uneasily with his captors, having been told that he would come to no harm and that he would be freed as soon as they were sure that the photograph they had released of him had made maximum impact. Di Stéfano has since claimed that he wasn't so sure about them, but the famous photo of him in the flat in a black t-shirt, his lined face turned sideways to the camera, half irritated, half worried, makes you realise that you are looking at a man approaching middle age – receding, still with a decent chin-line, but getting on nevertheless.

> I spent hours staring at my white shoes. After a day passed I
> thought they were going to kill me. They played cards, chess –
> they said they were students. They kept asking me what I wanted

to eat, but I had no appetite . . . When they let me go I ran around a few streets to put them off the trail, then I headed for the Spanish Embassy. In the afternoon I gave a press conference, then later I played for a while in the final game of the tournament against Sao Paulo.

His captor, Commandante Canales, is now a fashionable painter in Venezuela, and still sticks to the invitation extended to Di Stéfano to dine with him one evening, to talk about old times and give him the opportunity to apologise, face to face. The Argentine responded, in an interview in *El País* in 2000, that although he couldn't really accept, he forgave his kidnappers and recognised that they were only trying 'to improve things'.

So were Real Madrid, and in the Argentine's swansong season they made a plucky attempt to win back their crown, with the young Amancio up front alongside Puskas, and Zoco, Müller, Felo and Di Stéfano working the midfield. Things were solid at the back, with Santamaría joined by Isidro, Miera and Pachín – a defence that only conceded 23 goals in the league that year. These were the best figures since Betis let in a mere 19 in 1935, but the Andaluz side played eight games less than Madrid. It was the attacking potency that was beginning to wane, at least as far as cutting it with the top sides was concerned. Or perhaps one can only really apply this to Helenio Herrera's Inter Milan side that year, because Madrid scored plenty of goals in the run-up to the final. Glasgow Rangers at last got their chance to meet Madrid in the opening round, and were dispatched without mercy, 7–0 on aggregate. AC Milan let in four at the Bernabéu in the quarter-finals, and in the semis, in the same stadium, Zurich's net was peppered six times. But Inter, with the ex-Barcelona star Suárez, Mazzola, Milani and company in the side, were made of sterner stuff. Again, the 3–1 win for the Italians that day in Vienna was stuffed full of historical significance. It was the first final, curiously enough, in which a neutral venue was almost wholly given over to supporters of the two participating teams. The possibility of reaching Austria by road and by train and the fact that several travel agents in both countries had finally seen the commercial potential of football travel (several 'specials' were put on from Madrid to counter the anticipated arrival of hordes of *tifosi*) lent the game a distinct atmosphere and signed the death-knell of those cloth-capped occasions on which goals were politely applauded by fan and foe alike.

From the Italian side, Herrera had persuaded President Angelo Moratti to encourage the formation of supporters' clubs at the San Siro, and make it a more intimidating place to visit – as the Camp Nou had been during his stay there. The game was also the first mass public exposition of *catenaccio* – Herrera's hated 'door bolt' defence, loosely based on Karl Rappan's system whilst in charge of the Swiss national team in the late 1930s. Putting in a sweeper behind four man-marking defenders and breaking out rapidly from midfield was not necessarily a method that would bamboozle a side of Madrid's pedigree, and the significance of this game has maybe been a little exaggerated – but Real's inability to function that day certainly had something to do with Herrera's tactic of marking Gento and Puskas out of the game, intimidating the young Amancio and allowing Suárez to roam freely on the right-hand side of midfield so that Zoco and Müller would pay too much attention to him. Di Stéfano, in his final game for the club, was suddenly shorn of people to supply, and when the ball came anywhere near him it was whisked away unceremoniously by some young Italian pup. There is also evidence that before the game things were less than hunky-dory in the Spanish camp, with the *Madrileño* press sneaking photographs of Di Stéfano and Puskas to see which one was the fattest, and the players complaining about the facilities at the hotel. Several of the rooms lacked blinds and curtains, and the team were pestered by the travelling fans and by the early 1960s version of the paparazzi. Many have also seen the game as Herrera's revenge on Real Madrid (they were to meet again in 1966) and the match that marked the death of attractive football, until Celtic came along in 1967 and scotched the snake. Inter's success (they won the European Cup again the next year) shifted the focus of power away from Real Madrid and moved it to the other side of the Mediterranean. From the pinnacle of their power in 1960, only Benfica had briefly threatened to pick up the crown, but Eusebio aside, the European press were unconvinced. Inter made for a more convincing case.

But more than anything, this was the final curtain on the age of Di Stéfano. In the summer of 1964 Miguel Muñoz had some thinking to do, and his final conclusion was that it was time to let his ex-teammate go. He'd knocked in a decent 11 goals that season, but the twin traumas of Caracas and Vienna had taken some spark away, stolen some fire from his belly. He was 38 that July, and Muñoz felt that his talents and experience would be better served away from the field of play by incorporating him onto the club's technical staff. At least, this is the version that has been passed down. But Don Alfredo did not agree. There is a curious sepia photograph of Di Stéfano in his kit outside the changing-rooms, pleading with Muñoz to change his mind over something. Madrid's photo archive makes the unlikely suggestion that Munoz' decision to not renew Di Stéfano's contract is being enacted in front of the cameras, but it makes good copy nonetheless. Whatever, Bernabéu backed Muñoz' decision, and Di Stéfano left under a cloud, deprived of his golden handshake because he had refused to accept the club's new conditions. His own declaration, that Madrid had terminated his contract '*con nocturnidad y alevosía*' (maliciously, under the table) was a sad finale to such a glorious drama. After 11 amazing years in which the Argentine had changed the face of Spanish football, probably saved Franco's bacon, become Europe's most famous player and revolutionised its football, Bernabéu, in a merciless act of apparent ingratitude, declared that Di Stéfano would not tread the hallowed grounds again whilst he, Don Santiago, was still alive. By 1967, when Celtic visited the Bernabéu for the player's testimonial, everyone had kissed and made up, but it was nevertheless a sour end to some glorious proceedings. In the same year in which the new kings Johan Cruyff and Franz Beckenbauer made their league debuts, the old monarch was bowing out. Sport has a poetic habit of turning up this type of counterpoint.

He went on to play 19 games for Español, Barcelona's rather more rogue outfit. Kubala, by then their manager, persuaded him over, and the two finally coincided outside of the previous orbit of the national team. And talking of poetry, the fixture list contrived an almost unbelievable first game to the 1964–65 season – Español v. Real Madrid. Puskas was still playing in the capital, and came up against his old mate for the opening game of the season. Di Stéfano could not understand why he had been allowed to leave whilst his tubbier friend had had his contract renewed, but he bore him no grudge. For the record, Madrid won 2–1, and Di Stéfano failed to score.

It was not to be the end of his association with the club, and almost 20 years later he would return to preside over the appearance of another great set of players, the famous *Quinta del Buitre*, subject of a later chapter. But for now, an era had passed.

8. SHE LOVES YOU

In July 1965, exactly a month before the release of 'Help!', the first of those Beatles' titles that told you that something might be a little awry in their world, the Fab Four had played at the Plaza de Toros in Madrid. Footage of the concert demonstrates clearly that whilst the Franco regime had decided to ease up a little on the cultural control, the Spanish were still wary of letting their hair down in public. There's a smidgen of screaming here and there, and one or two youths stand on their chairs and wiggle their hips, but the scene is almost funereal compared to the hysterical reception the group had received in the USA the previous year. The audience seems vaguely bemused by it all, until Lennon launches into 'She Loves You'. The song was two years old by then, but had assumed something of a cult status in Spain for having been one of the few foreign pop songs to get a consistent airing on Spain's surprisingly lively radio network. Besides, the lyrics of the chorus were easily learned by Spain's youngsters, desperate as they were for some 'alternative' fare. The last three words of the opening line *'She loves you yeah yeah yeah'* were to become forever associated with the Real Madrid players that succeeded the side of the golden era – the so-called 'Ye-Ye' team, the spelling of which remains as a permanent testament to Spain's stubborn belief that all languages of the world can be happily reduced to their own phonetic fantasies.

This was the team that snatched the crown back in 1966, for one glorious year. This was a year, remember, when people discovered sex, England won the World Cup and there was a summer of love, but it was also *La Sexta* (the Sixth) for Real Madrid and it possesses a curious resonance in the club's particular culture, like the last sigh of the Moor on departing his beloved Spain. The period after 1966 also has a name, inevitably, referred to rather dramatically as *La época del desierto* (The wilderness years), nonsense of course, but logical if you have just spent ten years winning six European Cups, seven league championships, a World Club Championship and a Generalísimo's Cup into the bargain.

Given this perspective, one can excuse the authors of this particular phrase their poetic licence. Real Madrid, after the win over Partizan that year, would have to wait until 1981 before appearing again in a final of their beloved tournament, by which time the city that produced The Beatles was ruling the European roost. The years in the wilderness, if that is what they really were, ended in 1998 in Amsterdam with a shot into the top corner by Predrag Mijatovic against Juventus.

But back in 1966 it must have seemed that this new squad, shorn of all the great names, save Gento, were about to usher in a new era of glory. Puskas was still around, but wasn't picked for the final against Partizan. He finally called it a day at the end of the 1966–67 season, at the age of 40. The other significant factor about this new generation of players was that they were all Spanish – one of the only times since the 1930s that one can say this of the club. They were not all *Madrileños*, nor were they all formed in the bosom of the club (a detail to be reserved for the *'Quinta del Buitre'* of the 1980s) but the all-Spanish aspect of the squad's strongest line-up became another string to Madrid's bow. However, one of the most infamous of all the photographs for the anti-Madrid lobby was taken at the Bernabéu the day after the 'Ye-Ye' team had returned from Brussels. The 20-man squad poses on the turf with the six trophies held high by the players to the front of the shot, whilst the other 14 stand square around the Spanish flag. The photo is taken from a raised position with the players looking up rather stiffly to the camera. It has remained unclear as to whether they really wanted to do the shoot, but there they are, rather glumly retained for posterity in a photograph eagerly quoted by anti-*Madridistas* as evidence that the club and all its acolytes were perfectly happy to toe the political line. Di Stéfano, who has since spoken out over this issue by claiming that the '50s side would have preferred not to have been associated in any way with the politics of the regime – is nevertheless not in the picture. He was over in Barcelona, sorting out the terms of the end of his final contract as a player. He played for Spain, of course, but one suspects that he might have been reluctant to have posed for the picture. Puskas did, but he's holding one of the cups, not the flag. Then again, for all true *Madridistas*, this was just a harmless show of patriotism.

'Harmless' seems to be a word that fits this period well. As Manuel Velázquez points out in an interview on the *Marca* centenary video, the 'Ye-Ye' side could not possibly live up to the technical accomplishments of the players they replaced, but they were difficult to beat, and they had spirit. All the players interviewed from that period coincide on this point, that there was a togetherness and feel-good factor to the club which may have been missing from the previous side that won such acclaim. Velázquez, during an articulate and honest series of reflections, even implies that the immediate post-1960 period was a difficult one for the club – simply due to the expectations generated. There is also evidence, though Velázquez does not say so (he made his debut much later, in 1965), that the domineering presence of Di Stéfano had begun to rub some people up the wrong way. In the end, the unthinkable happened, and he fell out with Bernabéu. This was ostensibly over the job offer, but things had been far from ideal for some time. Besides, Di Stéfano has never enjoyed being old. You can see it in his frown in every photograph taken of him during the centenary celebrations. Back then, as his powers began to wane, he had become increasingly tetchy, and the younger players were allegedly terrified of him. Amancio Amaro, another of the major 'Ye-Ye' figures, first pulled on the white shirt in Ghana, on the summer tour of 1962. Before walking out onto the pitch he noticed that his shirt had no shield on the breast pocket, and commented on the fact to Di Stéfano as he was passing. The curt reply – '*Primero hay que sudarla chaval*' (You've got to sweat in it first sonny) – has become legendary in Madrid circles. But apart from illustrating the obvious fact that Di Stéfano considered the club to be special, one can also imagine the negative side of this oppressive little put-down.

Age has not mellowed him. When I tried to interview him for this book, I was told by his secretary that he would meet me at 11.30 a.m. in the '*Veteranos*' (Veterans' Room), a sort of bar-cum-social gathering place in the Bernabéu for some of the ex-players. When I walked into the room, it was exactly one hour after Argentina had been knocked out of the 2002 World Cup, a game that he had obviously been watching. 'I don't fancy talking now,' he snapped. 'Besides, I'm busy.' When I informed him politely that I had flown down to Madrid that morning from San Sebastián to speak to him, he barked 'San Sebastián? And I've come from Patagonia!' That was that. There was no point in arguing, although to be fair to him, I could have picked a better day! Puskas had his moments, but was – swipes at Germans notwithstanding – a more affable character. Gento was very much one of the boys, and was to continue playing until 1971 anyway.

Things seemed to lighten up after 1964. This jauntier feeling coincided with Spain's unexpected victory in the 1964 European

Nations Cup, to date their only major trophy. Spain beat the Russians, Yashin and all, in the Bernabéu in front of Franco and Don Santiago on a red-letter day for the two of them. Apart from the fact that Zoco and Amancio were in the side, the relationship between national success and Madrid as willing hosts was very much cemented that day, especially when the right-wing paper *ABC* hailed the victory as a new dawn for the country:

> In this quarter of a century there has never been displayed a greater popular enthusiasm for the state born out of victory over communism and its fellow travellers . . . Spain is a nation every day more orderly, mature and unified, and which is steadfastly marching down the path of economic, social and institutional development. It is a national adventure.

Stirring stuff, although to be fair, the economy was indeed on the up and the war years had been left behind. In truth, this period is seen as the beginning of the 'decomposition' of Francoism, in that the leader resisted all attempts for political reform and wider representation and guaranteed that the country would still be lagging behind when he died in 1975. But on the surface at least, things didn't look so bad. The 'Ye-Ye' phenomenon was a faithful reflection of this relatively upbeat feeling.

In fact the whole 'Ye-Ye' thing arose from a prank that with the hindsight of postmodern eyes seems a bit corny, but which has characterised this sense of mid-'60s innocent fun to perfection. Some three months before the sixth final, played against Partizan, Felix Lázaro, a prominent football journalist at the time, made his way with a friend to a hotel on the outskirts of Madrid in which the players were gathered before an evening game. In the days before top players hired personal secretaries to protect them from over-exposure and security guards to protect them from the outside world in general, men like Lázaro could simply turn up at the team hotel and wander up to the rooms, such was the easier relationship that existed then between press and players. Lázaro had come up with the idea of getting some of the players to wear Beatles-style wigs and pose for a shot that they would publish the next day, asking the public to guess their identities. Velázquez, De Felipe, Grosso and Pirri volunteered their services, but Lázaro could not run the shot the next day for lack of space in the paper. The photo was filed away and forgotten, until two days before the final when Lázaro remembered it and *Marca* ran the picture on its front page. The 'Ye-Ye' phrase was effectively born that day.

Velázquez also pointed out that the team did not feel under any great pressure because the Bernabéu faithful did not really expect them to win anything. The aspect of 'follow that' actually played into their hands and they performed with a lightness of approach that had been conspicuously absent between 1960 and 1964. The four great names from the period are Pirri, Velázquez, Grosso and Amancio. Pirri – José Martínez Sánchez – scores highest in the Top 100 poll, coming in at number 18. This is probably a vote for longevity, for he was to play from 1964 until 1980. He is usually described as a forward, and knocked in 170 goals over the 16-year period, but in truth he played everywhere, moving back to midfield in the early 1970s, then finishing up as a centre-back – the way of all flesh. After his retirement, he stayed on as club doctor, and later worked as the club's Technical Director. Amancio is next at number 22 and was the first of the four to arrive, from Galicia in 1962. The player that Pelé most admired of the '60s side, he was a goalscorer but a provider too, lending a certain status to the number 7 shirt that was later to be worn with such distinction by Butragueño and Raúl. Ramón Moreno Grosso (number 30), who died a month before the centenary date, is remembered as the player who took over Di Stéfano's number 9 shirt, which probably marks him out as having had the most difficult job of any footballer in the history of the game. During Di Stéfano's testimonial game in Madrid against Celtic in 1967, when the Argentine left the field in the first half, he picked up the ball and handed it to Grosso, who was already wearing number 9. The handing over was a symbolic act almost masonic in its ritualism. Grosso, to his eternal credit, was to live up to the shirt – to 'sweat it' as Di Stéfano would have said. He played in the 'hole' with great distinction, and even better, he was born and bred in Madrid. So was Manuel Velázquez (number 35), an intelligent midfielder who made his debut in the December of 1965. Grosso replaced Di Stéfano, but hardly ever played alongside him. Velázquez, on the other hand, did play alongside Puskas, and although he operated in a more withdrawn position, his attacking instinct earned him the distinction of being considered the Hungarian's successor.

All four of these players were in the final in 1966 against Partizan in the Heysel Stadium, and Amancio scored Madrid's first goal with a wonderful dribble, attacking the defender Jusufic on the edge of the box as if to pass him on the right then suddenly switching direction with a crafty little nutmeg that left the goalkeeper exposed. Soskic races off his line but Amancio tucks the ball exultantly to his left and the 'Ye-Ye' babes were about to come of age. The side that lifted the sixth trophy that early summer evening were all Spanish. In the quarter-finals against Anderlecht in Belgium, Puskas, despite playing wonderfully in the previous two rounds, looked tired and was left out for the second leg. He had made his last European appearance for the club. In the previous round, in the second leg at home to Kilmarnock (5–1), Muñoz had actually played the all-Spanish card for the first time, fulfilling a promise he had made to the press. Puskas took it well; *'Hay que tener fe en los chavales'* (You have to show faith in the young 'uns) and Velázquez got his chance. In the semi-finals, it looked as though this almost whimsically gathered side had met their Waterloo when they came up against the old foe, Inter Milan, again. Manchester United, who had famously destroyed Benfica 1–5 in Lisbon, were playing Partizan Belgrade in the other semi and, according to a Belgian newspaper, both sides had already paid a deposit on hotel rooms for the final. It was an interesting turnabout for Madrid to be seen as the underdogs, but Inter were on for a hat-trick and had clearly shoved the Spanish side off the podium. A goal from Pirri settled the April encounter in the Bernabéu, but the Italians had looked menacing, and an injured Betancort had limped around under the goalposts for the final half-hour praying for the whistle. Herrera, as generous as ever, parted with the shot 'Madrid will burn in the San Siro'. He should have known better than to motivate them with such a clichéd remark, and a record crowd at the Italian stadium were silenced by a famous strike from Amancio. Pirri was still in his attacking phase, but was under instructions to man-mark his compatriot Suárez, still the player Madrid most feared. Muñoz was taking a leaf out of Herrera's manual, but it worked a treat. Fachetti equalised, but Madrid held out strongly for a famous draw, going on to win the final. The famous *Sunday Times* exposé of Inter's attempts to bribe referees during this period suggested that Madrid's annoyance with the referee, Dimitris Wlachojanis, in the first leg may have had some justification. The Austrian had added on five minutes at the end of the match for no apparent reason, but the Italians had failed to capitalise. In the San Siro, it would appear that Real were fortunate enough to have had the Hungarian Gyorgy Vadas refereeing the game – one of the few, it would seem, who refused to take the bribes on offer. Madrid got through on merit. So did Manolo Santana a fortnight later in London, making him the first Spaniard to take the Wimbledon singles title. Santana, born in Madrid, wore the Real Madrid shield on his shirt in the final and dedicated the trophy to the team. 1966 was a good year for *Madridistas*.

The following season, Inter would get another crack at their third European Cup after coming up against Real for an amazing third time in four seasons. This time Suárez ran the show, particularly in Madrid where he scored in the 2–0 win that effectively began the rather dramatically named 'wilderness years'. Jock Stein's Celtic provided the Spanish (and most of Europe) with some comfort later in that tournament, winning a wonderful final in Lisbon and putting Herrera's hated system to the sword. But it was to be 14 long years before Real would return to dispute a final of the competition they had once considered their own.

Summarising what remained of the 1960s, it is worth pointing out, once again, that Real's consistency in the league was not something easily maintained. No longer able to rely on automatic qualification as European champions, the domestic competition was as important as ever. Besides, the winner mentality was very much in place by this period, despite Velázquez' insistence that the team felt under no particular pressure. This remark has to be seen in the relative context of Madrid, where 'no particular pressure' probably referred to the obvious fact that no team was going to win five consecutive European trophies again. But we know enough about *Madridismo* now to suspect that there was a need, in the guts of the club, to snatch back the dream. As they say, 'what you never have, you never miss' – but true longing arises from a state of grace attained. As Proust observed, '*A la recherche du temps perdu*'. To the club's immense credit, it has never allowed the *hazaña* (feat) of the 1950s and early 1960s to weigh as heavily on the club as did, for example, Manchester United's golden period around the same time. United were to suffer 25 leagueless years, and 31 years would pass before they lifted the European Cup again. Charlton, Best, Law and Busby cast a shadow that saw their successors scurrying around in the dark. Madrid had to wait a long time for another European Cup too, but in the meantime, they were nevertheless dominating their domestic league and participating in various European trophies. They were very much alive. Manchester United's pretensions to greatness seem absurd when you compare them with Real Madrid's so-called 'wilderness years'. Remember, this is a team who walked off the Bernabéu in April 2002 without so much as a wave to the crowd, even though they had just qualified for the Champions League final in their centenary year and beaten their old friends Barça on aggregate. Reasons to be cheerful? Not a bit of it. Iñaki Cano, one of Spain's more respected roving journalists, thrust his mike under manager Del Bosque's nose and asked why there had been no lap of honour. '*Solo celebramos los trofeos*' (We only celebrate winning trophies) was the curt reply.

In the 1966–67 season, Madrid lost only twice in the league, to Barça and Zaragoza, and set themselves up for another journey into Europe the following season, with Puskas finally retired. In the reduced terms of 'a good campaign', it was to be their last until 1973 when the great Ajax side of Cruyff, Neeskens *et al.* snuffed them out in the semi-finals. Two games stand out from that season – the wonderful semi-final against Manchester United and the opening round, curiously enough against Ajax. Rinus Michels had established an interesting-looking set-up in Amsterdam, and Cruyff's growing reputation was a cause for worry. Even more so when he scored a rather untidy goal after 17 minutes of the opening leg in Amsterdam. Although Pirri equalised before half-time and Madrid went home with a creditable draw, Muñoz was worried by what he had seen – the serene, rather arrogant touch of the Dutch side, their fitness, their 4–2–4 system and the lanky young Cruyff practising a similar art to the one that Di Stéfano had perfected a decade earlier – playing in a vertical central channel, breaking from midfield to attack with control and speed. It was a preview of things to come, but fortunately for Madrid that year it wasn't quite the finished article that they met. Pirri, interviewed for the *Marca* video documentary of the centenary, claims that Muñoz told Zunzunegui to 'follow Cruyff everywhere'. There are plenty of apocryphal tales of man-markers following their quarry to the toilet etc, but in this case it appears to have been true. At half-time, as Muñoz began his pep-talk, he asked Zunzunegui why he had allowed Cruyff the room to get in the shot that had opened the scoring for Ajax. When no one answered, Muñoz' rant was cut short by the phrase 'He's not here boss'. Pirri, himself one of the practical jokers in the camp, suggested to Muñoz that the defender might have taken his advice to follow him everywhere seriously. When Muñoz told Pirri to go and look for him, Pirri walked across to the Dutch dressing-room, knocked on the door and walked in. Sure enough, a straight-faced Zunzunegui was sitting on one of the Dutch benches next to a laughing Cruyff.

But it was kind of the fates to draw these two teams together back then, the young princes paying a visit to the castle where the old kings had reigned. In the second leg in the Bernabéu, the other young pretenders opened the scoring in the second half against a curiously defensive Ajax, but Grot soon equalised, majestically heading in Cruyff's cross and silencing the *Fondo Sur*. The news programme *El Nodo*, Franco's chief medium of propaganda, was by then so in favour of all things Madrid that it might as well have been entitled 'Whitewash', and its report on this game is something of a sociological treasure. When Gento opens the scoring for Real, the camera zooms in on a coloured Ajax supporter, glumly drawing on his cigarette as he contemplates the glee around him. The narrator chips in with: *'Marca Gento el primer gol y el moreno parece preocupado!'* (Gento scores the opening goal and the darkie looks worried!). It gets worse. When Grot equalises, the cameraman decides to focus on him again, at which point the jolly narrator informs us that *'Y el moreno explota de alegría!'* (And the darkie explodes with joy!). Of course, our Dutch hero cannot get away with this for too long, and when Veloso scores a wonderful winner for the hosts, evading three tackles and blasting in a shot from some 25 yards, we are told that *'Y ahora, el moreno está triste'* (And now the darkie's sad). The word *'moreno'*, which actually means 'brown', is not a seriously racist term, but the casual use of the word in a news programme from that bygone period is an interesting reminder of the days before commentators were limited by a greater awareness of these issues.

In the semi-finals, the defeat at the hands of Manchester United is possibly a greater legend in English football circles than in Spanish ones, but by any standards it was an epic encounter. Ten years after the Munich disaster United were on the verge of lending some substance to the theory that they were Europe's top side, 11 years after Real Madrid had cut them off in their prime. The 'Ye-Ye' side were, however, a fearsome unit by then, and could have written themselves into the Madrid history books with a little more of their own substance had they managed to hold onto their 3–1 lead in the Bernabéu, but they blew it and would have to settle for one further European final – the Cup-Winners' Cup against Chelsea in 1971, that would also end in tears. Of the 1968 game, Manchester United's official website says that Real Madrid were 'swept aside' on the path to Wembley, whereas Real Madrid's official centenary book gives the game the title *'La suerte de Manchester'* (Lucky Man Utd). Make of that what you will. On 24 April at Old Trafford, George Best gave United a slender lead to take to Madrid, and it looked slender indeed when United found themselves 3–1 down in an electric atmosphere at the Bernabéu – Pirri, Gento and

Amancio knocking in the goals – Zoco scoring a curious own goal for United. But Madrid seemed to relax in the last 20 minutes and United staged their famous comeback, Sadler pulling one back and then the unlikely figure of Bill Foulkes steering home a low cross from Best. The scenes at the end, as a euphoric United try to make a dignified exit whilst the Madrid players walk off stunned, is definitely one for the Manchester scrapbooks only.

Things got even worse for Real in early June when they reached the Generalísimo's Cup final, again scheduled to be played at the Bernabéu. Rigo, a Catalan referee, was chosen to officiate in the final, a decision much lamented by various centenary histories, all of them unquestioningly accusing Rigo of having been bent (he was a Catalan after all!) and none of them mentioning the awkward little fact of Madrid's home advantage. No matter, Barça won 1–0 and there is a precious shot of Franco glumly handing the cup to José Antonio Zaldua, Barça's captain. Not only is Franco's face evidence of what the Catalans had long since suspected to be the case, it seems that the dictator did not fancy a repeat of the scene – the reason, according to the conspiracy theorists, for the great refereeing scandal of 1970, the so-called 'Guruceta affair', in which a young Basque referee was accused of accepting bribes before the second leg of the Generalísimo's Cup quarter-final in 1970 in the Camp Nou.

In the end it is impossible to draw a firm conclusion on the matter of whether Real Madrid were 'helped' by Franco. The phrase itself is meaningless in practical terms, and could only be manifested in the general sensation that out on the pitch, especially at the Bernabéu, the referees were either bribed or intimidated into favouring them. But how does one draw the line between illegal intimidation and the simple fact that any big club such as Real Madrid will come to represent something of the nation by mere dint of the fact that they play in the capital? Almost all countries have similar tales to tell, but not all countries have the Madrid–Barcelona problem. Barcelona have never accepted Real Madrid's hegemony as a genuine football fact, an attitude that *Madridistas* insist is a result of the region's 'victim complex'. There is some truth in this, and it should not be forgotten that Real Madrid themselves have had cause over the years to also question several referees' decisions. Barcelona, particularly from the late 1960s until quite recently, have been if anything the richer of the two clubs – or the one least in debt, whichever way one wishes to put it. Do the *Catalanistas* seriously wish to suggest that it is only the *Madrileños* who are capable of corruption? Barcelona themselves would have had ample reasons down the years for slipping a few payments under the table. Franco's otherwise efficient centralised control of the country could not have prevented this, however much it might have wanted to. Did the police state really mean that only Madrid could bribe and get away with it? As a neutral observer, I find this thesis vaguely absurd.

Of course, it is in the nature of these two clubs, and to some extent Spain, to give no quarter, to show neither mercy nor admiration for the foe. So Madrid were cheats and fascist stooges, and Barcelona were bad losers, spoilsports with a victim complex. The fact that neither of these clichés is true is of no consequence. The Spanish are happy to go along with these traditional views, whilst the rest of the world draws a similarly twisted conclusion – that Madrid are the 'baddies' and that Barça are the 'goodies'. The baddies, in this context, won the 1968–69 league campaign by nine clear points from Las Palmas, and went the first 27 games of the season undefeated – but of course, the refs were all on their side . . . Three games from the end they went down 1–0 at Elche, but still won the title at a trot. However, it was during the next season that Madrid were supposedly exposed as the cheats that so many had accused them of being, with the core of their empire exposed as rotten.

The 1969–70 season seems to have marked another watershed in the history of the club, because their failure to win the league that year and the early home defeat to Standard Liege in Europe meant that the next season would see them watching from the sidelines for the first time since the first edition of Hanot's baby in 1956. Fourteen unbroken years participating in the European Cup. Quite apart from the six wins, it is an astonishing record. The Spanish league has never been a cakewalk, and Madrid's domination of it has been due to factors largely connected with football, not political influence. Of course, once they had the money (and even before) they practised an aggressive policy of buying the best in the domestic market, but this still falls short of explaining why the combinations of players who resulted from these purchases almost always turned up trumps. And as for the international signings, Barcelona signed Cruyff and Maradona in the '70s and '80s respectively – the former, as we shall see, preferring the more 'politically correct' choice of clubs – but they only managed one paltry league title between the two of them. Short of launching an attack on Barça's curious interpretation of Madrid's history, the evidence rather suggests that the Catalans themselves have simply failed to get the chemistry right, and that when they did, Real unfortunately came up with one of the best teams in the history of the game.

Nevertheless, by the time the quarter-finals of the Generalísimo's Cup had come around that year, it was obvious that Real were going to have their work cut out to stop their neighbours Atlético from winning the league. For a change, things had gone awry in the big games. Grosso, Amancio and Sanchís had all picked up injuries, and in the second half of the season they had lost at Barça, gone down 5–0 at a muddy and hostile San Mamés in Bilbao, then lost their next two away games 3–0, at Sabadell and at Atlético. As a consequence their goals conceded tally at the end of the season (42) was their worst since the 50 let in for the 1951–52 season – in which they managed to score 72 goals. In 1969–70, they only managed to score 50. In Europe they had started auspiciously, putting 14 goals past poor Olympiakos de Nicosia before stumbling badly in the next round, losing 1–0 in Liege and then losing 2–3 at home, after twice clawing back and drawing level. The unthinkable had happened. No trophies in an entire season! For the record, this had not occurred since 1954 and for anyone else it could have been considered a year of rest, a time to take stock, to reflect and to fine-tune. But not in Madrid. Something had to come home to the trophy cabinet. The spoilt brats of European football were not about to undergo some strange metamorphosis of character.

Generalísimo's Cup ties being two-legged affairs, the first game was played in Madrid, the hosts winning 2–0. In the scandalous return match at the Camp Nou, Rexach scored early on and Madrid began to wobble. On a rare counter-attack, Velázquez was tackled outside the area by Rifé, but his forward motion took him into the box. The Basque referee, Guruceta, yards behind and unaided by his linesman, gave a penalty and then sent off Eladio for protesting. The mood of the crowd turned ugly and Vic Buckingham, the English manager at the time, had to sweet-talk his players into returning to the pitch after they had walked off in protest. Velázquez has since admitted that it was not a penalty, and that the foul did indeed occur outside the box. Nevertheless, he has also been at pains to point out that the linesman, up with the play, could have intervened. As he had not flagged (a fact confirmed to me by the linesman in question, in a bar in San Sebastián in 1999), it was curious that Guruceta's decision was allowed to stand at least without some consultation, especially given the furore that broke out. Amancio eventually took the penalty and scored – and Madrid went on to beat Bilbao, then Valencia in the final, ironically in the Camp Nou. Given the public order implications of the Camp Nou riot, Franco at first decided to give the final a miss, but was persuaded (correctly) that his absence might be interpreted as a sign of weakness. Real Madrid kept him happy and won 3–1.

In the final five minutes of that quarter-final, the crowd had begun to chant anti-Madrid songs and a small section invaded the pitch. When bottles and other objects began to fly, Guruceta decided that discretion would win out against valour and blew his whistle, two minutes short of the full 90. He and the two linesmen (also Basque) ran the gauntlet of the baying fans and then spent the night in police cells 'for their own safety'. Guruceta was later suspended by the Spanish Federation for allowing the situation to get out of hand, but the whole of Barcelona was more concerned with what they saw as an obvious case of bent refereeing.

No one has ever proved that Guruceta was bribed, and the English historian Duncan Shaw, resident in Madrid, investigated the case exhaustively as part of his PhD thesis, but could turn up no hard evidence. However, the fact that Guruceta was later found to be guilty of taking bribes for the Anderlecht v. Notts Forest UEFA Cup semi-final of 1984 might seem to hand the benefit of doubt to the Catalans. Guruceta, by then an international referee, had opened up a sports shoe business in the south of Spain and had got into financial difficulties. Constant Vanden Stock, the Anderlecht president, also had money worries, and on finding out about Guruceta's needs, allegedly bought him off. The referee was never tried since he died in a car crash in 1987 on his way, ironically, to refereeing a game between Osasuna and Real Madrid. One can guess what the jury would make of all this, but the only question that one can seriously ask is 'Once a cheat, always a cheat?' And of course, it is irrelevant. To most Spaniards of that generation, the *Asunto Guruceta* (Guruceta affair) represented unequivocal evidence that Madrid could buy off referees when the fancy took them.

The incident is also very famous because it was one of the first public manifestations of discontent with the Franco regime, five years before it died its official death. Using the incident as an excuse, the pent-up years of oppressive police-state bullying and cultural prohibition came to the fore, not to mention the feeling that in football-related matters Barça had always been handed the shitty end of the stick. The times they were a-changing, and an ageing Franco probably knew it. Three years later his right-hand man, Admiral Carrero Blanco, was assassinated by ETA in a car bomb in Madrid, putting paid to the line of succession. But by 1970, there seemed to be some perceptible shift in the air. Real Madrid were not in the European Cup, regionalist sentiment was gathering voice and strength, and the defence of De Felipe, Zunzunegui and Sanchís did not quite convince. There was some trouble at the mill as the new decade began.

One of the most common phrases about the 1970s is that it was 'forgettable', a judgement usually based on the state of male hairstyles at the time, and much of the popular music. Spain was initially spared much of this, but watered-down versions of stack-heeled boots, flares and shoulder-length hair inevitably filtered through – the drip-down effect of popular culture. Besides, Spain had opened up a little. Although it was impossible to persuade Franco and those closest to him that some type of parliamentary democracy might be worth considering, when it came to more obvious sources of income he was more easily swayed. The late 1960s and early 1970s saw a construction boom in the south of Spain, fuelled by the new tourist invasions from the UK and Germany. The suspicion towards intellectuals and the stifling cultural regulation to which Spain had been submitted since the Civil War found its apotheosis in the invitation to northern Europe to come and share in the keg beer delights of the once beautiful Costa del Sol. Between 1959 and 1973 the number of visitors to Spain leapt from 3 million to 34 million, and footballers no longer needed to sport wigs in order to participate in this new era of erudition and learning. The British took Julio Iglesias back home with them, whilst the Spanish adopted Noddy Holder haircuts. Franco was probably getting too tired to care, but it would require his death to set Spain back onto the more interesting roads of democracy and the *movida madrileña* (Madrid scene) that came in its wake.

Two photographs sum up the period nicely. One is of Paul Breitner, who along with Stielike and Netzer embodied Real Madrid's 'German period' of the 1970s. Breitner, a left-wing intellectual and much else besides, was not quite the sort one expected to find in Real Madrid in the dusk of the Franco period, but in purely visual terms his Afro perm bore witness to the aesthetics of the time. The other shot is of José Antonio Camacho, Spain's former manager who retired from international duty immediately after the 2002 World Cup. The young Camacho (sixth in the top 100 poll) stands menacingly in the foreground, his foppish, shoulder-length hair contrasting with his hard-man frown. Cruyff is behind him, waiting for a free-kick to be taken.

The shot is a famous one, and seems to mark out the period well. Madrid's new hero is a hard young defender, Barça's an arrogant Dutch artiste, outspokenly critical of Madrid's right-wing associations. Madrid hated Cruyff, not only for the famous *noche negra* (black night) in 1974 when he presided over a 0–5 result in the Bernabéu but because of his immediate identification with the Barcelona scene and his obvious sympathy towards their sense of cultural superiority and regionalist fervour. The photograph, for some, is of beauty and the beast – but depending on which side of the fence your sympathies lie, the interpretation as to the identities of those two polarities remains an open one. Camacho and Cruyff were both working class – but there the similarities ended. Camacho was from the small provincial town of Cieza in deepest Murcia, and Cruyff from swinging Amsterdam. In the photo, Camacho's left hand is clutching his own balls, although it's unclear why. The picture is always used in biogs of Camacho because it presumably reflects his 'ballsy' character, but it adds to the contrast with Cruyff. The Real Madrid team of the 1970s was changing. Muñoz had gone, and whilst the core of the 'Ye-Ye' side was still around, players like Camacho, Santillana and Del Bosque had formed the first wave of newcomers, soon to be joined by the Germans. By 1977, Grosso, Velázquez and Amancio would all be gone. It is not a period remembered with massive affection by the Chamartín faithful, although it was to have its moments. Besides, the 1970s saw changes in the club and in the country that were not to be positive for all comers. Franco died in 1975 and was followed three years later by Bernabéu. The Madrid of that period seems to be a place associated with death and fascist nostalgia, whilst over in Barcelona everyone seemed to be having a great time. Those tourists who took time out to visit the cities and not just the beaches were generally attracted to Barcelona's trendier air, as opposed to Madrid's more stifling atmosphere.

What happened to Real Madrid in this period was that the political and cultural direction of the country moved away from the Bernabéu and began to flower to the east in Catalonia and to the north in the Basque Country. The sudden liberation that these two important communities felt on Franco's death could not help but shift attention onto them, and both communities had, of course, strong footballing traditions that had been jackbooted into the shadows in the early days of Franco's regime. Madrid's subsequent ruling of the roost was for this author, at least, a relatively sporting matter, but there are always those who would find it more comforting to disagree. ETA by then was the prominent front line of Basque nationalism, but in Catalonia the folk had just been getting on with building a fairly prosperous community, whilst toeing the line to Franco as much as their pride would allow them. Jordi Pujol, who was to become the President of the Generalitat, was back then the head of the old Banca Catalana, whose monetary links with Barça helped to finance the signing of Cruyff. The transfer was recorded by the bank as an 'agricultural import', which entitled its terms to be fixed on a low credit basis. Whilst Real Madrid have been accused for years of having had the Generals and the major Madrid banks in their pockets, no one has ever seen any problem in Barça's similar underground machinations. Besides, it is good proof of the fact that Franco could not control everything. The idea of the Catalans as poor, oppressed, disenfranchised citizens is hardly sustainable after the mid-1960s. The fact that between 1970 and 1980 Real Madrid won six league titles and Barça only one is also further proof of the fact that whilst the Catalans can indeed boast a dynamic and original society, they have never been able to get it quite right where it matters most – in the football trophy room.

Nevertheless, Real Madrid are a little reluctant to talk about this period, despite its six league championships, four Generalísimo's Cups and two UEFA Cups, as if the darker side of that decade's street were somehow more significant. The 1970s first setback came with the club's first entry into the Cup-Winners' Cup, a competition that Bernabéu always considered second best to the real thing, populated by fly-by-nights who were unable to withstand the pressures required to win a league championship. Worse, Atlético Madrid had already won it, back in 1962 against Fiorentina. The Italians had won the inaugural competition in 1960 having actually lost their domestic cup final to double winners Juventus – a fact that blotted the trophy's copybook in Bernabéu's eyes. But scathing though he was, Real had little choice but to dip their toes into its more brackish waters in 1971 and experience some of football's pond life. In truth, the campaign probably did them good, bringing them down to earth and enabling them to compete against some different, more swashbuckling styles. After dispatching Hibs in the opening round and the wonderfully named Wacker Innsbruck in the second, they came up against the Welsh Cup winners Cardiff City in the quarter-finals. Madrid, wearing an unusual all-red strip, faced a Second Division Cardiff side in front of a 50,000 crowd at Ninian Park. The BBC showed highlights of the Welsh side's famous 1–0 victory, Brian Clark's thumping header being one of the first occasions on which Barry Davies' voice rose in alarming ecstasy only to suddenly break at the point where it could go no further. Again, Real's history books are quiet on this one, and mention it in passing, as if it were of no real consequence. One of the books even refers to Cardiff as 'English', but there you go. In the second leg, the Spanish brooked no nonsense and won the game 2–0, but the Ninian Park encounter showed that they were by no means invincible.

In the final played in Athens, Real came up against a side that encapsulated everything that England seems to have lost in its football. Several of Chelsea's maverick characters from that time also embody some of the 1970s more forgettable features, but if my memory serves me correctly, Chelsea were an extraordinarily popular side in England amongst the younger element. The classy swagger of Osgood, Charlie Cooke's enticing wing play, Hudson's vision, Harris and Webb taking no prisoners at the back. And Bonetti in goal. Everybody wanted to be Bonetti in the playground, probably because he had such an exotic surname. None of this, of course, cut much ice with Real Madrid. The game went to a replay in the same stadium, after Zoco equalised Osgood's earlier opener in the dying seconds of the game. Madrid dominated the extra-time period (mavericks are never very concerned with fitness) but failed to score, and lost 2–1 in the replay two days later. Dempsey scored first with a spectacular volley after the ball had been bobbling about following a corner, and Osgood scored a clever second, beating Borja at his near post when there seemed no room to shoot. Fleitas got one back, but it was a sad night for Madrid, Gento having decided beforehand to hang up his boots come the final whistle. After 18 seasons with the club, the Cantabrian called it a day, but deserved to go out on a happier note. The aristocrats of England had proved just a little cleverer than their Spanish counterparts, and the defeat had dealt a blow to Real's morale.

Rumblings in the press and discontent in the bars led to some chopping and changing that same summer. Along with Gento went Sanchís, Betancort and De Diego, to be replaced by three players signed in the *'operación Santander'*, the most important of them being Carlos Santillana, a young 19-year-old attacker who had knocked in 17 goals for Second Division Rácing de Santander the previous season. Santillana was to stay until 1988, by which time he had been replaced by another great legend, Emilio Butragueño. But the ability of the club to find the right sort of players at the right time has been uncanny. Amancio was not really an out-and-out striker, Grosso was more comfortable in the hole, and with the loss of Gento, the creative side of the show would also need restructuring, with Velázquez given more freedom to roam. Santillana played in every game of the newly extended season – the top division now containing 18 teams – and scored ten goals. Pirri did the rest with 11 from midfield, and Real got their title back, leading from the second game to the last. Muñoz, having grown tired of the constant criticism of his team's lack of style and goalscoring ability, sent a few barbs back via the press, asserting that no one had given them a chance that season, and yet they'd won it fairly easily. Looking at the league table that year, only four points separated the top three (Real, Valencia and Barça) but Muñoz was having his say anyway.

The signing of Santillana throws an interesting light on the way that the club improvised its operations. During the summer, vice-president Antonio Calderón was asked to travel down to Alicante to watch a friendly game between Hercules and Santander that would feature a centre-back in which Madrid were vaguely interested. Calderón phoned Bernabéu to ask if he wanted to go to the game with him, since the president was down at his summer retreat in the coastal town of Santa Pola, not far from Alicante. Bernabéu apparently turned him down, citing the local fiestas and the fact that he was hopeless anyway at judging defenders. Calderón, not wishing to sit it out alone, eventually managed to persuade him and the two sat discreetly in modest seats to watch the game – a tedious 0–0 draw. On returning to Calderón's car, the ex-referee and deputy Mr Fixit asked Bernabéu what he thought of the centre-back. After all, he enthused, Santander had failed to score. 'That's true,' sniffed the president. 'But neither would you have scored if you'd been kicked to death like that centre-forward was for Santander. The centre-back's a donkey, but that kid who he was marking, I like him. He just got on with it, despite the fact that he was being kicked to death. He never retaliated once. He just got on with it, and he had a nice touch. I like people like that. It's dignified. Forget the centre-half. I'd sign the kid.' And on the following Monday, whilst Calderón waited for the strip-lights to flicker on in his office, he picked up the phone and rang Santander, to enquire about a certain Carlos Santillana.

That season saw another first for Madrid in their participation in the newly named 'UEFA Cup'. Again, Bernabéu had shown his contempt for the competition in its original guise of the Inter-Cities Fairs Cup. This was translated into Spanish as *La Copa de Ferias*, prompting Don Santiago to declare that he would never submit to his team playing in a tournament whose name was synonymous with 'circus'. But by 1972 he had little choice, although fortunately for him, it was renamed that very year. Another reason for Bernabéu's reluctance was that the Fairs Cup had Barcelona's stamp on it, the Catalans having won the opening two editions in 1958 and 1960. Indeed, whilst Real Madrid had been setting Europe alight in the European Cup, the smaller edition trophies had also been going to Spanish clubs – since in the first ten years of the Fairs Cup it was won a total of six times by three different clubs – Barça (3), Valencia (2) and Zaragoza – and had seen three all-Spanish finals. These facts are little known outside of the clubs' own circuits, and many neutral Spanish fans would be hard put to tell you, for example, when Valencia first won the trophy (1962). Such was the newsworthiness of Real Madrid's feats – another reason why they are accused (justifiably in this case) of having enjoyed a media monopoly during the second half of the Franco years. If the image of an all-powerful Madrid had been of political use to Franco, then why not make at least some fuss about the Fairs Cup events? Such questions fell on deaf ears.

Whatever, Real failed to distinguish themselves in the UEFA Cup either, and fell in the second round to PSV, courtesy of the away goal that the Dutch scored in their 3–1 defeat at in Madrid. Real lost 2–0 in Eindhoven, making for a brief first acquaintance with this particular cup. Thirteen years later, with the European Cup a distant memory, Real were to win a couple of editions with considerably more enthusiasm, but for now, the ghosts of Di Stéfano and the 'Ye-Ye's were still clanking their chains and shaking their wigs.

The next season, 1972–73, was something of a false dawn, because although the club returned to the European Cup with some distinction, going out in the semi-finals to Cruyff's Ajax, they dropped down the league table again and finished fourth, their neighbours Atlético waking up and pipping Barça for the title. They also went out of the Generalísimo's Cup to Sporting de Gijón, a modest mid-table outfit, after which the first cries of 'Muñoz fuera' (Muñoz out) were heard from the terraces. Santillana, whose uncanny ability to leap high into the air and 'hang' became a famous sight at the Bernabéu, finished top scorer with ten again that season, but the Ajax experience had finally convinced the technical staff at the club that the team needed a new cerebro (brain) to direct operations on the field like Cruyff.

Madrid had come up against poor sides that season until Dynamo Kiev in the quarter-finals, but Ajax – six years down the line from their original meeting – were the finished product, a sublime combination of tactical innovation and technical ability. The kings were dead, long live the kings. The two games were proof, as if proof were needed, that Real had dropped down the ladder of the European rankings, both in style and achievement. Muñoz had been a loyal servant, first as player then as manager, but something new was needed – not a clean sweep, but some new elements to reawaken the giant. In Amsterdam, Ajax turned on the style from the off and were 2–0 up after half an hour. Madrid were chasing shadows, a rare experience for them, but they still had sufficient quality and temperament to pull a goal back before half-time, from the ever-reliable Pirri. It stayed at 2–1, but in a packed Bernabéu in April 1973, Cruyff again took the plaudits and engineered a famous 0–1 victory, the goal scored by Muhren. The *Madrileño* press, so famously biased and happy to be so, were sharp enough to recognise what they had just seen. Relatively scathing of the Inter and Manchester United legends that had passed through Chamartín beforehand, now they were doffing their hats. It says a lot for that Ajax side that they were able to both silence the Bernabéu and draw praise from its absurdly one-eyed acolytes in the Fourth Estate. Santillana himself had no doubts either, and sounded like Charlton when he'd first seen Real Madrid in the flesh:

> Kiev were good, and I thought we were quite lucky to escape with a draw over there, but Ajax were something else. Cruyff was everywhere – we couldn't handle him – and the whole team demonstrated enormous quality. We couldn't get it together in front of goal in either game, and we had the chances, but we didn't deserve it really. We knew we'd lost to a special team.

Rare words, brave world. But Santillana knew too that Cruyff was already in Barça's orbit, and the rumours sent shock waves through the Madrid faithful. The embargo on foreign players had been lifted, and the Catalans had proved the cannier. Bernabéu was getting old, but he was still smart enough to suspect that 20 years on, the folks he hated the most were preparing to sign the new Di Stéfano, and that this time, there was no General Moscardó to pull the strings and stop them. That said, Cruyff did encounter some mysterious bureaucratic obstacles, and could not play for several games at the beginning of the 1973–74 season. Rinus Michels, Cruyff's original tutor, was at Barcelona by then, his international pedigree again contrasting with Muñoz' rather more homely appeal. Cruyff had in fact fallen out with everyone at Ajax by then (a pattern to be faithfully repeated over the subsequent years), and the negotiations with the Dutch club were by no means simple, with the Catalans at first balking at the one-million-dollar, three-year contract that Cruyff wanted. As soon as negotiations seemed to be breaking down, Bernabéu had Saporta and Peralba look into the possibility of making an outrageous snatch for the player – but Cruyff was not interested. Barcelona struck him as a cool place, and Michels was the manager. As soon as the Catalans got wind of Real's interest, they coughed up the money, and Cruyff's long relationship with Barcelona had begun.

The signing of Netzer looked like a tit-for-tat reaction to the Cruyff coup, but it was a coherent signing in terms of what the team needed. Netzer, his enormous legs and long blond locks making him look like a hip version of the Aryan supermodel, was in fact a wholly new type of player for Madrid, and in his three seasons there failed to convince, an experience that would also befall the rather more awkward Bernd Schuster in the late 1980s. Netzer was from the new thoughtful school of German football, a school that admired the player who could make time for himself, stroll around the middle of the park and orchestrate the play, without breaking too much sweat. Beckenbauer was, of course, the role model, but Netzer was very much his own man, requiring the pace of the game to be played at the speed that he had decided on. Brought up in the Borussia Mönchengladbach school – supposedly the 'rebel' face of German football, like Cruyff, he had already fallen out with his tutors by the time he moved to Spain. Netzer's outwardly casual approach to the art of midfield was all a bit Greek to the Bernabéu, accustomed to the 'control with speed' types that had been lifting the faithful out of their seats from the 1950s onwards. Samitier was the closest to Netzer that the club had possessed in its ranks, but he had joined Madrid in his later years, when the condition of 'stroller' had been more forced upon him by circumstances than by choice.

Netzer's laid-back approach to both football and life were not quite what the Chamartín had been demanding, and neither did they expect their beloved team to finish eighth in the league, the lowest finish since the traumatic season of 1947–48. Málaga and Granada finished above them that season – perish the memory! Muñoz finally left in the January of that year, replaced by another old warhorse, Luis Molowny, a temporary replacement until the beginning of the new management era of the two Yugoslavs, Mijalnic and Boskov. Muñoz had been holding the reins since 1960, and, despite the grumblings from the crowd, accepted, himself, that change was needed. He himself had had no say in the signing of Netzer, and there were rumours that the German was quietly scornful of his management techniques and philosophy, but Muñoz was of a different generation, and he knew when his time was up.

Not long after Muñoz' departure, with Madrid having won a measly five games by New Year, came Real Madrid's darkest day. Things had at last begun to pick up, with a couple of wins against Murcia and Bilbao, incredibly their first 'run' of the season. Pirri and Netzer at last seemed to be understanding each other, but the goals were not exactly flowing. Barça, to make matters worse, were top. They arrived at the Bernabéu knowing that their opponents were short on confidence, and convinced that their problems in the middle of the park would play into their hands. What happened was beyond the dreams of the most rabid *Catalanista*, and the 0–5 result immortalised Cruyff in the chronicles of the club. Barça took Madrid apart, Cruyff scored one himself and set up three of the other four. His own goal was a classic, beating several men in a gawky, speedy dribble before cracking a left-foot shot past García Remon. It's not a goal you'll see played too many times on Real's centenary video series. In fact it's not there at all. The result warrants two lines in Everest's *Cien años de Leyenda* book of the centenary, and in the photo book that accompanies it, the only evidence of the game is a snap of Cruyff consoling Netzer at the end. Well he might have done, for the German was a mere spectator for most of the game. The *New York Times* reporter wrote that Cruyff had done more for the spirit of the Catalan nation in 90 minutes than most politicians had achieved in almost a century's struggle. That was going a bit far, but the result – far more valid than the 11–1 farce that *Madridistas* insist on peddling out as their finest moment – has stuck in the craw of the Bernabéu ever since. It guaranteed that *el clásico,* never a game between friends, would increase in temperature with every subsequent year. And incredibly, just as the season concluded in mourning at Barcelona's triumphal romp to the title (they finished 16 points ahead of Real), the two met again in the final of the Generalísimo's Cup in late June. With neither Cruyff nor Netzer on the field (both rested for World Cup duties) Madrid took their revenge, scoring four without reply at the Vicente Calderón across the city. In a season that had been one to forget – their second foray into the UEFA Cup had seen them beaten 1–0 at Portman Road by a splendid but unknown Ipswich side, who then forced a 0–0 draw in the Bernabéu – they had at least exacted some revenge at the final gasp. But these were traumas unknown up to then by the majority of the crowd at Chamartín. Nostalgia was the new emotion in Madrid. When was the suffering to end?

For some, it was to end on 20 November 1975, when the plug was finally pulled on Franco. It is said that on that same night, it was impossible to find a bottle of champagne in any shop in Catalonia or in the Basque Country. That is not to say, of course, that there was mass mourning on every street corner of Madrid, but in some ways the death of Franco meant that Real Madrid could breathe more easily and just get on with being a football club. Bernabéu was not well, but he was still sufficiently *compos mentis* to keep the vultures from circling over him just yet. Nevertheless, Real Madrid were passing through an odd period, one in which the change in management at club level was ushering in a new period of football style, and one in which the death of the Head of State was changing the scene at city level, with the slow drama of the transition to democracy being acted out in the buildings of the capital.

Real Madrid, like it or not, were going to be caught in the face by at least some of the popping champagne corks, and there were certainly a few flying around the Camp Nou on 28 December 1975, almost two months into the post-Franco period. Seven hundred Catalan flags were smuggled into the ground, and when the players came out they were greeted by the sight of the yellow-and-red striped emblems of Catalonia, in a mass demonstration of nationhood. Whether or not the Madrid players cared two hoots mattered little, for they understood full well that they would have to be on the receiving end of a cultural raspberry that had been poised on the lips of Barcelona's citizens for 36 years. One wonders how Paul Breitner must have felt, signed the previous year from Bayern Munich. The German full-back, employed by Real in a more central midfield role, was university educated and a self-confessed Maoist, whatever that meant. His politics had raised some eyebrows in the more stuffy corners of the Bernabéu, but they were prepared to tolerate what they saw as his oddball politics if he performed well on the pitch. Breitner was a man of conviction both on and off the field, it would seem, and confessed in a recent interview that he did indeed think twice about playing for Real, but that he could never really believe that a football club was as political a phenomenon as some people would like to have turned it into. Coming from an ex-Bayern Munich player such a sentiment sounds almost naive, but Breitner was only expressing what Di Stéfano had been saying for years – that Real Madrid's players were as apolitical a bunch as you could get.

So to walk into the howling gale of *Catalanisme* that December evening must have been something of a torrid experience for a man who was anything but apolitical. For 90 minutes at least, he must have been regretting his decision to move to Spain. The result wouldn't have been to his liking either, Barcelona winning, of course, with the clincher scored by Charly Rexach, one of the club's legends and willing carrier of the flag. The roar must have awoken the ghost of Franco, and the fact that the Guardia Civil had made no attempt to suppress the flag waving indicated the way that the country was inevitably moving – towards autonomous regionalism, and the sort of federal democracy that the previous centralist regime had regarded as a mortal sin.

But political demonstrations apart, things had been looking up on the football scene. Muñoz, after the interim period with Molowny, was replaced by Miljan Miljanic, a coach who had built up a reputation for hard physical slog and discipline at Red Star in the early '70s. He brought with him Red Star's physical trainer, Felix Radisic, then brought in Breitner. The German was Miljanic's kind of player. As Maradona remarked of Breitner, he was never sure in which position he was playing, since every time he looked up at any part of the pitch Breitner was there. The contrast with Netzer was interesting, to say the least, but at least the blond architect now had someone to fetch and carry for him, although it would be wrong to view Breitner as the hod-carrier. There was much more to his game than that, but there is no doubt that he was signed in order to help get the best out of his worryingly laid-back compatriot. Camacho was there as well – perhaps the fiercest character to ever wear the great white shirt.

In the 1974–75 season, Real won the league back in impressive fashion, finishing 12 points above second-placed Zaragoza. They took the cup again as well, beating Atlético Madrid on penalties after a 0–0 draw in the Vicente Calderón – the first time that a Spanish cup game had been decided in such a way and the only time since the mid-'40s that Real had won two consecutive domestic cups. But the following season saw two firsts – the team were knocked out of the domestic cup by Second Division Tenerife in Madrid, at the end of which various groups of supporters began a *pañolada* (hanky waving) against the team, the manager and Bernabéu himself. Bernabéu's defence of Miljanic was typically decisive, claiming that he would prefer to be the target of insults than the manager, but it was a significant moment in the club's history, two years before the big man's death. The crowd were unhappy with Miljanic's 4–3–3 system, and the sudden introduction of the *balonazo* (big hoof up front), a style of play with which the team had never previously been associated. Although Netzer, for one, was perfectly capable of knocking a 40-yard pass onto the head of Santillana or Martínez, the faithful were more accustomed to the possession game, to the *olé* approach. These were the first voices ever raised in anger against Bernabéu, and they marked a change in the atmosphere of the club. A new generation of followers, less respectful of reputations than the previous, had joined the bandwagon – and Madrid now had its 'hooligan' element, congregating in the South Stand behind the goal, the *Fondo Sur*. During the season, the Spanish FA had also issued an edict obliging clubs to put up fencing behind the goals, and the era of *El Nodo* documentaries, with every male in the ground with a suit and tie, was as good as dead.

The other development that year was the birth of the so-called *miedo escénico*, a phrase later attributed to Jorge Valdano after a 6–1 home win against Anderlecht in 1984, but a phenomenon that began with the remarkable European Cup tie against Dave Mackay's Derby County. The phrase does not translate easily, but means something like 'the cauldron effect', whereby the sheer noise and hostility generated by the home supporters is enough to put the visitors off and enable the home side to turn an adverse situation on its head. These *remontadas* (comebacks) became a feature of the next few seasons, and though they were impressive, it has to be said that the Real Madrid of Di Stéfano and its 'Ye-Ye' successors were simply better at scoring first. But one should not be churlish. The fact is that a good *remontada* is exciting. It's everything that you could wish for in a football match. Real had had its period of arrogant domination. Now was the time for more heart-stopping stuff. In the second round that season Real drew the Derby County of Charlie George, Gemmill, Lee *et al*. They were a fine side, and the midweek *Match of the Day* where Charlie George ran scruffily riot was a classic. Real Madrid wore all blue, and despite knocking the ball around smoothly, were simply caught out by Derby's speed and directness. George scored a hat-trick, his first one a magnificent volley from outside of the box after Gemmill had knocked in a low cross. At 2–0 Pirri got one back, pulling away from Nish, chesting down Amancio's cross and tucking the ball neatly home. Even in 1975, applause rang around the baseball ground as in the *Pathe News* days. In the second half, with Madrid 3–1 down, Pirri scored what looked like a perfectly legal goal, but it was disallowed – a decision that seemed particularly crucial when Netzer gave away a penalty and George completed his hat-trick. The tie seemed as good as over, but they packed into the Bernabéu on Guy Fawkes Night, 1975, to see if miracles might happen. The new, more hostile atmosphere seemed to freeze Derby, and the gunpowder blew up in their faces. The game went to extra time, when Santillana scored a famous winner, controlling the ball on his chest, flicking the ball over Nish then volleying it home with his left foot in exultant style. Derby sent a telegram the next day, preserved in Madrid's archives:

> Excellent game of football. Stop. Good for all football fans in Europe. Stop. Congratulations. Stop. Good luck and all the best.

In the next game, Derby's wishing them good luck seemed to pay off against Borussia Mönchengladbach, the 2–2 draw in Germany effectively taking them through when the return tie in the Bernabéu finished 1–1. In Germany, when the teams were announced, the crowd whistled at the mention of Breitner, but reserved their real ire for Netzer, who was subsequently booed every time he touched the ball. The Dutch referee, De Kroft, disallowed two of Borussia's goals, inevitably sparking some barbed comments in the German press the next day. That season was to end on a German note too, since Bayern eliminated Real in the semis, drawing 1–1 in Madrid and winning 2–0 in Germany – with an inevitable brace from Müller. Vicente Del Bosque recalled that as the teams were walking onto the pitch, Sepp Maier was eating a sandwich. His interpretation of Maier's action (which he considered to be a lack of respect) was that it implied that Madrid were *pan comido* (eaten bread) – a Spanish phrase that means something like 'lambs to the slaughter'. Maier was more than likely unaware of this, and was merely hungry, but the two games had various controversies. In the Bernabéu, the sense that the supporter base was changing, the fences were going up and the hankies were being waved at Don Santiago were all crystallised by '*el loco de Chamartín*' – the unnamed fan who ran onto the pitch in the second half and attacked the Austrian referee, Linemayer, after he had ignored a rough tackle on Santillana in the penalty area. Amancio was sent off in Munich for petulantly kicking the ball away, the sum of which was that UEFA issued a tough edict banning Real Madrid from European competition for a year – a sanction reduced to a fine and three league games to be played away from the Bernabéu (minimum radius of 200 km) after the ageing but still charming Saporta once again worked his magic at a meeting with UEFA officials and succeeded in persuading them to reduce the terms of the punishment.

Looking back, the season of discontent of 1976–77 was probably the one that finally broke Bernabéu, so much did he take the club's fortunes to heart. The drop in the team's form and the 53 goals conceded were the worst ever, the team finishing in ninth place. In the 1970s, it was either glory or death. There was nothing much in between. A series of uncharacteristically heavy defeats saw the end of Miljanic and the return of Molowny, this time for a slightly longer stay of two years, before Boskov took over and re-established the Yugoslav line.

Amancio retired and Netzer left, claiming that he was 'too old to play in the best team in the world', but that he would miss Spanish football and the people of Madrid, whom he felt had been 'more than fair' to him. Significantly, Real signed Ulrich Stielike from Borussia, a *todo terreno* (four-wheel drive player) who could help to shore up the defence and give the whole team a bit more steel than the young Camacho alone could provide. Up front, on the right side, Amancio was replaced by Juan Gómez, 'Juanito', a rough diamond from Burgos who nevertheless proved to be an extraordinarily popular player, playing up until 1986 when he was transferred back to Málaga. He was later to die in a car crash and was much mourned at the Bernabéu. But the presence of the German and Juanito had an immediate effect and the league came back to the capital, a month before the death of Bernabéu. Struggling with cancer, the 82-year-old's health had been failing for some time when he made his last appearance at the stadium that bore his surname – fittingly at a 4–0 win against Barcelona towards the end of the season. His wave to the crowd is captured on film, before he shuffled off to die on 3 June 1978, a month before the World Cup in Argentina. For the inaugural match between the hosts and Hungary, the players wore black armbands and a minute's silence was observed. The act was a fitting testimony to his status and fame in the game, and few club managers can build up the sort of reputation that can earn them such homily. *Marca*'s cover on 4 June declared '*Bernabéu ha muerto*' (Bernabéu is dead), echoing the headlines that were offered to the Spanish public the morning after Franco had passed away. The various implications of these words would not be lost on the paper's readership, particularly in those provinces where the president had been considered an ogre, second only to the dictator himself. But politics aside, there had never been anyone quite like him, and we have certainly not seen his like since. His association with the club was extraordinary – spanning a period of nearly 70 years, from 1909 when he made his debut for the boys' team, to 1978. He lived through republics, dictatorships, civil war, world war – and survived to be given the freedom of Madrid by the first President of the new government installed by Juan Carlos, Adolfo Suárez.

Bernabéu was not to everyone's taste, and there are those who maintain that he stayed too long, delaying a further modernisation of the club and ensuring that the 'wilderness years' lasted longer than they need have. He had his enemies, which his own secret police, Saporta and friends, always kept at arm's length. Practically 70 years at the club! Did he have nothing better to do? Was Real Madrid the organ through which he could play out his own dictatorial fantasies, and enable him to continue crushing Catalans to the end of his days? It is not the remit of this book to come up with any decisive conclusions regarding these other aspects of Bernabéu, and his life is best analysed in a separate book from this. But he is a unique figure in the game. And without him around, things were bound to change.

The new president, Luis de Carlos Ortiz, had taken over as treasurer from Saporta in the mid-1950s, and was by 1978 no spring chicken himself, having just celebrated his 71st birthday. Saporta, three days after Bernabéu's funeral, insisted that he would not be taking over, and that a single candidate should be decided upon by the committee. This was, however, unconstitutional, since a club with 60,000 members was obliged by statute to hold elections. Maybe Saporta just thought that Don Santiago would go on forever, or that no one was eyeing the throne. Whatever, neither of the two candidates amassed sufficient votes, defaulting the job to Luis de Carlos. He was never considered as much more than a stop-gap, although he was to last until 1985. In his book about the love-hate relationship between Madrid and Barcelona, the journalist and writer Julián Garcia Candau refers to De Carlos' presidency as '*los primeros años de la democracia*' (the first years of democracy), but this is a deliberately sarcastic reference to the post-Bernabéu era, not necessarily the larger political arena. Saporta stepped down and ceased to hold any executive office at the club, but below this new umbrella of so-called democracy, vice-president Ramón Mendoza was forced to resign after an article in the right-wing newspaper *ABC* linked him and his business interests with the KGB. Mendoza would get his chance, and finally took over in 1985 – but for the time being, the forces of tradition prevailed.

In retrospect, the years that followed Bernabéu's death seemed like a transitional period between the fag-end of the 'Ye-Ye' years and the beginning of the new dawn of the 'Vulture', Butragueño. It was, as mentioned before, characterised as the period of the *remontadas*, where desperate second-leg comebacks at the Bernabéu created a new atmosphere at the ground and contributed to the *miedo escénico*. Various teams succumbed after Derby County: Celtic (3–0) in 1980, after the Scots had won 2–0 in Glasgow; Anderlecht (6–1) after losing 3–0 in Belgium; Inter again, after losing 2–0 in Italy; Borussia (4–0) after being thrashed 5–1 in Germany and Inter again in 1986 after losing 3–1 in the San Siro. As Butragueño was to famously remark, even though he missed out on several of the most famous ones, *'No hay nada como una buena remontada en el Bernabéu'* (There's nothing like a good comeback in the Bernabéu). It sounds like an advertising slogan, almost as if the players preferred to lose away so that they could set up a good heart-stopper for the home crowd. And they were exciting years, remembered with fondness by that generation – but years which were ultimately a celebration of heroic failure, something with which the club normally prefers not to associate itself. By creating this legend it takes on its own force, and rubs out the awkward fact of European failure.

A decade of *remontadas* led to four finals, only one of which was in the tournament that really mattered to them. In 1981, with Boskov at the helm, they reached the final in Paris after two epic struggles against the old foe, Inter Milan. It was a full 15 years since the 'Ye-Ye' triumph, but the Liverpool of Souness, Kennedy, Hansen and Dalglish were on for their third European Cup. With Madrid parading Lawrie Cunningham (85th in the Top 100 poll), Juanito and Santillana up front, Stielike in his prime in midfield and Camacho snarling at Dalglish and McDermott, the English champions never really got into their stride, and were grateful for Alan Kennedy's delicate little chip which won them the game. Real still moan about this game, and have written it into their records as 'unjust'. To rub salt into the wound, they lost at home three days later in the domestic cup to Sporting Gijón, and their magnificent run of five league titles in six seasons came to an end when Sporting Gijón, their Nemesis from the cup elimination, conceded a last-second goal to Real Sociedad up in Asturias and handed them the title on goal average. Madrid, having beaten Valladolid 3–1 away, had finished their match two minutes earlier and were celebrating the title. Juanito had promised that he would return to the dressing-rooms on his knees in the event of winning the league, and had just reached the near touchline when the transistors picked up the apocalyptic news from Gijón – Jesus Zamora had equalised and the Basques were champions. 1981 was not a good year for the club.

9. THE VULTURE SQUADRON

A curious season of fits and starts sees the 22nd game of that campaign being played on 5 February 1984, down at Cádiz on the south coast. Real Madrid lie second in the table. Cádiz, promoted the season before, are struggling, second from bottom. Real have only scored twice in the last four games, and Alfredo Di Stéfano, in his second season as manager, is under pressure from the press and the public alike. Worse still when Cádiz are 2–0 up at half-time and Santillana has been looking tired, making little headway against the gale blowing in off the Straits. Di Stéfano turns to the cherubic 20-year-old, Emilio Butragueño, and tells him to get changed. The youngster is to get the chance to join two of his old mates from the reserve side Castilla, already promoted to the first team earlier that season. The slight youngster trots on for the second half, tip-toeing as if in ballet shoes, head back like a dressage horse. By the end of the game, Madrid have won 3–2 and Santillana, looking on from the bench, knows that things will never be quite the same again.

Butragueño's two goals that winter's afternoon in Cádiz bore all the markings of the player who was to emerge from the chrysalis of that first season. Both goals are classic Butragueño, from his limited but practised repertoire. Nothing was left to chance for the 'Vulture', as he came to be known. None of his goals were random, lucky efforts. His first for the club (he was to manage another 159) was the art of minimal expression – the illustration of the simple act of being in the right place, then reacting with the minimum of fuss. Juanito receives a ball from wide on the edge of the penalty area, his back to goal. He spins to shoot but the ball bobbles slightly from his foot as he pivots. In an instant, before he can regain his poise, Butragueño appears and whips a low shot into the goalkeeper's right-hand corner. Four minutes later, and the ball falls invitingly to Juanito again in the box. He shoots, but the ball bounces off a defender and rolls to the right of the goal, sticking in the mud. A ruck of huge Cádiz defenders poise their limbs to converge

173

on the ball and clear the danger, but before they even manage to move, before the message from their brains has quite reached their leg muscles, Butragueño has sprung from nowhere, cracked the ball into the gaping net and hared off to the left in an instant of ruthless vitality. The defenders' legs seem weighed down by ponderous forces. Butragueño looks like Peter Pan, whizzing off to the bottom left of the picture to be met by his jubilant lost boys.

And lost they were, for if there were truly a period of wilderness, this was surely it. Di Stéfano, after spells back in Argentina and a decent enough period at Valencia, had returned to the nest, 15 years after his testimonial game against Celtic. But his return coincided with a four-year shift of power in the Spanish league, from both the capital and from Catalonia up to the Basque Country where an extraordinary generation of home-grown players brought the title back for two consecutive seasons to Real Sociedad and then over to Javier Clemente's hard-man Athletic Bilbao. As if the loss of the 1981 European Cup final to Liverpool had not been enough, the next three years were to see a series of blows to the club's morale and self-esteem. It was neither the fault of Boskov nor of his successor Di Stéfano, but rather a temporary caprice of the gods of fortune, who had clearly decided to experiment with the club for a period, to see how they might react to a little run of adversity. The Liverpool defeat had come on the heels of Real Sociedad's last-second theft of the league title, but the Basques were to hold on to the title the next year and prove themselves to be no flash in the pan, setting the new tone by beating Madrid 3–1 in the opening game of the season. And if the truth be told, Madrid's title win in 1979–80 had been somewhat unexpected. Real Sociedad, already underlining their quality, had gone the whole season unbeaten, only to lose in Seville on the last day. Madrid, dogged to the last, beat Bilbao on the same day and took the title by a point.

When Sociedad began to go off the boil, Bilbao took over, and after an epic struggle with the two Madrids won the 1983 title by a point – the same year in which Real reached the Cup-Winners' Cup final again, 12 years after the Athens fiasco. It was British opposition again, this time in the guise of Alex Ferguson's Aberdeen, played up in Gothenburg. Juanito, having equalised Black's opener and taken his team into extra time, showed a certain weakness of judgement in attempting to nutmeg Miller during a move in which he had plenty of passing options. Miller set up a swift counter, which Hewitt finished off. It seemed typical of the time. A combination of a lack of luck and a lack of discipline, despite the presence of Stielike and Camacho. Juanito himself was a hero of sorts, probably for his bullish behaviour and anti-Barça sentiments as much as anything, but the Madrid faithful could never quite look him in the face, nervously aware as they were of his capacity to self-destruct. And if 1981 had not been a good year, then 1983 finished off in funereal fashion with another defeat, this time in the final of the King's Cup to Barcelona, of all teams. Cruyff was long since departed, but the Catalans now had Maradona and Schuster, financed by a canny new president (Nuñez) who had already announced that he was 'running a business'. Real Madrid were not quite sure what their new(ish) president was running, but there was already plenty of nostalgia being expressed for the good old days of Bernabéu, when a spade was a spade and everyone knew where they stood. As in the earlier case of Cruyff, Madrid took the signing of any big-name players by Barcelona as a snub to their own cause. Maradona was the biggest thing in world football, and Schuster had been hugely impressive in West Germany's European Nations Cup win in 1980. Just to rub further salt into the wound, Barça's Nuñez suggested to the Spanish Federation that they set up a 'League Cup', a smaller version of the English competition. It began in the summer and ended in late autumn when, surprise surprise, the two friends met again in the two-legged final again, Barça winning 4–3 on aggregate.

Di Stéfano knew only too well that he was no untouchable, and when Real lost 6–2 at Málaga in the second game of the 1983–84 season, the calls for his head began to multiply. Neither did it help when they were knocked out of the European Cup in the opening round by Sparta Prague. Probably the only reason why he lasted the season was his faith in youth and his gradual introduction of the five players who were to make up the famous 'Vulture Squadron'. These five – Emilio Butragueño, Miguel Pardeza, José González (Michel), Martín Vásquez and Manolo Sanchís – were all products of the youth system – *the cantera* (quarry) as it is called in Spain. Although Madrid had been conscious for some time of the need to make things a little more rootsy, the abiding impression one gets from the post-war period onwards is that given the opportunity, the club always preferred to spend its money on outsiders – as if it were terrified of the consequences of a fallow period, where it might have to wait too long for its more promising seeds to reach the point where they could actually be harvested. Madrid's supporters demanded instant trophy fodder, with the obvious consequence that apart from Velázquez, few of the greats had actually been developed by a thriving youth system. It was perhaps the only piece missing from the club's otherwise bulging curriculum vitae. However, in 1980, one of the most extraordinary events in European football took place, a treasure for trivia merchants and a sure sign that Real Madrid were at last getting to grips with the youth development problem. The King's Cup final that year was played in the Bernabéu – which was just as well because the two participants were Real Madrid and Real Madrid Reserves, *aka* Castilla. Castilla, now defunct in name, were then in the Second Division 'A' and were indeed the reserve team. This system still exists in the Spanish league, but all the sides are named Real Madrid 'B', Barcelona 'B' etc. They cannot join their big brothers even in the event of winning the Second 'A', and the principle further extends down to the lower reaches of the professional and semi-professional leagues. That year, Castilla had knocked out Real Sociedad, Sporting Gijón and Athletic de Bilbao, all from the top flight, but were shown no mercy by the first team in the fraternal final, getting whacked 6–1. But it was all smiles at the Bernabéu, in a both unique and significant event. It brought to the supporters' attention the fact that the club were working the 'quarry' better, proof of which were the promotions of five of the Castilla players to the first team for the next season. None of the Vulture Squadron were in the Castilla side that day, but the signal was clear to the younger players. There was a way through now if you could prove your worth. The more cynical view is that the club were forced to rely on more home-grown talent because of over-investment in the years of European plenty, replaced by a drying up of the river of income that had been flowing so abundantly over the decades. Whatever the truth, for the record, Castilla still qualified for the Cup-Winners' Cup the next season (the First Team were in the European Cup) and beat West Ham 3–1 at the Bernabéu, a game in which the charming behaviour of the Londoners' fans earned their club a stab at the second leg behind closed doors at Upton Park, which they nevertheless won 5–1.

Butragueño was promoted swiftly through the ranks of the youth sides by Amancio and made his debut for Castilla in 1982. He comes in at number 11 in the Top 100 poll, but he scores much higher in my own personal hierarchy – probably in the top five. Of course, men are particularly fond of rankings and will defend their top ten albums and footballers with embarrassing commitment, though at the bottom of our cheesy souls we know that it is all subjective, all too determined by the generation to which we belong. For my generation, the choices are obvious and uncontroversial – Pelé, Maradona, Cruyff, Best and any one from a rump of half a dozen. But there should be room for a more quirky choice, and Butragueño fits my bill perfectly.

I first became aware of him when I was living in Peru, during the 1986 World Cup. There was a tiny 'bar' down the road from my flat, a small hut propped up by four poles, with a slab of corrugated iron balanced on the poles. The proprietor slept behind the counter in the day and kept a large dog on a lead to discourage thieves from walking off with his stock of bottled beer. At night, a group of men would meet and sit on the pavement outside talking into the small hours, drinking from the bottles. The bar collapsed in late '86 when an earth tremor dislodged one of the supporting poles. The dog survived, although the sleeping owner was not so lucky. But during the World Cup in Mexico, the nightbirds would congregate to discuss the games played in the afternoons or early evenings. The Peruvians were perceptive about football. They spoke poetically about it, in their curiously formal, florid Spanish. They liked to see it played with a flourish so that they themselves could talk about it in style. But teams that were all running and commitment – the work ethic? No. That wasn't half as interesting. Which is precisely why they were stunned by the Danes, a side they had expected to exemplify all the most tedious puritan traits of the severe northern Europeans. The evening after their 6–1 trouncing of Uruguay, an enormously fat and friendly customer was particularly enthralled, and in full gut-wobble mode, kept intoning: *'De puta madre! De puta madre!'* (Absolutely fucking brilliant!), banging his beer glass onto the counter in rhythm with his own insistence. 'That Elkjaer! Did you see him. Cut through them like a bull! They were trying to chop him down, hacking at him, but still he keeps going – then bang! Bloody Uruguayans! Good riddance I say!' And then a phrase that has always stuck in my head, spoken more quietly, as if he had been describing a lost lover to his friends – *'Que tal futbol . . . que tal futbol!'* (What wonderful football!) as if his otherwise problematic life had been blessed by what he had witnessed.

In the second phase, Denmark drew Spain. The Spaniards had been slowly improving, having looked quite useful in the group stage, losing unluckily to Brazil, scraping past Northern Ireland 2–1 then beating the weaker Algerians more convincingly, to the tune of 3–0. But I sincerely thought that Denmark were going to win the World Cup that year. They were indeed so wonderful in those first three games that it was difficult to see who was going to stop them. I didn't know much about the Spanish, beyond my general interest in the tournament, but I wasn't in any way prepared for what was to happen – and I remember the game as one of the most disappointing I have ever experienced, for the simple reason that I wanted to see more of the Danes. I hated the Spanish for what they did to them that day. The northerners had taken the lead but then Jesper Olsen, Manchester United's winger, played a calamitous back-pass to his keeper, and the Vulture appeared. Butragueño, with his baby-faced assassin's neutral expression, saw the mistake coming. He seemed to glide onto the ball as if on a cushion of air and stroke it past the onrushing keeper, as calm as you like. And so it continued. Every time the ball broke down in Denmark's midfield, Spain counter-attacked ruthlessly, and every time they did Butragueño seemed to score. And what I remember is that he looked as if he should have been doing something less strenuous than football, like a latter-day Billy Elliot. He ran with a ballet-dancer's poise, with a curiously nimble prance. He looked too feminine for the striker's art. His fourth goal was a penalty that he took himself, after turning Olsen in the penalty area in classic Dalglish style – turn the back, move to go one way, but feint in the opposite direction, flicking the ball through his own legs.

Denmark went tumbling out, as suddenly and as spectacularly as they had appeared. Butragueño was the first man to score four goals in a World Cup game since Eusebio had managed it against North Korea in 1966. In the next match, the Belgians played a cannier game, marking the Real Madrid striker so closely that he hardly touched the ball. Spain went out and, curiously, Butragueño never scored in a World Cup game again. He scored four several years later, in a 9–0 trouncing of Albania in Seville in 1990, and played his last game for Spain in 1992, against Ireland. Up until recently, his 26 international goals were a record for his country, first broken, curiously enough, by the defender Hierro but now also by Raúl.

Emilio Butragueño appeared on the international scene that summer just as the BBC were getting used to pronouncing the phonetic nightmare 'Severiano Ballesteros'. Proud as they were for finally getting to grips with the golfer's name, they had terrible problems with the new star from Real Madrid, insisting on pronouncing his surname 'Butragwaynyo'. In fact, they never got it right. The notoriously tongue-tied David Coleman was indeed happy to learn that the player's nickname was the 'Vulture' (*el Buitre*), and used the easier alternative whenever he was assigned to commentate on a game featuring Spain.

The period best known and cherished by a large proportion of *Madridistas*, that of the *Quinta del Buitre*, is a curiously resonant one. The Spanish – not just the Madrid variety – have a curious penchant for naming eras and periods of time, as if they had some national need to all agree on what was happening, at any specific moment in time in their history. Since Real Madrid have set the template for Spanish football since the 1950s, their periods, as we have seen, have all been named, signed and rubber-stamped into folk consciousness. And of course the quinta appeared after a period of relative crisis at the club – like a new lover who benefits from the 'rebound'.

'*La Quinta del Buitre*' means roughly 'The Vulture Squadron', but does not easily translate. The scavenger in question was thus called for his habit of arriving and finishing off the kill that others had set in motion. He was to gradually replace Santillana as the king of the terraces up until the mid-'90s when he was in turn replaced by the present monarch, Raúl. The word *quinta* is borrowed from military service, and refers to the group of buddies with whom you coincided during this potato-peeling year and with whom you might have remained in contact afterwards. With the appearance of this group of friends, Madrid could at last boast that one of its great periods stemmed from local roots, all five of the original *quinta* having done their Castilla apprenticeship. More importantly, they were all *Madrileños* apart from Pardeza, who was perhaps the least important figure of the five.

The *quinta* restored the concept of *Madridismo* and repositioned it at the centre of things, within a heady mix of popular culture and sport. The phenomenon turned up at the right moment, just as the *movida Madrileña* (Madrid scene) was flowering – a period of musical and cultural dynamism that was diverting attention away from Barcelona and back to the capital. It rekindled Madrid's self-confidence, converting the phrase into something strangely magical for Real Madrid supporters. It has also lent Butragueño legendary status, one that certain detractors claim he does not deserve on the basis that the *quinta* has been lent a mythical status above and beyond the sum of its parts. There may be some truth in this, but as we shall see, the main factor for the doubting Toms was the squad's inability to endorse the period with a European Cup, with the elusive *séptima* (seventh Cup).

When I interviewed Jorge Valdano for this book he was equally effusive about his ex-teammate Butragueño, and it was obvious that he meant it. In answer to my question about whether Madrid's supporters had always tended to perhaps over-appreciate 'gutsy workers with skill', he made the interesting point that Butragueño represented the death of this concept at the Bernabéu, replacing it with a more sensitive feel towards the football aesthetic.

> For many years Spanish football was associated with 'La Furia' [the fury], a kind of sentiment that associated it with aggression and directness. Those were the qualities most respected and sought after, but it was difficult to convert it into a style. There was no beauty to it, but it predominated for decades. Then Emilio came along and was an instant hero despite representing the total opposite of the *furia* stuff. The *Madridistas* do indeed have a certain weakness for players who give 110 per cent, but now they also like the stylists – and that's because of Emilio. He seduced the Bernabéu. He won them over completely, maybe because he was so unique. Nobody has ever played quite like him. He changed the way the Bernabéu viewed the game, and the legacy has grown.

As far as the five are concerned, the one who ranks highest in the Top 100 centenary poll is Michel, at number 9. Butragueño comes in second at number 11, Sanchís third at 16, then Vásquez at 48. Pardeza does not figure, perhaps due to spending his best years at Zaragoza. The first two to be promoted from the ranks of Castilla by Di Stéfano were the defender Manuel Sanchís and the midfielder Martín Vásquez, in a 0–1 win at Murcia in 1984. Sanchís, who managed 40 goals in a record 689 appearances for the club, actually scored his first that evening in Murcia. He was to become the only member of the *quinta* to soldier on and finally lift a European Cup in 1998 and 2000, dedicating the first trophy to his four squadron friends, by then all retired. Though Sanchís was a hero in Madrid circles, John Toshack, on the final day of his first spell as manager of the club in 1991, was to say of the veteran defender that he was, 'The worst person it has ever been my misfortune to meet'. It is not known what Sanchís thought of Toshack, but the Welshman was taking the lid off the alleged darker side of the group, in an acid reference to the power that the *quinta* were supposed to have established by then in the dressing-room of the Bernabéu, as well as in the presidential corridors and in the national side. Toshack had cause to regret his little speech when he returned to the club eight years later, and Sanchís was still there. Toshack had been brought back from Turkey by the stressed-out President Sanz, desperate for results and searching for a hard-man to sort out the swollen egos in the astronomically expensive squad. Sanchís' nearest contemporary, Vázquez, went on to play in Italy for Torino, a rare example of a Spaniard who travelled well. He had, nevertheless, left the club under a cloud, arguing with the old president Mendoza after the latter had refused to pay him more money. On returning to Spain he ended up at Deportivo de La Coruña, managed inevitably by John Toshack.

Pardeza, originally from Huelva, was the third to appear, followed by the Vulture, who lent his name to the group. A falsely mythical status he may have accrued, but he figures in the other *Marca* poll as one of the members of the all-time Real Madrid top 11. One of the players alongside him in this pantheon of greats, Di Stéfano, must take much of the credit for the appearance of the *quinta*, though he has always been at pains to play down his role in their emergence, claiming that it was just a case of good luck for him to have been around when the eggs were hatching. Though his period as manager of Madrid was brief and unsuccessful in terms of trophies, he did indeed see to the nurturing and development of the *quinta*. When Butragueño joined the club in 1980 as a 17-year-old apprentice, he went to training every day on his motor scooter. Di Stéfano, on spotting him driving in one morning, told him that he would have to come by some other means, given that a player had to look after his main asset, his body. The young Emilio did as he was ordered, but one Saturday evening took his Vespa down town to see some friends. Hearing the blare of a horn behind him, he glanced into his mirror to see a red-faced Di Stéfano, shaking his fist and cursing at him from behind the wheel of his car. He sold the bike soon after.

Butragueño, now employed by the club in a PR role, still looks as if he goes home every night to his mum. He still has the delicate looks, the boyish Peter Pan face, the curly fair hair and the slight frame that once made him look more like an angelic schoolboy than a footballer. No footballer had ever looked quite like him. Born and raised in the centre of Madrid, he helped out in his parents' perfume shop and played football at the weekends with family and friends, never really considering himself to be a potential professional. His father was a paid-up member of Real Madrid, but had not played to any significant level. When it was suggested that Emilio go for a trial to Atlético Madrid after scoring 8 goals for his school team at the age of 15, he almost fell into the clutches of the red and white rival, a fate that almost befell Raúl ten years later. His father was on the point of signing an agreement with Atlético when a family friend (Juan Gallego), who was also manager of the Real Juniors side persuaded him to hang fire until he had given the youngster the once-over – just in case. Butragueño, a humble youth, told his father on returning home that he had played *fatal* (badly), but the official report on him that day noted that,

> . . . technically he holds the ball up well, with both feet. He has the vision of a midfielder, and passes perfectly into spaces such that his colleagues were often too slow to anticipate his intentions.

Three days later he signed apprentice forms, and in a friendly match at San Lorenzo, Luis Molowny, ex-player and manager, wandered along to see the game. After half an hour he sought out Gallego and exclaimed, 'Who the fuck is that weird-looking kid playing up front? Where did you find him? He's a genius.'

Perhaps more ruthless than genius, if only in the goalscoring sense, for he never hurt a fly, was rarely booked, and his ability was based more on avoiding physical contact than actively seeking it. He must have been the perfect five-a-side player, the man to have on your side during the one-touch training sessions. Michel recalled that he could always rely on Butragueño to read his intentions. Michel, rated as one of Spain's best ever crossers of the ball, pointed out that it was the Vulture's art of the *desmarque* that was his greatest virtue – the ability to hang square in a line with the defence then suddenly break for the space when the ball was delivered. Watching a video of Butragueño's career, it is remarkable the number of times Michel knocks the ball forward and the Vulture sprints out from the ruck to score. But the goals are never hammered home, never scrambled in untidily. He keeps his head and places the ball carefully home, or feints subtly to one side and taps it in. They are almost all unspectacular goals – a flick here, a chip there, quiet little efforts that became his killer's trademark. He managed 140 goals in 340 league appearances, 25 in 71 European appearances and 15 in 39 King's Cup games, plus 26 for the national side. He won six leagues with Madrid, two UEFA Cups and two King's Cups – not a bad haul.

Michel, now a commentator on Spain's *TVE 1*, was in fact the senior member of the group, and by 1984 was alarmed to see that his mates had all been promoted to the first-team before him. Not one to hold back even in his younger days, he approached Di Stéfano one morning outside the training ground and asked him why he was still with the reserves. Di Stéfano, never one to suffer cocky youths gladly, dismissed him with the celebrated, 'You can play when your balls have dropped.' Once this auspicious event had taken place, the team was under 'new' management, with Luis Molowny asked to step into the breach for a fourth time. In 1985 Michel joined his pals in the first team, and went on to a distinguished career with both club and country. But his international career slowed down after 1992 when the Basque, Javier Clemente, took over as national manager, since his strategy was to break up the *quinta* and limit their influence on the national squad. Michel, intelligent, smooth talking and very much the man with the officer qualities, never forgave Clemente, and spent the rest of the '90s attacking his management strategies from behind a microphone.

But apart from the *quinta* there were other important parts that constituted the whole. Apart from the promotion of Michel, in the season 1984–85 Jorge Valdano, an experienced Argentinean forward at Zaragoza, was signed by Molowny to provide alternatives to the Santillana–Butragueño pairing. He quickly made his mark and scored 17 in a first season which saw Madrid still fall short of regaining the league title, a five-season wait the like of which they had not seen since the early 1950s. To further salt the wound, Terry Venables' Barcelona side, without the departed Maradona, had won it by a mile, finishing ten points above their nearest rival, Atlético, and a full 17 above Real. It was Stielike's last season after almost 300 games, but on paper, the squad looked as though it could absorb his departure, with Michel and Martín Vásquez having looked promising all season, and the young Butragueño having delivered, with ten goals under his belt in his first full season. The season had not been altogether dry, however. The team did recover some European glory, albeit in one of the competitions that they had initially looked down on as unworthy of their presence. But time can change the most snobbish of attitudes, and by 1985, Bernabéu was no longer around to cast aspersions on competitions such as the UEFA Cup. After defeating old rivals Anderlecht along the way, knocking out Spurs in the quarter-final and then defeating the old foe Inter in the semi-finals, they took on the Hungarian part-timers, the curiously named Videoton, in a two-legged final. Winning 3–0 in Hungary in the first leg, they relaxed rather too much in the return game and lost it 0–1, somewhat muting the celebrations surrounding their first European title since 1966. They were to win it in rather more style the following year against Cologne, but the win against Videoton hinted at some steel in the side and suggested that this transitional period might begin to bear fruit.

On 24 May 1985, two days after the Videoton game, Luis de Carlos resigned as president and Ramón Mendoza was voted in as his replacement. After being forced to resign from the board in 1978 after he was accused of working for the KGB by the right-wing paper *ABC*, he had finally ascended to the throne. Despite the political rumours that were always to surround him, the election of Mendoza was greeted with enthusiasm in *Madridista* circles, chiefly because it restored to the job a man with charisma, a man known to be a brilliant wheeler-dealer, and a *Madrileño* to boot. Apart from these factors, he was one of Spain's best-known public figures, having married into Spanish *alta sociedad* (high society) in the 1960s and having wheedled his way into the monied corridors of horse-breeding and racing. He was a witty, attractive man, linked with dozens of rich and beautiful women and never seen in public without a cigarette in his hand. Mendoza was self-made, but he was cool. He hadn't turned himself into a rags-to-riches right-wing boor, and he seemed sharper and more sophisticated than Nuñez over at Barcelona, a tiny man with an unfortunate expression locked into a permanent sneer. In terms of his public persona, Mendoza was the antithesis of Nuñez, and although the little president at Barça was despised by the Bernabéu faithful, they nevertheless harboured a sneaking feeling that he was sorting the club out and putting it onto a firmer financial footing. Mendoza, of course, was to take the club to the brink of bankruptcy, but history has largely forgiven him because of the *quinta* – with whom he is permanently associated – and because he was cool. The Spanish will forgive any rogue his crimes, just so long as he carried on in his everyday life with a certain amount of hauteur and style. Men liked Mendoza because he had so many of the things that most of them aspire to – money, wit, women – and the presidency of the world's biggest football club. Women liked him because he was a quietly strong individual who excelled in the art of the cutting one-liner, and because he made no secret of his weakness for the opposite sex.

Mendoza died in the Bahamas in 2001 at the age of 74. He was not mourned in the manner of Bernabéu, since by then the nature of his reckless speculation in the club's collateral was part of *Madrileño* folklore. But he was mourned by the *quinta*, for whom he was something of a father-figure, and by the section of the Bernabéu that likes to think that the club upholds the spirit of caste (*castizo*) quoted in the original '*Hala Madrid!*' song which was penned in 1952:

Of all the sporting glories
That excel throughout the country
See Madrid with her white flag flying
Clean and white that never fades
Club of noble descent and generous spirit
All nerve and heart and sinew
Young and old, young and old
Never forget her honour . . .

In truth, with Mendoza it could well have been the red flag flying as opposed to the white one, but his dealings in Russia were simply an early example of his entrepreneurial nose, seeing a market for the importation of Soviet oil, caviar and vodka, all on the cheap. What the Soviets got in return were cheap shoes and oranges, but they weren't complaining. His gradual but inevitable rise to the throne of Real Madrid marked another change in the club, as if it were looking for someone to redirect it towards a new image. Mendoza was not only the antithesis of Nuñez, he was also a vastly different character to Santiago Bernabéu – scourge of the Commies, family man and Spanish *caballero* – a complicated idea of manhood at the heart of older Spain – cigar-smoking, paternalistic and patriotic. Mendoza preferred cigarettes, and seemed less interested in the diversions of patriotism. He was in it for himself, but because he made no secret of this he was admired.

He got straight to work. In the summer of 1985 he signed Antonio Maceda from Valencia, Rafael Gordillo from Betis and Hugo Sánchez from neighbours Atlético Madrid. The three signings reinforced defence, midfield and attack respectively, and perhaps apart from Maceda – whose promising start with the club was truncated by a series of injuries – these arrivals were to bring to the boil the new elements of the squad that had up to then been merely simmering. The figures speak for themselves – five straight league titles between 1986 and 1990, one King's Cup and another UEFA title. But the European Cup eluded them, a title that the style and power of this team surely deserved. The *quinta* reached three semi-finals and lost them all, a bridesmaid's story in an otherwise successful period. One writes 'the *quinta*', but it was really the whole team. The curious fact about the Vulture Squadron is that the five only played together as first-team choices on one occasion – in the 1987 season, on 3 June in the King's Cup semi-final against Atlético. Pardeza, now a journalist with an elegant turn of phrase, left at the end of that season for Zaragoza, leaving his four *Madrileño* friends to become the principal parts of this newly dominant squad.

Michel, interviewed as part of *Marca's* centenary series video, describes the team as:

> . . . a jigsaw that just fitted together – a sort of complicated dance where everyone knew the steps by heart. It was uncanny. If you played the right ball, Emilio or Hugo [Sánchez] would get on the end of it. If you carried on running, they'd give it back to you. Always. They never got it wrong. Rafa [Gordillo] would just run all day. He had four lungs. The crowd loved him. It was weird – I can't quite explain it to you. It was just that certain players came together at a certain time, and I was lucky to have been a part of it. It only happens every now and then. But I'll tell you what – that side had one of the most awesome forward lines of all time. Attacking power? You tell me a better one.

There is a fine photograph of the signing of Hugo Sánchez, preceding one of the rare occasions that a player crossed the city. Mendoza sits in a Madrid restaurant, cigarette inevitably in hand, holding forth to a leather-jacketed Sánchez, who sports a rather alarming mid-'80s bouffant hairstyle, whilst Atlético's president Vicente Calderón, now also immortalised in the name of the club's present stadium, looks on with a wide-eyed expression. It is as if the amounts that Mendoza is quoting are good news to Atlético's main man, but Sánchez was to prove good news for Real Madrid. He'd already finished as top-scorer in his first season in the Spanish league with 19 goals, and his move to Real, questioned at first by the press who mistrusted his flamboyance, was the spark that ignited the proverbial. Sánchez is 14th in the Top 100 list, with 205 goals in 279 appearances. He topped the Spanish charts for three consecutive seasons between 1985 and 1988, then equalled Zarra's all-time league scoring record of 38 in a season under Toshack in 1990. He was the striker supreme, finishing off his goals with the famous *Huguina* backflip. His left foot was also capable of delivering precision passes, but it is his deadly stuff in the box for which he is best remembered. Butragueño's goal-scoring record, though thoroughly decent, pales in comparison to Sánchez' achievements – but it was all part of the mix. The two seemed to understand each other perfectly, and never trod on each other's toes. Their subtle interpassing was a joy to behold, and should be standard viewing for any would-be strikers who want to add a bit more to their game. Butragueño was different in that he was not quite so obsessed with scoring as was Sánchez, and could satisfy himself with a little touch, a flick, a little wall-pass that set up the goal. Sánchez just wanted to get on the end of the move and finish it. He looked like a bullfighter, with an upright stance and a repertoire of jinks and shuffles based on his extraordinary athleticism. His success at the club seems all the more remarkable considering the fact that he and Michel were rumoured to have disliked each other, an item of hearsay that seems unlikely, given the fact that they finished off their careers together in Mexico – but you never know. Neither of them was over-burdened with the weight of humility. During the 1986–87 season, with the Dutchman Leo Beenhakker now installed as manager, Sánchez told the press that he belonged to the '*Quinta de Los Machos*' (The Real Men's Squadron) implying that he was fed up with all the Vulture stuff. He added that he had had offers from all over the globe, and that Inter were prepared to pay a king's ransom for him. Mendoza ignored him, and the storm passed over – but it has never been altogether clear how well the disparate elements of this squad got on with each other away from the field of play.

But the style and the results were what the folk had been waiting for, and this is why the *quinta* has become so legendary, above and beyond the sum of its parts. That first season, Sánchez ran riot and scored 19, Valdano managed 16 and Butragueño 10. Santillana and Juanito, lest they be forgotten, were still there to provide the experience, and managed 28 and 27 games between them respectively, but they were no longer the only source of the goals, and the following season would see them share just a couple between them. The kings had once again been replaced, but this time more slowly, more sensibly.

The European Cup semi-final against PSV Eindhoven in 1988 remains the event which most stuck in the craw of the *quinta* since it was the one that they most felt they could have won – to give them a crack at the *séptima*. The other two semi-finals, against Bayern Munich and AC Milan, were both fairly traumatic affairs, accompanied by heavy aggregate defeats. Besides, it seemed auspicious that the team had overcome every obstacle placed in its way that season. The opening tie of the competition against Maradona's Napoli was played behind closed doors – *el partido del silencio* as it has come to be called – because of incidents the previous season in the semi against Bayern. Madrid were picking up a reputation for being bad boys, but Mendoza was of Oscar Wilde's opinion that 'It doesn't matter what they're saying about you, as long as they're talking about you', and instructed Beenhakker to prepare for the game by practising behind closed doors against Castilla, the reserve side being instructed to wear Napoli's blue shirts. Scarves and banners were draped around the terracing, and it seemed to do the trick, Madrid winning 2–0. Maradona, accustomed to baiting the Spaniards after his previous life over there, declared that Real would not win in Napoli even with Puskas and Di Stéfano playing. As so often in his life, he got it wrong, and Butragueño earned them a 1–1 draw. Having disposed of Bayern Munich in the quarter-finals – another *mini-remontada* after the Germans had won 3–2 at home, the club were reasonably confident of beating PSV. A disappointing 1–1 draw at home was the real cause of the failure, but in Holland it was the nature of the defeat that proved to be most upsetting for the *quinta*. The 0–0 draw was clear evidence to them of the missed opportunity, in a game where Sánchez came agonisingly close on three occasions to breaking the deadlock. But it was not to be. The next season, at the same stage, Gullit's Milan destroyed them, and Leo Beenhakker resigned. He knew that the league runs were not enough to satisfy the Bernabéu's cravings.

Mendoza turned to John Toshack, who had been making a name for himself up at Real Sociedad. Although the new incumbent did no better in Europe, the team losing again to Milan in the second round, the league season was to be more memorable. Ironically, the *Madrileño* press, who mistrusted the outspoken Toshack from the off, decided to ruffle him in the early stages of the season by implying that he was over-cautious and defensive-minded. The only empirical proof of this was the fact that the side failed to score in their first two away games, but unfortunately for the journalists things soon picked up. Both the macho and the scavenger *quintas* reached the zenith of their powers that year, and Real scored a record 107 goals, with only 38 conceded. The amount of goals conceded by the excellent new goalkeeper Paco Buyo was the same amount as those scored by Sánchez, equalling the 35-year-old record set by Bilbao's Zarra. In the last match against Oviedo he scored the 38th, then missed a sitter late on which would have written him more firmly into the record books.

But there was *sombra* (shadow) as well as *sol* (sun) that famous season. Bernd Schuster had been brought over from Barcelona by Mendoza to annoy the Catalans as much as anything, but they were actually quite happy to see him go. He had fallen out with Venables and been at loggerheads with the club for over a year, and had actually begun legal action against them for their refusal to allow him to play.

Predictably, he failed to get on with Toshack either, complaining that he was being misused as a *libero*, but the Welshman was by then famous for his own stubborn resolve and his failure to toe the party line at Madrid. The hacks, so favoured by previous regimes, were given short shrift by Toshack, and there were the inevitable rumours that the *quinta* were trying to have him removed from office. The King's Cup defeat that season at the hands of Barcelona can hardly have helped his cause, despite the record haul of goals in the league, but one might conclude that Toshack was unlucky to have begun his period in Madrid just as Johan Cruyff was planning his next step on the ladder to immortality, this time as manager of Barcelona. He was putting together the wonderful 'Dream Team' that were to take the next four league titles and silence Madrid for half a decade. It was a killer blow for Toshack, sacked in the November of the following season – and the final decade of Spain's first footballing century was to prove a killer blow for the *quinta* too, accustomed as they had grown to at least ruling the domestic roost. Butragueño, Michel and Sanchís had plenty of football left in them, but it would be a callow youth, training over at Atlético Madrid, who would really bring back the smile to the Bernabéu.

10. RAÚL MADRID

In the Bernabéu on 4 February 2001, Raúl González' second goal against Málaga, a simple tap-in, was celebrated as if the scorer had done something truly exceptional. But even those who do not dedicate themselves to a life of statistical gathering will have known the reason. Raúl – one of the select band of players in the Spanish league who has earned the right to refer to himself permanently by his Christian name – had just scored his 113th goal in the Spanish league, thus overtaking the man playing out the twilight of his career in Pamplona, '*Cuco*' Ziganda. By the end of that game, Raúl had scored more goals than any other player currently performing in the Spanish league, and had managed his first 113 in just 6½ seasons, whereas it took Ziganda 12 seasons to score his. And where Ziganda was looking forward to retirement at the end of that season, Raúl has a good ten years left in him yet, injuries permitting. By keeping up his strike-rate, he should easily overtake the league record established by the Athletic Bilbao legend Zarra, 47 years ago, who had managed 240 in the league by the time he hung up his boots. And then there's the little matter of the national team where he has already overhauled the record number of goals scored by his club colleague and captain Fernando Hierro, who retired from international duty after the 2002 World Cup. The magical 31st goal arrived on Mallorcan soil, rather spookily in the 31st minute of Spain's friendly with Germany in February 2003. Fittingly, Raúl stroked it past Oliver Kahn, in most people's judgement the world's best goalkeeper.

It seems appropriate to focus an entire chapter of this book on Raúl, not only because he is the latest embodiment of Madrid's famous continuity factor but because he stands out in a period that has seen numerous stars passing through the club, many of whom have left their mark more in the pages of the gossip columns than on the field of play. In the postmodern age of the mercenary, where clubs like Real Madrid have been at the forefront of the fashion for breaking the bank and swelling their squads with stars innumerable, the story of the home town boy comes as something of a balm to this ungainly scene, where players come today and are gone tomorrow – versed in the arts of kissing the local shirt and shaking the bank manager's hand with justifiable enthusiasm. But there are other factors too.

Raúl appeared on the scene just as Ramón Mendoza's relationship with the club had reached the point of no return. His attempts to re-model the stadium had ended in accusations of corruption and financial incompetence, and his witty sangfroid was no longer so appreciated. The Catalans were exultant, having won their first European Cup and put together a side that even the most rabid *Madridista* was forced to admire. Cruyff was once again the ogre, lording it over the Bernabéu and aiming well-directed barbs at every little fissure of Madrid's seemingly crumbling empire. The worst thing of all was that the so-called Barça 'Dream Team' were as lucky as they were undeniably attractive, and of their four consecutive titles, two had been won on the final day of the season in dramatic circumstances, Real gifting them the title in 1992 and 1993 by losing both times at Tenerife. The extraordinary circumstances surrounding these two final games were lent even more significance by the fact that Jorge Valdano was manager of Tenerife at the time. His apprenticeship over, he returned to manage the club in 1994 where four members of the ageing *quinta*, all of whom had played alongside him in the 1980s, were still active. More significantly, he was quick to notice Raúl González, a skinny 17-year-old forward who had taken his eye in a friendly game against Karlsruhe. When Martín Vázquez was injured in a home draw against Compostela, Valdano surprised the press and just about everyone else by pencilling in the young forward for the away game at Zaragoza – another of the manager's ex-clubs. Despite Zaragoza's 3–2 win, the youngster did enough to keep his place for the local derby the following week against Atlético in which he scored the third goal, set up two, and was the cause of the other when he was fouled in the area. Suddenly, Valdano's various signings seemed to make sense. Uninterested in the complicated and moody Robert Prosinecki, he had managed to sign two midfielders very much in keeping with his idea of 'footballing intelligence' – the Argentine Fernando Redondo and the Dane Michael Laudrup. The former had been with him at Tenerife, but the latter had been the chief architect of the 'Dream Team's' aesthetic at Barcelona. He had fallen out with Cruyff, saying that he could 'take no more'. Laudrup, a courteous fellow, had grown tired of the Dutchman's whimsy and his passable impression of a mad dictator. Valdano was much more his type, and despite the problems associated with moving between these two clubs, he had no hesitation. His function that first season was to supply the Chilean striker Zamorano, which he was to do with telling effect. But no one had really anticipated the appearance of Raúl.

Raúl González was born in 1977 in a working-class suburb of Madrid. His father was an electrician, and the son was bound for the same trade until Atlético Madrid took an interest in the scrawny boy and drafted him into their junior side in 1988. Four years later, Jesus Gil, always keen on saving a few pesetas whenever it was possible, made one of the worst decisions of his presidency when he decided to scrap the Atlético youth team set-up, and sack all the personnel who had been involved. What he saved in money that year he lost in terms of future investment when Raúl, already spotted by Real's chief scout Paco de Gracia, decided to move across the city to the Bernabéu – not the ground he had gone to with his Atlético-supporting father as a boy. After a year playing for Real's 'C' team, he moved up to the 'B' side in 1994, and after making his debut for the Spanish Under-18 team that same year, Jorge Valdano, as mentioned, decided to blood him in the first team.

Raúl was fortunate in two senses. Firstly, he was lucky to have encountered a manager of Valdano's vision and intelligence so early in his career. Had he stayed at Atlético he would have been subjected to the usual monthly rounds of managerial *coups d'état* and ritual executions around which his talents may not have blossomed so easily. Valdano's rather complex ideas of 'football intelligence' were always more easily understood in the concrete terms of players like Raúl, for he clearly had these qualities in abundance. Secondly, Laudrup's midfield orchestration always required perceptive forwards to get onto his wavelength, and Zamorano would be the first to enjoy a fruitful season up front, scoring goals by the bucketful and returning the title to the Bernabéu after the four-year drought. Raúl played a bit-part, a supporting role that year, but it was clear that he was no mug. His ability to hang in close to defenders then burst into space was the perfect foil to Laudrup's imaginative and sometimes supernatural passing abilities. By the same time the next year, Zamorano was gone and Raúl was the new undisputed king. Moreover, by the end of Raúl's first full season (1994–95), it was clear to all concerned that Butragueño's previously exquisite services were no longer needed. He played only eight games during the campaign, and was given an emotional send-off on 15 June 1995 in the Bernabéu in a friendly against Roma. The Vulture was gone, replaced by an equally unassuming assassin. Like the first successful handing-over of a democratic regime to another after a period of political instability, the succession at long last of one Madrid-born king to another was cause for celebration. It papered over the cracks of the club's worrying financial situation and coincided with wresting the initiative back from Barcelona – with one of their ex-players to boot. Things were looking up.

And things have continued to look up, especially on the European front. In the five-year period between 1998 and 2002 Real Madrid won the European Cup three times, on the last occasion winning it in their centenary year in Glasgow, 42 years on from the 7–3 final. Raúl's role has been crucial in this restoration of the monarchy, the interregnum having lasted a full 32 years. He has scored so many vital goals and has saved the team's bacon on so many occasions that it is difficult to pick out his most significant contributions – but one of them is easily recalled by the British TV audience on an April night in 2000 when Real Madrid once again visited Old Trafford in a European tie. The first of his two goals in that Champions League quarter-final said everything about his various virtues. With United a goal down as they came out for the second half, the expected tidal wave of English attacks had begun. In the 50th minute, however, a United attack broke down and Redondo slipped a sudden pass from the centre into a space on the right that Irwin, the United full-back, had left as he had pushed forward. Raúl latched onto the ball and hared down the right flank, angling himself slightly inside so as to line the ball up onto his favoured left foot. The main camera was perfectly placed in the stand and was focused right behind Raúl as he began to lean to the left. If you'd been watching him every week in Spain, you knew exactly what he was going to do. Johnsen, rushing up to tackle, did not, and the Spanish forward stroked the ball with just the right amount of curve so that it arched around Johnsen and the advancing goalkeeper and flew into the only section of the net visible to the television spectator. It was the perfect finish, but this time on the European stage. Three minutes later, Redondo left various United defenders on their backsides over on the left, knocked the ball across the goal, and Raúl appeared, as ever, to tap it home. United, virtually unchallenged in the Premier League week in week out, were not used to this sort of quality and seemed unable to cope. Two months later and the same player was setting up the first and scoring the second in his team's eighth European Cup victory, against fellow Spaniards Valencia in Paris. Three years later, *plus ça change*. Sir Alex Ferguson, commenting on Raúl's sublime performance for Madrid in their 3–1 dismantling of Manchester United in the Bernabéu during the 2003 Champions League quarter-finals, was moved to say that he considered the Spaniard to be the world's best player, and could some immigration official be persuaded to refuse him entry to the country on the occasion of the return leg in Manchester? In the end, Raúl was injured for the game in question, but Ronaldo scored a hat-trick anyway. Well might Ferguson have looked long-faced at the end of proceedings. The game was to take on even more significance for the future, since the manager's decision to leave Beckham on the bench was interpreted as a symbolic gesture in the direction of Madrid, as if to say 'It's over for us. You can have him now'. Beckham's wave to the Old Trafford crowd at the end of the game did not go unnoticed by the Spanish press, and the following morning was effectively Day One in the saga that was to become the mother of all transfers.

Fernando Redondo, the other Valdano baby, was voted the top player by journalists in that season's Champions League, with Raúl taking the prize for best forward. The fact that to date Raúl has missed out on the seasonal European top player awards is something of a mystery. Good though Michael Owen is, his being voted above Raúl in the 2001 awards seemed like a nasty outbreak of collective *northern Europeanitis*, for Raúl is a much more complete player, a much more sophisticated model. It is difficult to see what more he has to do to be given the award.

When talking about the model of player Raúl conforms to, there seems to be no exact prototype to which he compares. Rather he is more of a hybrid, a composite of various greats that have come before. Like Gerd Müller, and his hero Butragueño, his style can best be described as 'concise'. He rarely hangs around on the ball for more than a second, and his goals are scored, like Müller's, with the minimum of fuss. That is not to say that he is incapable of the spectacular – far from it – but the majority of his goals are the product of quick-thinking, perfect exploitation of space and an almost unnatural coolness under pressure. Like many of the great goalscorers of the past, he can sometimes fade completely from a game for long periods, only to suddenly emerge and score the winner. In a sense, it is this ability to drift in and out of games that makes him doubly dangerous, for his lack of physical presence makes him more difficult to mark.

It is difficult to fault him. Despite his slight build, he rarely gets injured. He is described as a 'striker', but in truth he often sits behind another front man, for example Morientes, and exploits the spaces that are often left in the upper sections of midfield to steal up front and arrive behind the zonal markers. His second goal against Manchester United was a classic example of this. Yet despite this typecasting, he also scores every type of goal. He rarely scores headers, but when he does they are executed with powerful grace and perfection. He has scored powerful shots from outside of the area, sudden dribbles in confined spaces culminating in a subtle finish, tap-ins, penalties – you name them, he's scored them. He can also tackle back and defend, and seems capable of fitting in with whomsoever he is partnered up front. It is said that he prefers his friend Fernando Morientes to anyone else, but despite the early rumblings in 2002–03 that he and Ronaldo were incompatible, the two eventually struck up a relationship. Apart from the latest partner, Ronaldo, he has accompanied a whole welter of big-name players since his debut in 1994, either complementing or leading them. After Zamorano left, Butragueño retired and Valdano was sacked, new man Fabio Capello brought in Pedja Mijatovic from Valencia and Davor Suker from Sevilla, two players who had been making waves with their respective clubs. Raúl just continued where he'd left off. In the 1996–97 season, after a wonderful nine-month struggle with Barcelona, Real won back the league surprisingly taken from them the previous season by Gil's Atlético. Mijatovic scored 14, Raúl 21 and Suker 24. Talk about instant chemistry. Even when things went less swimmingly, as in the previous season (1995–96), Raúl still scored 19, the only one to reach double figures. His efforts failed to save his mentor, however, and in the January of that year, after a defeat to neighbours Rayo Vallecano, Valdano was dismissed by new president Lorenzo Sanz.

In the national team, he has blended perfectly well with the big burly centre-forward Urzaiz, the more cerebral Alfonso, the more selfish Tristán – or whoever he is asked to work alongside. He appears to be able to adapt to other players' strengths, and so improves their performances as well. But as this book draws to a close, it is worth re-emphasising the fact that all the truly great *figuras* (stars) who have turned up during the last hundred years at Real Madrid have been more than mere footballers. In almost every case they have been characters who have represented one of the individual building blocks that constitute the current edifice of *Madridismo*.

Although Raúl was an Atlético supporter as a child he has been forgiven this accident of his upbringing. The fact that he is the highest-paid Spanish footballer in the league has nothing to do with his dedication to the cause. It is impossible to think of him in any other colours than those of Madrid, something which he has repeated ad nauseam when even the tiniest rumour of a possible move has surfaced. In the summer of 2000, when it became clear that Luis Figo really was coming to town, there was speculation that Raúl might be sold to raise the cash, or even – horror of horrors – be used as part exchange and go over to Barça. For several days during that astonishing summer, when the realisation that Figo really was changing clubs began to sink in, anything seemed possible. But when the drums began to talk about Raúl's possible departure, even the most imaginative of Spain's citizens found it impossible to envisage him in a Barça shirt. Jesus Christ had returned, and was alive and well and working in a bar in Badajoz? Fine. Raúl to Barcelona? Tell me another one! Besides, Raúl himself scotched the rumours, declaring himself to be happy in Madrid, a city which he described as 'like no other'. If he were not already canonised in the eyes of the worshippers, that statement finally bestowed on him the sainthood that his brief but spectacular career had merited to that point. Similarly, when David Beckham's transfer to Madrid was confirmed, the rumour began to circulate that Raúl was unhappy with the simultaneous dismissal of the faithful old manager Vicente Del Bosque and the termination of Hierro's contract – and that he was prepared to listen to offers from Manchester United. A couple of weeks later, just before Beckham's official presentation, president Florentino Pérez reiterated to the papers that although the Englishman was an important star in the firmament, Raúl would always be Madrid's icon, the living symbol of the club's greatness. He wasn't going anywhere.

Perhaps uniquely among Madrid's pantheon of greats, he is something of *un niño bueno* (a good boy). Butrageuño was not exactly a rabble-rouser, but in nine years of high-profile prominence Raúl has failed to provide the press with even one decent soundbite. This is the man who, on being gifted a Porsche as best player in the World Club Championship final in 2000, promptly sold the car and gave the money to charity. After being awarded his first official contract with the first team, he went out and secured a mortgage on the amount and bought his parents a new flat. He lists as his extra-curricular interests 'Charity, and visiting children's hospitals', devours biographies of Mother Teresa and confesses to a weakness for Julio Iglesias' music – but he did at least play for Real Madrid.

The satellite channel Canal Plus runs a nightly series of caricature puppet characters under the title *El Gran Guiñol* in a spoof news presentation programme. Players come and go, but Raúl has been featured almost from the start of his career. The puppet, with a grotesquely long nose and large sticking-out ears, mouths nightly platitudes like they are going out of style, rather like his human equivalent. When the puppet is asked his opinion on anything, he always replies with statements along the lines of 'It's a question of application and hard work. I'm just thinking about the next game and I'm really happy to be playing.' Rather like the gardener played by Peter Sellers in *Being There*, he uses this phrase whatever the question, so that he has at times been mistaken for saying something of interest. 'Raúl – what did you think about Rivaldo's goal that they disallowed last week?' 'Well,' he will reply, 'it's just a question of application and hard work . . .'

Raúl, then, is no Cantona when it comes to the charisma countdown, but footballers are not obliged to be fascinating characters, especially ones as brilliant as Raúl. As the old cliché goes, he lets his feet do the talking. And just as he is a decent God-fearing chap off the pitch, so is he a sporting player on it. He rarely gets booked, never talks back to referees, and refrains from that tendency endemic in his fellow countrymen of sniping at the opposition through the papers. The famous gesture of him putting his finger to his lips after scoring at the Camp Nou in 1999 was the furthest he has ever gone in the provocation stakes. And anyway, he was asking them to stay quiet. Later that same season there was righteous indignation steaming from the Bernabéu camp after FIFA decided to fine Raúl 5,000 dollars after he 'did a Maradona' against Leeds in the Champions League, punching the ball into the net for Real's opening goal in their eventual 3–2 win. In typical style, he was honest enough to own up to his sin (as opposed to Maradona), and when asked by the Polish referee at half-time whether he had handled the ball or not, replied immediately that he had and that he was sorry. The referee went directly to the Leeds changing-room and also apologised for his mistake. Of course, having admitted the sin, FIFA were absurdly obliged by their own ground rules to make an example of Raúl – which brought forth protests not only from Real Madrid but from much of Spain. Almost uniquely among Madrid players in recent years, Raúl is universally acknowledged as a decent guy and a sporting performer, even by the Catalans. Valdano, reinstalled as Real's Director of Football, drafted the letter of protest to FIFA in which the main thrust of the complaint centred on the fact that Raúl's disciplinary record was impeccable (only two bookings in his career – almost supernatural in Spain) and that it was like 'making an example of John the Baptist'.

Almost alone among Real Madrid's Spaniards, Raúl has never attacked Barcelona and their attendant *Catalanisme*, although he has had plenty of opportunities to do so. Despite the Madrid press's attempts to cast him in the role of the anti-Catalan, Raúl has never sunk to their pitiful level. He always has the good grace to praise the opposition (even Barcelona) when they win. The fact that he likes Mother Teresa rather suggests that he might not be the best of company down at the pub, but he'd rather just be a straight young chap rather than give the journalists something to write about. Indeed, when rumours began to circulate in the society magazine, *Hello*, that all might not be well in his marriage to the model Mamen Sanz, the paparazzi were onto it in a flash, despite the player's almost embarrassing decency towards the press in general, and his reputation for always making himself available (even if he subsequently says nothing of any interest). And there remains the distinct possibility that Raúl decided from the beginning that the less said the better. As Stephen Spender observed:

> I fear I cannot make an amusing speech. I have just been reading a book which says that 'all geniuses are devoid of humour'.

So what of the period in general? What has happened around this emblematic figure, the player who was voted as the second greatest of all time at the club, behind Di Stéfano? Quite a lot, it has to be said, but most of it centres around Europe, enormous transfers and presidential comings and goings. Amongst the clutter it is Pedja Mijatovic's goal in Amsterdam on 20 May 1998 that gels the decade, that lends it coherence and which repositioned Real Madrid at the centre of the footballing universe. For those of us unaccustomed to the luxuries of a trophy-laden history, it is difficult to understand the significance of that goal. Just as older Manchester United followers will find it hard to forget the importance of those two late goals against Bayern Munich, Mijatovic's strike was equally memorable, ending an almost identical period of drought – 32 years as opposed to United's 31. The goal arrived in the 66th minute of the game against Zidane's Juventus, in Amsterdam, and it has seen its fair share of replays since. It was a good one too, worth the wait. Roberto Carlos, in his second season with the club, belts a shot at goal which Iuliano blocks and unwisely tries to control. The ball squirms free in the area and Mijatovic resolves the mess in two touches – stretching his right foot out to take the ball beyond the prostrate defender then delicately stroking the ball with his left foot into the top corner before the angle runs out on him. It all seems so simple – a two-touch resolution to end the 32-year wait. A week later, Lorenzo Sanz and his directors visited a Madrid cemetery with the cup, to place it briefly on Bernabéu's grave.

But they had only finished fourth in the league, and the German Jupp Heynckes' brief but significant reign ended in the summer. He remains the only manager in the modern game to be sacked within one month of his team winning the European Cup. The event smacked of trouble at the mill, despite the win in Amsterdam, a suspicion confirmed when José Antonio Camacho, the legendary ex-defender, was offered the job but only stayed 22 days, the briefest rule in the club's history. After a fight with Sanz's 'number three', Juan Antonio Onieva, over the club's future transfer policy, things were said that made it clear to Camacho that his appointment had not been greeted with universal enthusiasm by the board. Suspecting (correctly) that he was unlikely to be given much support for his initial plans for restructuring the team, he walked out, saying that it was better to do so after 22 days than after three months. In less than six months he was manager of the national team and the Dutchman Guus Hiddink was installed in the vacant hot-seat at the Bernabéu.

When Ramón Mendoza gave up the crown in 1995, the club's members decided to vote in Lorenzo Sanz, a property speculator who had acted as Mendoza's treasurer. Looking back, this was not an entirely sound reason for handing him the top job, but in presidential elections it is often a case of Hobson's choice, as Barcelona found to their dismay when Nuñez retired and presented them with the virtually unchallenged candidature of the controversial Joan Gaspart. Sanz, committed though he was to the job, never quite managed to convince the *Madrileño* public, suffering poorly in comparison to Mendoza for a lack of style and an unfortunately shady appearance. There were also rumours during his presidency that the taxmen were on his trail, and that some of his dealings outside the orbit of the club had been less than honest. Nothing was ever brought to light, but the constant rumours and allegations did nothing to enhance the image of the club, weighed down by an accumulated debt of some 170 million pounds – although official figures quoted always placed the figure at 60 million. In late 1999 Sanz survived a boardroom coup brought about by the financial problems and the deteriorating image of the club, where the accusations centred around the so-called 'Ferrari' boys in the squad. The fingers were being pointed at Seedorf, Karembeu, Suker and Panucci, with Seedorf the alleged gang-leader. The phrase *'Menos millones más cojones'* (Less money, more commitment) had been heard echoing around the stadium after Toshack, brought back from Turkey for a second spell to sort out the dressing-room, had failed to get the European Champions beyond the quarter-finals. Toshack had begun his second spell at the club by announcing that he was in no way 'worried' by the job he faced, since according to him:

> It's the people on the dole queue who are worried. People like me have it easy. I don't have to pay for anything. I fly for free, the club pays my car and my rent. I get up late in the mornings and saunter down to the training ground, do a couple of hours and then that's it. Footballers have an easy life. They've no idea what it's really like out there.

The press loved it, leading with headlines the following day on how Toshack was defending the poor and how he would bring back the work ethic to the club. Sanz had been smiling by his side during the press conference, but the grin was soon wiped off his face when it became clear that Toshack's hard-man approach was simply making matters worse. When Davor Suker flew to London for the weekend and brought back a teddy bear for his high-profile actress girlfriend Ana Obregon, Toshack joked to the press that on his wages, the Croatian could have been a little more generous. Suker took offence, but when the players spoke out publicly in his defence the image of solidarity amongst them was immediately dispelled when Ivan Campo and Seedorf were involved in a punch-up during training. Toshack had to go, and when he was reported by the tabloid *Marca* as having criticised the presidential regime at the club for incompetence, he refused to go back on what he had said, producing the famous phrase *'Habrá cerdos volando sobre el Bernabéu antes de que yo rectifique'* (You'll see pigs flying over the Bernabéu before I take back what I said). Sanz, on reading this quotation in *Marca*, called Toshack into his office. The conversation between the two men, later narrated by Toshack, was in many ways the catalyst for a new beginning at the club – of happier times to coincide with the millennium and the subsequent centenary celebrations. Sanz, in a classic case of misinterpreting a foreign idiomatic phrase, showed

Toshack the headline and asked 'John. Did you really say this?' Toshack, laconic as ever, replied 'Yes, boss. That's how we say it in Welsh.' Sanz pulled out a letter of resignation from the drawer, already typed up and ended the conversation with 'Sorry, John – but you'll have to go. Would you mind signing here?' Of course, Toshack signed nothing, and later won considerable damages from the club on the grounds of premature dismissal (as opposed to resignation).

So ended a curious period in Real Madrid's history, but one which was also conditioned by the tendency of the postmodern football scene to blow up every single fissure in the club with the dynamite stockpiled by the press. Spain's football tabloid scene, though dominated by a Madrid-friendly pack, is also split down the middle by the claims and counter-claims, insults and counter-insults, that are swapped daily by *Marca* (Madrid) and *Sport* (Barcelona), or by the Madrid-based *As* and the Catalan *El Mundo Deportivo*. Of course, what they report can also be accurate, and in the case of the mid- to late 1990s it has to be said that Real Madrid, Raúl excepted, were not exactly demonstrating their famous *casta*, in spite of the celebrations surrounding the 1998 victory. The club was unused to washing its dirty linen in public, Bernabéu having famously kept all bitching and disputes within the walls. But since Mendoza's flashy star had begun to fade, the problems had been steadily mounting. To cap it all, when FIFA announced in 1999 that clubs entering the Champions League would subsequently have to prove their financial sea-worthiness, the prospect of Madrid being barred from the competition in whose waters most of their money could be made was to prove decisive. And the fact that Lorenzo Sanz had once accused Barcelona's Luis Figo of being 'the best actor outside Hollywood' in reference to his alleged tendency to dive, was to prove even more decisive. Figo, one of the main reasons why Barcelona had taken the league title back in 1998 and 1999, was approached in the early summer of 2000 and asked whether he would consider a move to Madrid. He allegedly replied that he would, just so long as Sanz was not there. And so the famous plot was hatched.

Figo watched Real Madrid win *La Octava* (the eighth) on television in May 2000, on the famous occasion in which two sides from the same country disputed the main European title for the first time. Madrid beat Valencia 3–0 in Paris in a game which spoke volumes for Spanish club football and in which Raúl once again excelled, sealing the game with the final goal after running alone from behind the halfway line, taking the ball around his former colleague Cañizares and squeezing the ball in from a rapidly narrowing angle. The smile on the face of the avuncular Vicente Del Bosque, brought in to pour oil on the waters of the post-Toshack storm, basically said it all. Del Bosque, the defensive midfielder who had played for the club with distinction up to 1984, had been brought in before as caretaker, but the win in Paris extended his contract and gave him the chance to settle down longer term. Though not strictly a local boy (he was born in Salamanca) he was considered Madrid through and through. Besides, the players liked his less confrontational approach and responded to his implicit trust of them. The young midfielder, Guti, after several weeks under Del Bosque's management, made the interesting remark that it was nice to play again in an atmosphere where the players were not automatically assumed to be little schoolboys in need of a regime of iron discipline. Del Bosque was from the *cantera*, the mystical Spanish football concept that confers a special status on those who are 'part of the local tradition'. These people, like Muñoz and Molowny before, are considered to be steadying influences, equipped with backroom knowledge and a locally flavoured savvy that temporary outsiders can never acquire. In times of greatest upheaval, they are sought out as calming influences, not as figures of radical new inspiration. Their days are always numbered, since the demands of powerful clubs like Madrid usually culminate in a high-profile signing to placate the impatience of the supporters. Del Bosque went on to win Real their 29th league title in 2003, but was then sacrificed on the altar of marketing. Everybody's favourite uncle no longer belonged in the new context ushered in by Beckham, and he was cast aside in a new sweep of the presidential broom. Del Bosque was a competent manager who was adept in his handling of the human side of the job, but president Pérez wanted someone new, choosing the Portuguese Carlos Quieroz, Ferguson's Number 2 at Old Trafford. Not exactly high-profile, but at least he knew Beckham.

Back in 2000, Figo had seen no problem in coming to a club that was managed by Del Bosque, particularly after suffering the rather less humane approach of Louis Van Gaal. There was also some evidence to suggest that he was less than keen on the new regime of Joan Gaspart. But his move to Madrid stands out in the recent history of the club and was easily the most significant hullabaloo since the Di Stéfano affair. Similar moves by Schuster and Laudrup had caused both players problems, particularly Laudrup, but Figo was considered the best player in the world at the time, and had the Catalans in his pocket. His move was considered to be an affront to their very soul. They simply could not believe it.

With Lorenzo Sanz on the ropes, one of the new candidates for the job, industrial property magnate Florentino Pérez, leaked to the press that if he were elected, he would bring Figo over to Madrid. It smacked of Mendoza's move for Schuster back in the 1980s, but Pérez was virtually unknown in football circles and thus unlikely to pull off such an outrageous coup. His second claim, that he would wipe off Real's debt if elected, also seemed to belong to the realms of science fiction, but, as is now known, the man was true to his word. Figo came, was treated with unprecedented hostility on his return to the Camp Nou that same October, but helped them win back the league from Deportivo. Only Bayern Munich stopped them from getting to the final of the Champions Cup that season, and the smile was back on the face of the Bernabéu. It got broader still when Pérez controversially sold off the old Ciudad Deportiva training facilities to the local council, wiping off the club's massive debts overnight. The facilities, which have various hectares of land, are to be developed by private speculators, an outcome which has led to various accusations that taxpayers' money has been used to eliminate a football club's debt. The complaints seem justified in the sense that the city of Madrid has at least two other football teams of substance, Atlético Madrid and Rayo Vallecano, two institutions that boast plenty of supporters between them. The fact that their taxes have in effect subsidised the building of the new training ground (nearer to the airport) and facilitated the purchase of Zinedine Zidane are political matters of some importance, but this book prefers to avoid the issue for the simple reason that it is not a short-term debate. The accusation that Real Madrid are 'the team of the government' seems to be once again in fashion, especially since the town council administration of Madrid belongs to the *Partido Popular*, the party in government whose president, José María Aznar, is a life-long supporter of the club.

Besides, it would be churlish to end the chapter on a sour note. After an agonising centenary year in which the fabled treble of League, King's Cup and Champions League seemed to be fading before the club's eyes, up stepped Raúl again to save the day. With the King's Cup stolen from the Bernabéu on the big night and the league title won by Valencia, the emotionally charged semi-final of the Champions Cup against Barcelona simply had to be won. In the opening leg at the Camp Nou, Barcelona were predictably doing most of the attacking, with Madrid on the back foot. Suddenly, Raúl, anonymous up to that point, received a pass to feet from his own defence. In one move, he swivelled and placed a perfectly angled ball into space on the right flank of Barça's defence.

Zidane, appearing from nowhere, hurtled forward and placed a looping shot over the goalkeeper and into the net. It was the killer blow, even before McManaman made things sure in the second half. In the return leg, Raúl himself sentenced the show, hammering in a wonderful shot from outside the area with unusual venom.

The final in Glasgow, which a 76-year-old Alfredo Di Stéfano was invited to attend, was a fitting arena for such an emotional send-off to the centenary. Raúl and Zidane did the trick again, and the story finished happily ever after.

11. BRAND IT LIKE BECKHAM

The season that followed the centenary, 2002–03, was expected to feature a few hangovers. Some saw it as a new beginning, a symbolic year zero – whilst others thought it might be the year in which the club's bloated sense of its own importance would finally cause the whole institution to begin to eat itself alive. But by the end of August Florentino Pérez pulled off the third coup of his mandate and signed the re-born Ronaldo, fresh from his World Cup triumph and apparently happy to leave Italy, despite the reluctance of his footballing wife to leave Milan and the rumblings in the Italian press regarding the player's lack of gratitude to a club (Inter) that had stood by him during his years in dry dock. There was quite a hullabaloo, most of it focusing on the dodgy knee, the size of the transfer fee (45 million dollars) and the more important fact that the club already had a decent centre-forward in Morientes with a very promising youngster, Portillo, also waiting in the shadows for his turn. Raúl, Morientes' best mate, was said to disapprove, and Spain's most respected journalists went into the usual frenzy of speculation as to whether the Brazilian and Raúl would be compatible. Significantly, Raúl was injured when Ronaldo finally made his debut, five weeks into the season at home to Alavés. Coming on in the 64th minute as substitute, he required exactly 40 seconds and two touches to register his first goal for Real. Chesting down Roberto Carlos' cross he thumped the ball into the Fondo Sur goal and ran up to the advertising boards in something resembling a state of ecstasy. Thirteen minutes later he got another one, and although poor Alavés were to finish the season with the league's worst defensive figures, back then it looked pretty impressive. The Madrileño press, up to that point more than a little worried by rumours of the player's lack of fitness, tubby appearance and alleged distress at all the question marks, simply exploded with incontinent relief at the reconfirmation that he could actually play football and score goals. The tabloid *Marca* led with a memorable header '*Debuta madre!*' ('The Mother of all Debuts!') but punning on the foul-mouthed phrase 'De puta madre', which can be either positive or negative, depending on your intonation. It was a headline worthy of The Sun in its heyday, and it ushered in the new Ronaldo era.

His season was to be far from an easy ride, however, with his contribution to the team's overall playing patterns constantly questioned by fans and press alike, added to the further pressure exerted on him by the resentment of Morientes and Portillo at their lack of involvement. The famous Argentine César Menotti, briefly brought back into the limelight as a possible replacement for Barça's Van Gaal, commented on Spanish radio that Ronaldo 'No tiene ni idea de fútbol' (Has no idea about what football is) and that Real had wasted their money. But by the end of the season he had scored 23 goals in the league – including two in the final game to clinch the title – and had scored a sublime hat-trick at Old Trafford in the Champions League quarter-finals in a performance that saw the Manchester faithful applaud him off the field when he was substituted near the end. So moved were the Spanish club by this gesture that Florentino Pérez proposed to the Spanish FA that they award the Old Trafford supporters with the medal of the Prince of Asturias for 'services to sportsmanship'. They didn't take up his offer, but the fact of the matter was that by the end of the season no-one was too worried about the so-called lack of understanding with Raúl, and as far as the initial expense was concerned, the happy news from the Bernabéu marketing department was that sales of the number 11 shirt bearing his name had comfortably covered the cost of his transfer.

Ronaldo, then, brought along with him a whole package of virtues that finally silenced the critics. However, not to put too fine a point on it, even the player himself has admitted that he is no oil painting – and back in the summer of 2002 this was still relatively unimportant. In the first seven hours of Ronaldo's shirt being put up for sale in the official Real Madrid retail outlets, 2,000 were sold. Flash forward ten months to 2 July 2003, and in the first four hours of trading in the same shops David Beckham's number 23 shirt shifted 8,000. Zidane, wonderful player though he is, only moved 300 on his first day – an obvious sign of how things were changing.

Beckham's was the face that launched a thousand articles. In a sense it is difficult to add much more to what has been said and written about his thermo-nuclear transfer, but certain things did stand out, particularly here on the ground in Spain. In the first place, the transfer contained echoes, albeit more muted ones, of the famous Figo snatch in 2000, when Pérez brought him over from Barcelona in a deal that stunned the Catalans and delighted *Madridistas* far and wide. It was the beginning of a new aggressive era of *Madrileño* dominance over their old enemy, both on and off the field. The history of the two clubs' rivalry is one of distinct phases in which one of the clubs has lorded it over the other, maximising the propaganda benefits and twisting the knife as much as is permitted within strictly legal boundaries. Within the particular synergy of the two clubs' mutual hostility, it has been logically impossible for one of them to be happy at the same time as the other was celebrating. Thus when the young Catalan lawyer Joan Laporta announced in June 2003 in the hustings for the vacant Barça presidency that he would sign Beckham if he were elected, the news catapulted him into pole position and eventually won him the job, precisely two weeks before Real Madrid announced to the world that the Englishman was destined to be wearing a white (Adidas, of course) shirt for the next four years of his career. Laporta shrugged off the news, claiming that it had been impossible to even talk to Beckham to discuss a deal, but that it was no problem. Other players would come along. In a sense, he had little room for complaint, since the prospect of Beckham had had the desired effect on his candidacy, but in Madrid the refusal of the Beckham camp to even consider the Catalans was seen as a juicy snub to the club not only for footballing reasons but for cultural ones too.

In pure sporting terms, Barça were not even assured of a UEFA Cup place during the period when they were attempting to woo Beckham. They subsequently qualified when Real Madrid clinched their 29th league title on the last day by beating Athletic Bilbao, thereby depriving their Basque opponents of a place and handing it ironically to Barcelona. After such a poor season, it was unlikely that Beckham – no fool when it comes to such matters, would fancy taking on the role of saviour for a club clearly in the doldrums. He is a team player, an occasionally brilliant but integral part of the type of unit represented by Manchester United. You can't expect him to start the revolution, and as such he was never going to dip his toes in the turbulent waters of Catalonia. Best leave that to Ronaldinho. Besides, the election of the new president did not necessarily mean that the club was about to either become solvent or cast off the image of internal warfare and instability that had characterised its lot during the 2002–03 season, despite their impressive showing in the Champions League. In contrast, the smooth PR machine that Madrid had in place, coupled with the sexiness of their financial whack and the gallery of superstars already installed could hardly have failed to tempt the Beckhams – Victoria having been present during each stage of the negotiations and clearly a player in the field, as it were. Nowadays it's no longer a case of the 'missus' packing the bags and meekly following her man to his new destination. In fact the Spanish press were fascinated by the influence that Beckham's wife clearly wielded, popping in an old-fashioned 'She wears the trousers' on the day after the official presentation.

This may well be true, but Beckham has never made any secret about the fact that the relationship involves, at best, joint decisions. And good for him. But the issue was a significant one when the more cultural questions over the transfer came into play. The Spanish have never been so class-obsessed as the British, but they have always been sensitive to imagery. The fact that both Beckham and his wife are products of London's working-class means little to them. Victoria's 'Posh' nickname has always confused them anyway, the Spanish logically assuming that she belongs to the middle-class. The fact that her father was an electrician who drove her to work in a Rolls Royce (hence her nickname) might not mean much to them either, but their instant sun-kissed glamour and the ease with which they handled the absurd fuss that was made of them during their brief, initial stay in the Spanish capital will have marked the Beckhams down in Spanish eyes as more Marbella than Madrid, as instant fodder for the centre-spread of the country's glossy magazine *Hola* (Hello), a publication about Spain's idle rich which is read exclusively at the hairdresser's. Barcelona is more about being cool, more about innovation and trends. The Beckhams may be many things, but they would be unlikely to describe themselves as 'cool', whatever the term means. The added complexity of Catalan society with its bicultural tensions (interesting though they may be) and its more politically demanding society might have exposed the English couple's frailties in ways that Madrid's straightforward, more patriarchal personality is unlikely to. Beckham's choice of Madrid seems a million years away from the fuss that was made over Johan Cruyff's explicit political rejection of the club, back in 1973 when Franco was still around. Madrid as a city and Real Madrid as a club have lightened up their act considerably since those darker days, and as mentioned in the earlier section of this book, the city is a friendly and welcoming place. Beckham is also a nice guy. The press noted straight away that he was *simpático* (affable), that he was a baby-kisser, a humble chap despite all the circus that surrounded him. This came as something of a relief, since the initial rumours were that the rest of the Madrid squad were none too chuffed at the prospect of his arrival, marketing army in tow. Despite the high-profile nature of Pérez' three previous signings, both Figo and Zidane in particular were quiet, unassuming men, little given to the soundbite or the late-night paparazzi shot. Even Ronaldo came married this time around, ensuring to some extent that he might throw off his previous reputation for being a bit of a lad. Significantly, Beckham was presented as a stable family man, holding the wife's hand and saying all the right things at the right time. All he had to do was to convince the more doubting *Madridistas* that he could play football too.

From the perspective of the summer of 2003, it is impossible to predict how Barcelona's fans will react to Beckham when he visits the Camp Nou, but jokes quickly appeared in the Spanish press regarding Beckham's tendency to take corners, thus relieving Figo of the job. One of the most notorious *derbis* in the history of the Spanish league took place in November 2002 when Real visited Barça and Figo was subjected to an even worse reception than on the occasion of his first return. *Marca*, once again the quickest off the mark, dubbed it 'The Derby of Shame!', and featured some of the objects hurled at the Portuguese international as he attempted to take a corner, an act delayed for a full ten minutes as Roberto Carlos led the players off the field in protest. The head of a suckling pig was the object that captured the most attention, followed by a bottle of JB Whisky, free advertising for which the company were no doubt grateful. Beckham's very affability may spare him the same reception when he lines up to take the first corner there, but you never know. Hell hath no fury like a Catalan scorned.

But the transfer was more about cash than culture. Manchester United, fearing that they would have eventually lost their prize asset to a Bosman in 2005 decided to liquidate their major asset, despite the further marketing opportunities that were likely to have come about from their summer tour of the States in 2003. Instead, Beckham's signing for Real Madrid was announced to the press exactly five hours before the famous couple took off on a promotional tour of the Far East, first stop Japan. The timing was a master-stroke in financial terms, changing in an instant the Japanese market from red to white. It suddenly looked as though Alex Ferguson's alleged dislike of Beckham's wife and his disapproval of the player's penchant for the catwalk had finally cost the English club its place at the top of the league – of the world's richest clubs, that is. And to twist the knife further, the eventual adoption of shirt number 23 – allegedly proposed by Valdano because it was the same number as worn by Michael Jordan – was another ingenious move designed to interest the Americans. It did of course, all the major American dailies featuring the '23' dispatch on their front pages the day after Beckham's army of advisers, apparently reluctant at first, finally gave the number the thumbs-up. Such media prominence for the theme of soccer, especially the European version, was virtually unprecedented in the United States. The subsequent outburst of absurd speculation as to the mystical properties of the chosen number, a phenomenon that reached its nadir at the discovery that the phrase 'David and Victoria Beckham' contained 23 letters, was best left to those who had nothing better to do. But it sold the papers, and probably kept us all happier for another day – the function, in the end, of the beautiful game itself. And when all is said and done, Beckham is better to watch in football kit than in Dolce & Gabbana.

Indeed, with regard to the matter of mere football, and of how the team will manage with such a surfeit of stars, the jury is unlikely to deliver any premature verdicts. Nobody really knows how the new story will develop. The blizzard that has been Real Madrid, the white storm that has raged for so long in the skies of Europe's football may one day be reduced to a whisper, a small breeze that once blew with hurricane force. It seems unlikely, but it is possible. Having been officially named 'Best Team of the 20th Century', Real Madrid may well have their work cut out to retain this title – won by a combination of accidents, luck, sweat, inspiration, political influence, brilliance and perhaps the most important aspect of them all – the sheer will to win. Loathe them or love them, it is difficult to deny the club their special twinkle in the firmament, their place at the top of the pile. They have given a lot of people a lot of pleasure, and long may they continue to do so.

Phil Ball, July 2003

TABLE OF STATISTICS

REAL MADRID: FACTS & FIGURES

Most appearances for club: Sanchís (710)
Longest serving manager: Miguel Muñoz
Biggest home league win: 11–2 versus Elche, 7 Feb 1960
Biggest league win away: 1–7 versus Zaragoza, 12 Sept 1987
Biggest domestic cup win: 11–1 versus Barcelona, 13 June 1943
Biggest home league win over Barcelona: 8–2, 3 Feb 1935
Biggest win in European Cup: 8–0 versus Sevilla, 23 Jan 1958

MOST APPEARANCES – TOP FIVE:

Manolo Sanchís	710
Carlos Santillana	645
Paco Gento	602
José Antonio Camacho	577
Pirri	561

MOST GOALS – TOP FIVE:

Alfredo Di Stéfano	307
Carlos Santillana	290
Ferenc Puskas	239
Raúl	210
Hugo Sánchez	207

EUROPEAN PLAYERS OF THE YEAR

Alfredo Di Stéfano	1957
Raymond Kopa	1958
Alfredo Di Stéfano	1959
Luis Figo	2000
Zinedane Zidane	2001
Ronaldo	2002

LEAGUE RECORDS

Most league titles won: 29

Most games won: 1,266

Most consecutive wins: 15 (1960–61)

Most goals in a season: 107 (1989–90)

Most home goals in a season: 78 (1989–90)

Player with most league titles won: Paco Gento (12)

Player with most European Cups: Paco Gento (6)

Highest scorer in a season: Hugo Sánchez, 38 (1989–90)

Most home wins in a season: 18 (1987–88)

Most consecutive away wins: 7 (1960–61)

Only team to play an entire season undefeated: 1931–32

President with most league titles: Santiago Bernabéu (16)

Manager with most league titles: Miguel Muñoz (9)

League won by the highest margin of points: 12 (1960–61, 1962–63, 1974–75)

All games in a season won at home on three occasions: (1959–60, 1962–63, 1985–86)

Highest scoring team in the league since 1928–29 (4,528)

Longest time undefeated at home: 8 years (121 games, from 1957 to 1965)

ALSO WITH MOST . . .

League titles (29)

European Cups (9)

League Top Scorers (22)

Best defence records (15)

European final appearances (16)

Spectators for the pre-season presentation of the new squad (120,000 in July 1996)

Goals scored in a domestic Cup final (6, against Castilla, 1980)

Most points in a league season (80, in 2000–01)

LIST OF MAJOR TROPHIES WON:

League titles (28)

1932, 1933, 1954, 1955, 1957, 1958, 1961, 1962, 1963, 1964, 1965, 1967, 1968, 1969, 1972, 1975, 1976, 1978, 1979, 1980, 1986, 1987, 1988, 1989, 1990, 1995, 1997, 2001, 2003

European Cups (9)

1956, 1957, 1958, 1959, 1960, 1966, 1998, 2000, 2002

King's and Generalísimo's Cups (17)

1905, 1906, 1907, 1908, 1917, 1934, 1936, 1946, 1947, 1962, 1970, 1974, 1975, 1980, 1982, 1989, 1993

Spanish 'Supercups' (6)

1988, 1989, 1990, 1993, 1997, 2001

Intercontinental Cups (2)

1960, 1998

UEFA Cups (2)

1985, 1986

League Cup (1)

1985

LOSING FINALISTS IN:

European Cup (3)

1962, 1964, 1981

King's and Generalísimo's Cup (14)

1929, 1930, 1933, 1940, 1943, 1958, 1960, 1961, 1968, 1979, 1983, 1990, 1992, 2002

Cup-Winners' Cup (2)

1971, 1983

Domestic 'Doubles' (4)

1962, 1975, 1980, 1989

League and European Cup 'Doubles' (2)

1957, 1958

OVERALL STATISTICS, 1929–2003

Played	*Won*	*Drawn*	*Lost*	*Goals For*	*Goals Against*
2,179	1,245	463	471	4,528	2,535

OTHER INTERESTING FACTS

- First player to score a goal in official competition for Real Madrid: Arthur Johnson, 13 May 1902 versus Barcelona
- First game between Real Madrid and Barcelona: Real Madrid 1 Barcelona 3, 13 May 1902
- Number of players who have turned out in official competition for Real Madrid between March 1902 and July 2003: Total 1,219
- Spanish region with most supporters' clubs (*peñas*): Andalucía (352)
- Spanish region with fewest supporters' clubs: the Basque Country (12)
- Oldest living *socio* (club member): Paula Carrillo (Born 12.1.1900)
- Worst league finish: 11th (from 14) 1947–48.
- Club's most capped player for Spain: Fernando Hierro (90)
- Teams most played against in European competitions: Internazionale (15), Bayern Munich (12), Anderlecht (10)
- Teams most played against in Domestic Cup: Athletic Bilbao (53), Atlético Madrid (35), Barcelona (28)
- Teams most played against in League: Barcelona (145), Athletic Bilbao (143), Espanyol (137)
- Overall league record against Barcelona:

P	W	D	L	GF	GA
145	63	27	55	242	219

- Teams defeated most times by Real Madrid: Espanyol (77 occasions), Valencia (71), Atlético Madrid (70)
- Team that have defeated Real Madrid most times: Barcelona (55 occasions), Athletic Bilbao (46), Valencia (38)
- Overall league classification, 1929–2002: (Top Ten – based on points accumulated playing in First Division)

  1. Real Madrid   (4,068)
  2. Barcelona   (3,022)
  3. Athletic Bilbao   (2,612)
  4. Atlético Madrid   (2,523)
  5. Valencia   (2,487)
  6. Espanyol   (2,116)
  7. Real Sociedad   (1,998)
  8. Sevilla   (1,929)
  9. Zaragoza   (1,692)
  10. Celta   (1,386)

BIBLIOGRAPHY

Burns, Jimmy, *Barça, A People's Passion* (Bloomsbury 1999)
Carr, Raymond, *Modern Spain 1875–1980* (Oxford University Press 1980)
Cresswell, P. & Evans, S. *European Football, A Fans' Handbook* (The Rough Guide)
Fundación Real Madrid, Archives.
García-Candau, Julian, *Historia de un desamor* (El País/Aguilar 1996)
Glanville, Brian, *Champions of Europe* (Guinness, Enfield 1991)
Gonzáles, Luis Miguel, *Alrededor de La Historia*, (Fundación Real Madrid, Everest 2002)
Gonzáles, Luis Miguel, *Cien años de Leyenda*, (Fundación Real Madrid, Everest 2002)
Hesse-Lichtenberger, Ulrich *Tor! The Story of German Football* (WSC Books 2002)
Hooper, John, *The New Spaniards* (Penguin 1995)
Inglis, Simon, *The Football Grounds of Europe* (Willow Books 1990)
Kuper, Simon, *Football Against the Enemy* (Orion 1994)
Malcon & Smith (eds), *The Real Madrid Book of Football* (Souvenir Press 1961)
Partington, Angela (ed), *The New Oxford Dictionary of Quotations* (Oxford University Press 1996)
Prados de la Plaza, Luis, *Real Madrid*, Centenario (Silex 2001)
Thomas, Hugh, *The Spanish Civil War* (Penguin 1990)
Varela, Andre Merce, *Josep Samitier* (Barcanova 1998)

PERIODICALS CONSULTED AND REFERENCES:
As
Classic Moments from a Century of Sport (Hodder Headline AudioBooks)
El Diario del Real Madrid (Supplement in *El Mundo*)
El Heraldo del Sport
El País
La Razón
Marca – Supplemento del Centenario
Nuevo Mundo
The Manchester Guardian

INDEX

ABC 146, 170, 184
Aberdeen 174
AC Milan 115, 120, 129, 140, 187, 188
Adidas 209
Agnelli, Umberto 138
Aguirre, Gonzalo 90
Ajax 150–151, 161–162
Alavés 22, 75, 83, 87, 207
Albania 178
Alcalá (Street) 46, 49, 50
Alcantará, Paulino 67
Alfonso XIII, King 53, 56, 69, 72, 80
Ali, Muhammad 82, 105
Alicante 160
Alonso, Carlos 91–92
Alonso, Juanito 119
Amancio 138, 140, 141, 145, 146, 147, 148, 152, 154, 157, 159, 167, 168, 169, 176
Anderlecht 115, 124, 138, 148, 155, 167, 171, 183
Anoeta 23
Antwerp (Olympics) 67, 88
Aranguren, Sotero 67
Aranzabal, Augustín 26
Araquistain, José 138
Arenas de Getxo 62, 64, 69, 71, 75
Argentina (country) 16, 56, 65, 72, 103, 106, 114, 169, 174
Argentina (team) 110, 145
As (Newspaper) 95, 202, 217
Asociation Sportiva Francesa 50
Athens 159, 174
Athletic Bilbao 43, 44, 45, 46, 52, 53, 56, 61, 62, 63, 64, 65, 67, 68, 74, 75, 76, 77, 78, 83, 84, 87, 88, 94, 95, 96, 98, 99, 109, 111, 122, 124, 128, 129, 154, 155, 174, 176, 209
Athletic de Madrid 69, 75, 76, 77, 80, 90, 93,
Atienza, Angel 129
Atlético Aviación 37, 89, 93–95, 97

Atlético Madrid 20, 29, 37, 61, 62, 70, 81, 89, 93, 105, 122, 131, 138, 154, 158, 161, 181, 185, 186, 189, 192, 193, 196, 203
Atocha 23
Aznar, José María 33, 204

Bahamonde, Ángel 46
Barcelona (city) 31, 33, 35, 36, 37, 44, 61, 74, 78, 79, 82, 85, 86, 88, 90, 91, 107, 157, 163, 179
Barcelona (team) 8, 9, 23, 31, 38, 43, 44, 54, 56, 63, 64, 75, 93, 97, 99, 107, 111, 113, 122, 131, 155, 164, 169, 175, 183, 189, 192, 196, 202, 209
Barinaga, Sabino 98
Basque Country 24, 33, 34, 53, 61, 66, 99, 157, 165, 174
Basques 20, 21, 23, 25, 35, 61, 64, 78, 86
Bastión 37
Bayer Leverkusen 27, 134
Bayern Munich 24, 165, 187, 188, 199, 203
Beatles, The 7, 132, 143, 144, 146
Beckenbauer, Franz 142, 163
Beckham, David 7, 76, 195, 197, 203, 207–12
Beckham, Victoria 210, 211
Beenhakker, Leo 187, 188
Belgium 65, 81, 171
Bermejillo, Luis 46, 53, 54
Bernabéu, Santiago
    attitude to Barcelona 74, 86, 92, 96, 97
    background, 64–65
    Civil War 82, 91–92
    death 15,16, 157, 169–171
    personality 65–66, 71, 74, 76, 77, 100, 104–105, 114, 118, 123–124, 128, 129, 142, 158, 160–161

player 66, 67
quotations 76, 92, 96, 104, 123, 135, 137, 160
with Franco regime 88, 91, 96, 118, 122
Bernabéu Stadium 9, 10, 13, 15–17, 22, 27, 29, 31, 33, 41, 50, 54, 98, 109, 120, 122, 125, 136, 144, 152, 162, 164, 168, 171, 180, 184, 191, 201
Berraondo, José Angel 68
Best, George 106, 149, 151, 152, 171
Betancort, Antonio Rodrigo 148, 159
Betis 29, 34, 75, 88, 140
Bilbao (city) 25, 36, 64, 69, 79, 80
Birmingham City 71
Blair, Tony 34
Blanchflower, Jackie 125
Boavista 29
Boca Juniors 109
Borussia Mönchengladbach 163, 168, 169, 171
Boskov, Vujadin 163, 169, 171, 174
Breitner, Paul 156, 165–166, 168
Bru, Paco 67, 87–88, 94
Buckingham, Victor 154
Buenos Aires 109
bullfighting 8, 9, 50, 127
Burns, Jimmy 95
Busby Babes 124, 126
Busby, Matt 125, 126, 149
Butragueño, Emilio 36, 66, 77, 106, 110, 147, 159, 171, 173–174, 175, 176–183, 186–188, 189, 193, 195, 196
Buyo, Francisco 188
Cádiz 173
Calderón, Antonio 100, 160
Caldéron, Vincente 106
Camacho, José Antonio 156, 157, 166, 169, 171, 173, 199
Camp Nou 22, 24, 37, 45, 81, 137, 154, 165, 203, 204, 211
Campo de Estrada 49
Campo, Iván 201
Canales, Máximo 139
Canal Plus 197
Canario, Darcy 136
Cano, Iñaki 150
Cano, José María 14
Cantabria 73, 113
Caracas 139, 141

Cardiff City 158, 159
Cardus, Neville 103
Carlos Ortiz, Luis de 170
Carlos, Roberto 16, 24, 199, 207, 211
Carniglia, Luis 128, 129, 134
Castaño, Heliodoro 119
Castell, Pepe 70
Castellana (Avenue) 14, 29, 41, 49, 62, 98, 131
Castile 73, 75
Castilla 173, 176, 179, 180, 188
Catalans 35, 46, 49, 74, 78, 81, 85, 152, 158, 170, 188, 198, 209, 210, 211
Catalonia 25, 34, 37, 73, 157, 158, 165, 174, 209
catenaccio 110, 140
Celades, Albert 20
César Sánchez Dominguez 26
Chamartín Stadium 70–71, 74, 76, 80, 92, 93, 94, 97–98, 115, 157
Chamberi 32, 34
Champions League 22, 23, 27, 36, 54, 150, 194, 198, 201, 204
Charles, John 138
Charlton, Robert 19, 106, 110, 126, 149, 162
Chelsea 17, 114, 115, 151, 159
Cibeles fountain 49, 70, 84
Cieza 157
Ciriaco, Errasti 83, 84, 87, 92
Ciudad Deportiva 127, 203
Ciudad Lineal 70
Civil War 71, 75, 76, 79, 82, 86, 88, 90–93, 156
Clark, Brian 159
Clemente, Javier 174, 183
Club Ciclista San Sebastían 62
Club Español de Foot Ball 53
Club Moderno 50, 60, 61
Club Retiro 50
Coleman, David 178
Compton, Denis 103
Conrad, Joseph 132
Copa del Generalísimo 93, 128
Corinthians 47
Cossío, Manuel 46
Costa Brava 40, 44
Cruyff, Johan
manager 189, 192
player 111, 142, 150–1, 153, 157–8, 161–4, 177, 210

Cuatro Caminos 68
Cunco, Julio 72
Cunningham, Lawrie 171
Cup-Winners' Cup 114, 151, 158, 174, 176

Dalglish, Kenny 171, 178
Daucik, Fernando 100
Davies, Barry 159
De Felipe, Pedro Eugenio 146, 156
De Gracia, Paco 193
De Paula, Oscar 27
De Pedro, Javier 26
Del Bosque, Vicente 26, 30, 77, 150, 157, 168, 197, 202–203
Del Sol, Luis 136, 138
Denmark (team) 177–178
Deportivo de La Coruña 9, 22, 45, 50, 54, 71, 181, 203
Derby County 167–168, 171
Didi (Waldyr Peréira) 136
Di Stéfano, Alfredo
   background 109–110
   early career 103, 104, 105, 109
   influence of 38, 55
   kidnapping 139–140
   manager 77, 114, 173–175, 180, 181
   personality 82, 105–107, 114, 117, 130, 134, 144–145, 183
   player 15, 16, 110, 111, 118, 120–121, 124, 133, 136, 138, 141, 147
   statistics 110, 129
   transfer scandal 86, 90, 108–109, 123
Domingo, Plácido 13, 21
Dream Team 92
Dynamo Kiev 161, 162

El Capricho 45, 49, 51
El Escorial 40
El Gran Guiñol 197
El Heraldo de Sport 52
El Nodo 111, 151, 167
El País 34, 92, 106, 119, 140
Elche 13, 135, 153
Ellis, Arthur 121, 136, 137
Escolá, José 88, 89, 95
Espanyol 23, 25, 27, 29, 37, 74, 80, 81, 82, 85
Espanyol de Madrid 47, 50
ETA 156, 158

Europa de Barcelona 75, 76, 78, 83
Eusebio 138, 141, 178

Fairs Cup 160, 161, 187
Federacíon Madrileña de Fútbol 61
Felipe II, King 40
Ferguson, Alex, 174, 195, 203, 211
Fernández, Enrique 113
Ferrol 40, 93
FIFA 8, 29, 108, 112, 135, 198, 201, 202
Figo, Luis 7, 16, 17, 18, 19, 20, 21, 24, 26, 72, 76, 82, 85, 196, 202–203, 209, 211
Fiorentina 125, 127, 158
Firth, Robert 84, 87
Foot Ball Sky 46–47, 53
Foulkes, William 125, 152
France Soir 121
Franco, General Francisco
   attitude to Real Madrid 15, 16, 33, 37, 40, 88, 94, 98, 104, 109, 113, 118, 127, 146, 152, 153
   death 69, 156, 157, 165–166

Galicia 40, 14, 40, 147
Gardel, Carlos 85
Gaspart, Joan 33, 36, 200, 203
Gemmill, Archie 167
Gento, Francisco (Paco) 76, 106, 113–114, 119, 120, 125, 127, 130, 138, 145, 151, 159–160
George, Charlie 167
Geremi 26
Getafe 29
Gimnástica 67
Giralt (Brothers) 60
Giralt, José 54, 59, 60, 63
Glasgow 124, 126, 132, 134, 171, 194, 204
Glasgow Celtic 126, 141, 142, 147, 149, 171, 174
Glasgow Rangers 133, 140
Gonzáles, Felipe 34
Gonzáles, Nacho 22
Gordillo, Rafael 185, 186
Gorostizaga, José 51
Granada 40, 163
Grasshoppers (Zurich) 127
Grimsby 17, 55
Grosso, Ramón 146, 147, 154, 157, 160
Guadarrama mountains 40

Guerra, Ricardo 37
Gullit, Ruud 188
Guruceta, Emilio 152, 154–155
Guti, José María 202

Hanappi, Gerhard 123
Hanot, Gabriel 112, 115, 117, 120, 153
Happel, Ernst 123, 124
Helguera, Iván 19, 26, 27
Heliodoro Rodríguez López Stadium 38
'Hello' (Magazine) 210
Hercules 160
Hernández, Pablo 83, 91
Herrera, Helenio 110, 131, 135,
    140–141, 148, 149
Hertza, Lippo 77, 83, 84
Heynckes, Jupp 30, 128, 199
Hibernian 15, 115, 120, 158
Hierro, Fernando 17, 24, 106, 110, 178,
    191, 197, 216
Hippodrome 53, 59, 62
Honved 112, 115, 130
Horn, Leo 127
Huracán 109

Iglesias, Julio 13
Infante Don Juan 70, 118
Institución Libre de Enseñanza 46
Internazionale 126, 140, 141, 148–149,
    162, 171, 183, 187, 207
Ipiña, Juan Antonio 128
Ipswich Town 164
Irureta, 'Chefo' 66

James, Rob 14
Japan, 211
Johnsen, Ronny 194
Johnson, Arthur 47–48, 50, 51, 52, 53,
    59
Jordan, Michael, 212
Juan de Borbón, King 118
Juan Carlos, King 106, 117, 170
Juanito (Juan Gómez) 169, 171, 173,
    174, 175, 187
Juventus 19, 29, 108, 131, 138, 144,
    158, 199

Kahn, Oliver 191
Kamper, Hans 44
Keeping, Michael 99, 100
Kennedy, Alan 171
KGB 184

Kilmarnock 148
King's Cup 50, 51, 59, 60, 63, 64, 67,
    69, 175, 176, 182, 185, 189, 204
Kocsis, Sandor 135, 136
Kopa, Raymond (Kopaszewski) 120,
    121–122, 125, 132, 136
Kovasevic, Darko 26
Kubala, Ladislao 22, 99, 100–101, 107,
    110, 134, 142
Kuper, Simon 110

La Taurina 51
Laporta, Joan 209
Las Palmas 13–22, 131, 153
Laudrup, Michael 82, 192, 193, 203
Lázaro, Felix 146, 147
Lazcano, Jaime 74, 76
Leafe, Reg 135, 136, 137
Leeds United 8, 9, 30, 198
Leganes 29
Lennon, John 143
L'Equipe 112, 121
Le Monde 121
Liverpool 171, 174
Lopez-Rekarte, Aitor 24
Loy, Egon 133

Mackay, David 167
Madrid (city) 14, 31–33, 35, 37, 46,
    210
Madrid FC 47, 50, 51, 53, 54, 59, 60,
    61, 62, 64–66, 68, 69
Madrid Foot Ball Club 47, 53
Madrid–Barcelona problems:
    corruption theories 135–137,
        152–153, 155
    culture 9, 10, 31, 33, 35, 49, 56, 80,
        82–83, 85, 87, 131, 157
    notorious games 22, 53, 67, 76, 78,
        84, 85, 88, 95, 128, 134–137,
        152–153, 204, 211
    politics 24, 33, 79, 81, 90, 93–94
Madridista (concept of) 31, 33–34, 38
Madrileño 31–32, 34–35, 39–41, 65, 70,
    79, 80, 138, 153, 179, 184
Madrileño press 79, 136, 141, 162, 188
Maier, Sepp 168
Maine Road 124
Manchester Evening News 125
Manchester United 14, 30, 31, 34, 124,
    129, 148, 149, 150, 151, 162, 178,
    199, 209

Maradona, Diego 106, 110, 111, 153, 166, 173, 175, 177, 183, 187, 188
Marca 84, 99, 106, 113, 144, 147, 169, 181, 201, 207
Maria Cristina, Queen 70
Marquitos, Marcos Alonso 120, 127, 129, 133
Marshall Plan 99
Mateos, Enrique 121, 125, 127, 132
Mazzola, Sandro 140
McIlvanney, Hugh 105
McManaman, Steve 20–22, 24
Meléndez, Adolfo 65, 68
Mendoza, Ramón 170, 178, 181, 184–186, 187, 188, 192, 199, 200
Mengotti, Adolfo 71
Menotti, César 208
Mestalla Stadium 74
Metropolitano Stadium 70, 93, 95, 97, 99, 131
Mexico 72, 106, 187
Michel (José Miguel Gonzáles) 175, 180, 182–183, 186, 187, 189
Michels, Rinus 150, 162, 163
miedo escénico 167, 171
Mijatovic, Predrag 144, 196, 199
Miljanic, Miljan 166, 167, 169
Millonarios (Bogotá) 103, 104, 108
Miró, Luis 97
Moleiro, José 95
Molowny, Luis 77, 99, 113, 114, 163, 166, 169, 182, 183
Moncloa 46, 49, 50, 61, 62, 89
Montjuic Stadium 78, 81, 85, 87
Moratti, Angelo 140
Morientes, Fernando 17, 18, 19, 20, 21, 22, 24, 195, 207, 208
Moscardó, General 96, 97, 108, 162
movida Madrileña 156, 179
Müller, Gerd 195
Munich (air disaster) 124, 126, 151
Munitis, Pedro 21, 24, 25, 26, 27, 195
Muñoz, Miguel
    manager 135, 141, 148, 150, 157, 160, 161, 162, 163, 164, 166
    player 77, 99, 109, 117, 121, 127, 131
Murcia 157, 164, 180

Nantes 129
Napoli 187, 188
Navarro, Joaquín 117

Nemes, Jorge Neufeld 99, 130
Netzer, Günter 156, 163–164, 166, 167, 169
New Foot Ball Club 47, 53
New Foot Ball Sky 47, 53
Newcastle United 71
Nice 86, 89, 90, 129
Norkoeping 104
Nottingham Forest 155
Nuevo Mundo 59, 67
Nuñez, Josep Lluís 175, 184, 185, 200

Obregón, Ana 200
O'Donnell Stadium 52, 65, 66, 70, 114
Old Trafford Stadium 14, 27, 34, 125, 127, 151, 194, 208
Oliva, Joaquín 117
Olsen, Jesper 178
Olympiakos de Nicosia 154
Onieva, Juan Antonio 199
Ortega, Antonio 92
Os Belenenses 98
Osasuna 76, 155
Overmars, Mark 113
Oviedo 75, 95, 98, 99, 135, 188
Owen, Michael 195

Padrós, Carlos 48, 49, 54, 60, 61, 63
Padrós, Juan 32, 48, 49, 50, 51, 52
Pahiño, Manuel Joaquín 101
Palacios, Julian 47, 48, 50, 52, 54
Palamós 44
Parages, Pedro 77
Pardeza, Miguel 175, 179, 180, 181, 185
Partizan Belgrade 115, 118, 119, 144, 146, 147, 148
Pathe News 30, 111, 167
Pedernera, Adolfo 104, 109, 110
Pelé 88, 106, 110, 111, 147, 177
Peña, José María 71
Peñarol 135
Pentland, Fred 79, 86
Pérez, Florentino 36, 45, 56, 197, 203, 204, 207, 208, 209,
Peternac, Alen 21
Petit, René 67
Pichichi (Rafael Moreno) 62, 64, 68, 78, 82
Pirri (José Martínez Sánchez) 146, 147, 148, 150, 151, 152, 160, 162, 164, 167

Portillo, Javier 207, 208
Porto FC 29
Primo de Rivera, José Antonio 68, 75
Proust, Marcel 149
professionalism 71, 73
PSV Eindhoven 115, 161, 187, 188
Puerto Del Sol 17, 33, 68
Puskas, Ferenc 76, 126, 129–131, 133, 134, 135, 136, 140, 141, 142, 144, 147, 148, 150, 188

Querejeta, José María 95
Quieroz, Carlos 203
Quincoces, Jacinto Fernández 80, 83–84, 87, 89, 93, 99
Quinta del Buitre
    definition 179–183
    components 180, 181, 192
    importance 142, 179, 183, 185–187
Quirante, José 77

Rácing de Madrid 67, 71, 80, 88
Rácing de Santander 73, 75, 77, 84, 109, 113, 121, 159, 160
Rácing Ferrol 93
Radisic, Felix 166
Rapid Vienna 123
Rappan, Karl 140
Raúl Gonzales 14, 15, 17, 24, 25, 26, 106, 110, 114, 147, 178, 179, 181, 191–199, 201, 202, 204, 205, 207, 208, 213
Rayo Vallecano 77, 93, 196, 203
Real Irún 64, 65, 84
Real Sociedad 21, 22–28, 37, 38, 69, 70, 75, 81, 99, 171, 174, 176, 188
Recreativo de Huelva 43–44, 63, 67, 181
Redondo, Fernando 192, 194, 195
Relaño, Alfredo 119
Revie, Don 9
Rexach, Carles 154, 166
Rial, Hector 114, 118, 120, 121, 125, 131
River Plate 103, 108, 109
Rivera, Valero 90
Roma 33, 193
Ronaldinho 209
Ronaldo 7, 76, 195, 196, 207-208, 211, 213
Rubio, Gaspar 74

Sabadell 154
Sadler, David 152
Salgado, Michel 26
Samitier, Josep 71, 79, 83, 85–87, 90, 93, 100, 104, 108, 163
Samways, Vinnie 16
San Mamés 52, 74, 83, 124, 154
San Sebastían 22, 24, 34, 35, 38, 40, 63, 64, 69, 145, 154
San Siro 120, 140, 148, 171
Sánchez, Hugo 30, 110, 185, 186–187
Sánchez, Rafael 90, 92
Sanchís, Manuel Martínez 154, 156, 159
Sanchís, Manuel (Jnr) 173, 180, 181, 189
Santa Cruz (Tenerife) 38
Santa Pola 160
Santamaría, José Emilio 127–128, 135, 139, 140
Santana, Manolo 149
Santillana, Carlos 157, 159–161, 162, 167, 168, 171, 173, 179, 183, 187
Santisteban, Juan 129
Sanz, Lorenzo 36, 180, 196, 199–200, 201, 202
Sanz, Mamen 198
Saporta, Raimundo 99, 100, 107, 108, 112, 117, 118, 124, 129, 130, 134, 163, 168, 170
Schuster, Bernd 82, 163, 175, 188, 203
Sebes, Gustav 112
Seedorf, Clarence 200
Segovia 40
Segovia, Andrés 60
Servette 117, 118
Seville (city) 40, 174, 178
Seville (team) 29, 67, 75, 88, 93, 128, 129, 138
Shaw, Duncan 155
Sochaux 122
Solari, Santiago 20
Soler, José María 97
Solich, Fleitas 135
Sparta Prague 175
Spender, Stephen 198
Sporting de Gijón 161
Sporting de Irún 66
Sporting de Lisboa 115
Spottorno, Alvaro 51, 54
Stade de Reims 115, 120, 131, 136
Stalin, Joseph 81

Standard Liege 138, 153
Stein, Jock 149
Stielike, Ulrich 156, 169, 1171, 175, 183
Suárez, Adolfo 170
Suárez, Luis 135, 137, 140, 141, 148, 149
Suker, Davor 195, 200, 201
Sun, The 208
Sunyol, Josep 90
Symon, Scott 133

Tenerife 38–39, 166, 192
Teus, Eduardo 95
Toledo 40
Torino 29, 181
Toshack, John 30, 180–181, 186, 188–201, 202
Tottenham Hotspur 16, 71
Triana, Enrique 74

UEFA Cup 155, 161, 164, 183, 209
Ultra Ultras Sur 14, 15, 16, 21, 25, 37, 36
United States, The 211, 212
Upton Park 176
Urquijo, Luis 77

Vadas, Gyorgy 148
Valdano, Jorge 25, 30, 33, 36, 55–56, 77, 130, 167, 179, 183, 187, 192, 193, 195, 196, 198, 212
Valencia 9, 13, 22, 23, 25, 26, 27, 54, 75, 87, 88, 93, 94, 111, 138, 155, 160, 161, 174, 194, 195, 202, 204, 216
Valladolid 21, 171
Van Gaal, Louis 203, 208
Vanden Stock, Constant 155
Varela, Enrique 50
Vásquez, Martin 175, 180–181, 183, 192
Velázquez, Manuel 144, 145, 146, 148, 149, 154, 157, 160
Veloso, José Luis 151
Venables, Terry 183, 188

Vendrell, Colonel 97
Vicente Calderón Stadium 29, 164
Victoria Eugenia, Queen 118
Videoton 183, 184
Vigo 63
Villalonga, José 113, 121, 126, 128
Vizcaya 53, 54, 61

Wacker Innsbruck 158
West Ham 176
Wiener Sport Club 131
Wlachojanis, Dimitris 148
Wolverhampton Wanderers 112
World Cup
    (1930) 88
    (1934) 83, 84
    (1950) 103
    (1954) 134
    (1966) 143, 178
    (1978) 16, 15, 65, 169
    (1982) 128
    (1986) 177
    (2002) 145, 156, 191

'Ye-Ye' 114, 138, 143, 144, 145, 146–147, 148, 151, 157, 161, 167, 171

Zaldua, José Antonio 152
Zamora, Jesus 172
Zamora, Niceto 82
Zamora, Ricardo 69, 71, 74, 76, 80–84, 85, 86, 88–92, 93
Zamorano, Ivan 193
Zaragoza 21, 131, 150, 161, 166, 180, 183, 185, 192
Zarra (Telmo Zarraonaindia) 10, 110, 186, 188, 191
Zárraga, José María 111, 117, 129, 132
Zidane, Zinedane 7, 16, 18–20, 21, 24, 26, 72, 134, 203, 204, 208, 211
Ziganda, Cuco 191
Zoco, Ignacio 138, 140, 141, 146, 152, 159
Zunzunegui, Fernando 150, 156